D1279384

BITTER ROOTS
TENDER SHOOTS

ALSO BY SALLY ARMSTRONG

VEILED THREAT: THE HIDDEN POWER
OF THE WOMEN OF AFGHANISTAN

BITTER ROOTS
TENDER SHOOTS
The Uncertain Fate of Afghanistan's Women

Sally Armstrong

VIKING
CANADA

VIKING CANADA

Published by the Penguin Group

Penguin Group (Canada), 90 Eglinton Avenue East, Suite 700,
Toronto, Ontario, Canada M4P 2Y3 (a division of Pearson Canada Inc.)

Penguin Group (USA) Inc., 375 Hudson Street, New York, New York 10014, U.S.A.
Penguin Books Ltd, 80 Strand, London WC2R 0RL, England
Penguin Ireland, 25 St Stephen's Green, Dublin 2, Ireland
(a division of Penguin Books Ltd)
Penguin Group (Australia), 250 Camberwell Road, Camberwell, Victoria 3124,
Australia (a division of Pearson Australia Group Pty Ltd)
Penguin Books India Pvt Ltd, 11 Community Centre, Panchsheel Park,
New Delhi – 110 017, India
Penguin Group (NZ), 67 Apollo Drive, Rosedale, North Shore 0745, Auckland,
New Zealand (a division of Pearson New Zealand Ltd)
Penguin Books (South Africa) (Pty) Ltd, 24 Sturdee Avenue, Rosebank,
Johannesburg 2196, South Africa

Penguin Books Ltd, Registered Offices: 80 Strand, London WC2R 0RL, England

First published 2008

1 2 3 4 5 6 7 8 9 10

Copyright © Sally Armstrong, 2008

LIBRARY AND ARCHIVES CANADA CATALOGUING IN PUBLICATION

Armstrong, Sally, 1943–
Bitter roots, tender shoots : the uncertain fate of Afghanistan's women / Sally Armstrong.

Includes index.
ISBN 978-0-670-06868-5

1. Women—Afghanistan—Social conditions—21st century. 2. Women—Afghanistan.
3. Women—Legal status, laws, etc.—Afghanistan. I. Title.

HQ1735.6.A744 2008   305.4209581'090511   C2008-902640-3

Visit the Penguin Group (Canada) website at **www.penguin.ca**

Special and corporate bulk purchase rates available; please see
www.penguin.ca/corporatesales or call 1-800-810-3104, ext. 477 or 474

FOR THE TOMORROW GIRLS

JULIA RISHOR, AGE THIRTEEN MONTHS; ALAINA
PODMOROW, ELEVEN YEARS; TAMANNA NAVEED,
SEVENTEEN YEARS

"TO YOU ... WE THROW THE TORCH"

CONTENTS

INTRODUCTION

WHO KNEW?

IT WAS 7 A.M. ON A MARCH MORNING in 2003 when my cellphone rang in the Red Roof Inn in Manhattan. I was in New York for the American launch of my book *Veiled Threat: The Hidden Power of the Women of Afghanistan.* The skyscraper next door was blocking the early morning light, so it was still dark in my hotel room when I fumbled around to find the phone and answered in a rather groggy, post-launch-party voice. The caller, from Radio Canada, asked if I would do an interview. "Probably," I replied. "But what's it about?" "The military has massed forces on the border between Pakistan and Afghanistan," she told me. "They're going after Osama bin Laden. They say he's in a cave near Kandahar. And some people here say you know exactly where he is."

I sat on the edge of the bed, listening with incredulity, and then remembered a speech I had delivered in Montreal a few months earlier. I had told the audience about a visit I made to Kandahar in January 2001 to interview a group of courageous women who shared the ghastly details of their lives under Taliban rule. They wanted their story to reach women outside Afghanistan who might help them with the human rights catastrophe they were living with.

In the course of our conversation, they told me about Osama bin Laden, a man who was hardly a household name at the time. They told me he was ruining their country, hijacking their religion, and feeding the Taliban a steady diet of medieval, theocratic dogma. They took me—all of us wearing all-enveloping burkas—to see his home in Kandahar. It was a palatial estate, with marble pillars, a grand tiled entrance, and lush gardens—a shocking contrast to the dirt-poor, drought-ravaged city around it. The women told me that bin Laden had four other homes such as this one in other Afghan cities. Then they said, "But he doesn't work in any of these houses. He works in a cave thirty kilometres north of Kandahar City."

When 9/11 forced the world to pay attention to Afghanistan, a country that had been abandoned by the international community at the end of the Cold War, I thought the invading armies would go directly to the cave north of Kandahar and capture the world's most wanted man. After all, if I knew where he was, everyone else must know, too. But the soldiers didn't go there. They went north, to Mazar-e Sharif and Kunduz, and to Gardez in the east. They tracked along the fractious border with Pakistan's North-West Frontier province. Not surprisingly, they didn't find the mastermind of the attacks on the World Trade Center.

I shared that story with the reporter on the telephone. "Oh," she said. "I wonder why no one ever looked in that cave." Why, indeed. Evidently even the CIA wasn't smart enough to ask the women where Osama bin Laden was.

Women always know what's going on in the village. They know who's dealing in drugs and arms. They know who's in power and who only pretends to be powerful. They know about clandestine love affairs and marriage woes. Not much gets past the women. But nobody ever asks them to share what they know. Except, of course, other women. They told me behind closed doors and in whispered, conspiratorial voices what was happening to them under the Taliban regime. And every time I return to Afghanistan, they tell me what has changed, and what hasn't. Who's stealing the international aid, who's sharing it, where the schools are operating, and why some are off limits. They tell me about the wins and the losses, the cultural and religious edicts that still are enforced. They name names and spell out the need for change.

I began reporting from Afghanistan soon after the Taliban took over in September 1996, creating a human rights catastrophe for women and girls. I followed the five years of Taliban rule, the subsequent arrival of the international community, the fledgling development projects, the sometimes disastrous setbacks, and the flickering hope for peace. Although I have reported on the military campaigns, and was embedded from time to time at Kandahar Airfield, my beat does not usually include interviewing generals and politicians. Instead, I write about the women and girls who live with the consequences of military and political decisions.

Recently, I heard a commentator claim that the coalition forces went into Afghanistan on October 7, 2001, to rescue the women. A lovely humanitarian thought! But I doubt very much that in recorded history the armed forces of any country have ever gone anywhere to rescue women. What the women of Afghanistan have learned, as women in North America and Europe learned during the sixties and seventies, is that if you want change, you have to make it yourself.

There is much to be said about where the women and girls of Afghanistan are in 2008, a dozen years after the Taliban took over and half a dozen years since *Veiled Threat* was published. I wrote that book because I felt it was important to chronicle what really happened to the women and girls when the Taliban were in power. If the facts weren't recorded, they would be forgotten. No one would believe that the soccer stadiums were used to stone women to death in a ghoulish display of misogyny. No one would remember the Taliban edict: "Don't throw a stone so big as to kill her quickly." The citizens of Afghanistan who were raped in the name of God, forbidden education because they were girls, and refused life-saving medical help because they were women would be written out of the history of the darkest days in that country. Even today, while the Taliban resort to suicide bombing and improvised explosive devices (IEDs), the public debate is about negotiation with, and accommodation of, these illiterate thugs who want to regain the power they held from September 26, 1996, until late October 2001. The headlines about their hateful treatment of women and girls are beginning to blur.

Without exception, the women I met during those five long years, while the world chose to look the other way, were valorous and determined to get their story out to anyone who would listen. Time after time they said, "We have no voice. Ask the women in the rest of the world to speak for us."

So how are they doing today? Immediately after the Taliban were ousted, the women were allowed to return to work. The professional women—doctors, lawyers, civil servants, and teachers—found their place in the workforce. For the others, the clerks, secretaries, and cleaners, jobs were scarce. Being paid on time, if at all, was another problem. But most felt it was early days and, with the world on their doorstep, a prosperous future was around the corner.

Within days of the arrival of the international community, women were seen on the street again. The Taliban decree that a woman could not leave her home unless she was accompanied by a husband, brother, or son was discarded. Slowly at first, but rapidly later, the women in the cities doffed their burkas.

Although some still wear a burka, most urban working women do not. In many rural areas, women never did wear them.

Some girls are back at school. Of the six million students registered, about two million are girls. There are another five million, half of them girls, who are not in school. The reasons are many. Reconstruction of the schools has been slow. Some schools that were rebuilt and re-opened were fire-bombed by the Taliban insurgency. The lack of security makes it difficult for some parents to risk sending their girls to school. Then there's the teacher shortage. The government doesn't have enough money to pay an adequate roster of teachers. And some teachers are simply too afraid to take the job because of the *night letters*—notes dropped on doorsteps under cover of darkness that carry a menacing message from the Taliban, threatening to kill them for teaching girls. But the number of girls in high school also reflects the complexity of the social and religious environment. By the time they are fourteen, most girls are told by their families to leave school and stay at home to help with the younger children or are married off to a cousin or an older man in another village. Education is an ongoing and contentious conundrum.

The first-ever Ministry of Women's Affairs was established in 2002. The new constitution included equal rights for women and reserved seats for women in parliament in 2004. While 30 percent of the women won their seats in their own right rather than by the reserved-seat option, sixty-eight women were elected in 2005, making up 27 percent of the 248-member Wolesi Jirga (the lower house, also known as the Peoples' Council). An additional twenty-three women were elected to the Meshrano Jirga (the upper house, also known as the Elders' Council).* Of eighteen government-appointed commissioners,

---

*For the sake of simplicity, throughout the text I often have used *parliament* and *member of parliament* in place of the Afghan terms.

three are women. One provincial governor is a woman. There are other signs of emancipation. The Afghanistan Independent Human Rights Commission chaired by Dr. Sima Samar is a stunning success story. The work to reform family law within the mix of civil, tribal, and sharia (religious) law has begun. Some women have been trained as police officers, and both the medical and law schools are flush with women students. Two Afghan women took part in the Olympic Games in Athens. Robina Muqimyar came seventh in her heat in the 100-metre sprint, beating the runner from Somalia. Friba Razayee lost her opening match in the judo competition. But both women said being there was the real victory. In 2008, one woman, Mahbooba Ahadgar, a 1,500-metre runner (pictured on the jacket of this book) was selected for the team going to the Beijing Olympics but just weeks before the games began, she went missing. As of late summer, it was presumed she was seeking asylum in Norway to avoid the death threats from fundamentalists who claim women athletes are anti-Islam.

Women and girls alike are better off than they were under the Taliban, and their situation continues to improve marginally each year. But there are immense problems that need to be addressed. Women trying to escape abusive marriages are still jailed. So are women who have been raped. Tribal law, which is often brutal for women and girls, hasn't budged. The suicide rate is soaring. Afghanistan is the only country in the world in which the suicide rate is higher among women than it is among men. Women are using self-immolation to escape the misery of village life and tribal law. Sima Samar says, "Violence is still part of every Afghan's home."

I have been following the trials of the women of Afghanistan for eleven years. I met the gentle women of Kandahar, who were confined to dwellings with windows that were painted over by the Taliban so no one could see them. The same women were made to wear identical wedge shoes because the Taliban declared that the tap, tap, tap of a woman's heels was un-Islamic. I also met the high-spirited teachers who pretended their schools were sewing centres and the little girls who were forced to toss their dolls in a bonfire because the Taliban claimed it was blasphemous to depict a living being other than the Prophet. There are also stories about individuals that still haunt me. I remember Lima, for example, a thirteen-year-old girl when I met her in 2002, who had witnessed her mother, father, and grandmother being killed by the Taliban the year before. Lima never smiled, hardly made eye contact, and to me was the saddest kid in the world. I remember also the urban women, the women who had been lawyers, doctors, professors, and civil servants before the Taliban tried to reduce them to faceless objects of ridicule and punishment. I met the feisty Dr. Samar, who, when threatened with death by the Taliban for educating girls, defied them to do their worst and never stopped what she was doing. I followed the Hazaras, Pashtuns, and Tajiks and learned of their centuries-old ethnic quarrels and their fierce pride in their country.

I also discovered the facts behind their veiled lives. Eighty-five percent are illiterate. A thirty-five-year-old woman I met at one of the literacy classes that popped up like kebab stands all over the country when the Taliban were ousted referred to her illiteracy as blindness. When I asked her to explain the connection, she said, "I couldn't read, so I couldn't see what was going on." Women's health was so severely compromised that the country had the highest infant and maternal mortality rates in the world, and *osteomalacia* (softening of the bones) was endemic, due to a diet that had been reduced to tea and naan (flatbread). Their religion had been hijacked by extremists who told them it was God's will that women and girls be denied education and health care. Their culture was similarly misinterpreted by men who drew on an astonishing combination of revisionist history and ancient myths to blame women for everything from the five-year drought that afflicted the country to its crushing poverty. The tribal law that ruled their lives was brutal and merciless. The tradition of *bad*, the giving of a young daughter, or sometimes two or three daughters, to settle a dispute—also known as "blood money"—was like something out of a medieval horror story. Similarly *badal*, the trading of daughters without a dowry into what amounted to slavery, was an incomprehensible violation of universally accepted human rights declarations and conventions. These abuses were endemic throughout the country during the five years of Taliban rule, but the international community looked the other way.

Except for other women. Before I travelled to Afghanistan in 1997, I was in touch with author Deborah Ellis, whose splendid children's books—*Parvana's Journey, The Breadwinner*—would later become bestsellers because of their poignant portrayal of life for children under the Taliban. She introduced me to Adeena Niazi at the Afghan Women's Organization in Toronto. These women were valuable sources of information for me when I started on this odyssey, and they continue to inspire and inform the work that I do today. Soon after I wrote my first story about the women of Afghanistan, I heard from two women in Calgary, Janice Eisenhauer and Carolyn Reicher, who said, "We want to raise awareness about this atrocity, and collect money to send to the women. Stay tuned." They started an organization called Canadian Women for Women in Afghanistan (CW4WAfghan). Today they have fourteen chapters across the country and have raised more than $2 million that goes directly to women's projects in Afghanistan. Rights and Democracy, the human rights centre in Montreal, got involved in distributing the funds so that 100 percent of the dollars raised goes straight to the projects CW4WAfghan supports, and donors receive tax receipts. Rights and Democracy also turned their internationally respected resources to the initiative by using their women's project, under the leadership of Ariane Brunet, to guide the Calgary volunteers. A movement had begun in Canada to give voice to the women in Afghanistan.

There was a man in their midst. The minister of foreign affairs at that time, Lloyd Axworthy, took up the cause, and vowed to bring it to the Security Council of the United Nations. Good as his word, he stood up at the United Nations on April 7, 2001, and spoke of the Taliban and the ongoing strife in Afghanistan. He said, "All aspects of this conflict are reprehensible. But some stand out more than others. Perhaps the most disturbing is the Taliban's systemic pattern of violation of the human rights of half the population—the women and girls—a violation that the Taliban misrepresent as having a religious foundation."

Similar movements began in the United States, led by the Feminist Majority Foundation; in Europe, led by Emma Bonino; and in Pakistan, led by Farida Shaheed and Shirkat Gah. And an association called Women Living Under Muslim Laws (WLUML) was becoming the leading voice for women in countries governed by sharia law. Meanwhile, cyberspace allowed women's groups from all over the world to stay in touch with one another while they worked on strategies for reaching out to their sisters in Afghanistan.

By the time *Veiled Threat* went to press, there was a lot of hope for the country. As ethicist Margaret Somerville says, "Hope is the oxygen of the human spirit." We were living in the traumatized aftermath of 9/11. The Taliban seemed to have slithered away. Billions of dollars in aid, thousands of soldiers, and countless volunteers were dispatched to Afghanistan to bring its thirty million people into the twenty-first century. The years 2002–05 were a heady period filled with puffed-up prospects.

But then something went wrong. The Taliban regrouped with al Qaeda and became a menacing force once more.

Security, or its absence, became the preoccupation of every Afghan. The warlords would not let go of their militias because the precarious state of the nation left an opening for them to take back the turf they once controlled. The government was exposed as a safe haven for war criminals. The international community started to put a brake on its commitment to reconstruction.

The insurgency in the southern provinces confounded both the international mission in Afghanistan and the Afghans themselves. Politicians in Canada began weighing the future of Afghanistan against their own ability to get re-elected. Protestors claimed we should leave the country and let the Afghans fight it out among themselves. Every single person I spoke to in Afghanistan was terrified that the world would abandon them, that the fighting would resume, and that the country would become a pariah state again within a week.

Meanwhile, women's groups in Canada doubled their efforts to keep the programs for women in Afghanistan going. And then, in the midst of the renewed darkness, a child held up a clear, pure light. In the fall of 2006, nine-year-old Alaina Podmorow stepped onto the stage in an auditorium in Winfield, in the Okanagan Valley of British Columbia. She and her mother, Jamie, attended an event put on by CW4WAfghan and sponsored by the B.C. Rotary clubs. I was one of the speakers at that event, and afterwards Alaina came to me and said, "Those are girls the same age as me. Everyone needs to help them." The next morning she announced to her parents that she would start another group called Little Women for Little Women in Afghanistan. She said she would gather kids her age; they would raise money through bottle drives and bake sales; and they would help the girls to get back to school. Her voice would ultimately be heard on national news broadcasts and by Prime Minister Stephen Harper at a meeting in Ottawa.

BY THE FALL OF 2007, the world had begun to wonder if Afghanistan could be moved out of its new dark age. That's when my publisher at Penguin called and asked for a book about the women and girls I had written about in 2002. I eagerly accepted the assignment and started making plans to return to the country to find the women I had been talking to during the last decade.

This is the sequel to their story. It's a story about roots—bitter roots that have tentacles reaching every facet of a woman's life—and it's the story of the tender shoots that are trying to bring the blossom of change.

CHAPTER 1

BITTER ROOTS

Whenever women protest and ask for their rights, they are silenced with the argument that the laws are justified under Islam. It is an unfounded argument. It is not Islam at fault, but rather the culture that uses its own interpretations to justify whatever it wants.

—Shirin Ebadi, Iranian lawyer, 2003 Nobel Peace Prize Laureate, excerpt from her presentation at Rights and Democracy, October 2004

IT IS AN OLD, OLD STORY but as modern as present-day Afghanistan. In the middle of the ancient city of Balkh, in front of the mosque, and just ten metres away from the road, a slab of cement two metres high marks a spot that has become a kind of holy sepulchre for Afghan women and girls. It is the tomb of poet Rabbia Balkhi.

Rabbia was a tenth-century Afghan princess. She was born Rabbia Kosdor but is now famously known as Rabbia Balkhi because of her association with the city. She was a beautiful girl according to the stories, and just twenty years old when she began writing the poems that ultimately would lead to her being known as the first female Persian poet. She wrote about nature and beauty but mostly about love—her forbidden love for a man called Baktash.

She lived during an era of prosperity, in what was then known as Bactria, the centre of the Samanid Empire, the greatest civilization of central Asia. It was a time, beginning around 900 AD, when architecture and the arts flourished along the Silk Road. The region's reputation was well established before Rabbia took quill pen to parchment, thanks to its many famous and infamous inhabitants. The Persian prophet, Zoroaster, reputedly died within the walls of Balkh. The city was conquered by Alexander the Great, and eventually would be sacked by the Mongol warlord, Genghis Khan. But at the turn of the tenth century, it had become a centre of study in mathematics, medicine, and astronomy, and the site of the first silver mines to produce coins. By any measure, Balkh sheltered an advanced civilization. Examples of its architecture can be seen today. The Nuh Gunbad (nine domes) mosque still stands in Balkh, as do the remnants of the city wall. But it was also an empire that kept its women veiled and out of the public eye.

Rabbia was prohibited from joining the discussions among the scholars, artists, and writers at court but often hid herself in a secluded part of the courtyard where she could see without being seen. She began to write her own poems but kept them carefully concealed, even from the women who waited on her.

The story of her love for Baktash has many versions, according to Professor Ekramuddin Hesarian in Kabul University's literature department. As the daughter of a Samanid king, Rabbia would have had slaves, and depending on which version of the story you hear, Baktash was either her slave or the slave of her brother Hareth. She fell in love with him, and began writing poetry about her passion for a man she was forbidden to see. It is said that Baktash responded with poems of his own declaring his love for the beautiful Rabbia. Then, the story goes, they were found out. What happened next also comes in two versions. In the first version, Baktash is banished from the empire but ultimately returns and kills Hareth before killing himself. Upon hearing the news, Rabbia decides she can't live without him and goes to the *hammam* (women's bath) and slits her wrists. The second version is equally gruesome. Hareth discovers the lovers' tryst, sends her to the *hammam*, and orders the king's barber to open her vein and bleed her to death (or does the grisly job himself), to preserve the family's so-called honour. In this version, Baktash finds the love of his life dead and kills himself.

Whichever account is correct, it was in the act of dying that Rabbia claimed her place in history. The oft-told story says that, while she lay bleeding to death, she used the blood dripping from her vein to write a poem, "Love," on the wall of the *hammam*. The English translation by Manouchehr Saadat Noury reads:

> I am caught in Love's web so deceitful
> None of my endeavors turn fruitful.
> I knew not when I rode the high-blooded steed
> The harder I pulled its reins the less it would heed.
> Love is an ocean with such a vast space
> No wise man can swim it in any place.
> A true lover should be faithful till the end
> And face life's reprobated trend.
> When you see things hideous, fancy them neat,
> Eat poison, but taste sugar sweet.

This Romeo-and-Juliet-style love story has been woven into the fabric of the lives of women in Afghanistan ever since

Rabbia's tomb was found in 1967 by Ghullam Habib Nawabi. He wrote a book about Rabbia, and she became part of the cultural history of contemporary Afghanistan. Although most of her poems have been destroyed, the few that remain have captured the attention of literary critics, as well as the women and girls who visit her tomb. Professor Hesarian, for example, rates the poems as excellent in terms of their contribution to literature; meanwhile, the women of this tortured country see them as the same story of forbidden love they struggle against today.

Rabbia's tomb, which is surrounded by a park where children play, is approached by the women and girls who go there with the devotion appropriate to a pilgrimage. They go to Rabbia to pray for the fulfillment of their own romantic dreams. Children climb over the tomb, while their older sisters and mothers squeeze into the narrow opening and drop to the floor below. In the damp, cold vault, the coffin is draped in fabric that displays the words of her poetry. When asked why her poems are so popular with women and girls who haven't been to school, much less studied ancient poetry, Hesarian says, "It's because she was a woman in love, she was an oppressed lover, and she's seen as a martyr because of the way she was killed."

The devotion of the women of Afghanistan to the poems of a tenth-century romantic poses a conundrum that is rarely addressed in any culturally correct discussion about their situation. While it is accepted that women are the heart of the Afghan family, that they are protected and, indeed, guarded by the men, neither tradition nor everyday practice allows them to fall in love. And yet they do. The attraction to one special man or boy; the giddy, heart-pounding enchantment; the charm and chemistry that accompany love—all are as old as the bathhouses and the village wells and as current as the high-tech offices in downtown Kabul. But romantic love is forbidden.

In January 2008, a thousand years after Rabbia was murdered for loving Baktash, a modern version of the story is playing out in the office of the women's project at the Afghanistan Independent Human Rights Commission in Kabul. Project officer Homa Sultani arrives with a girl who looks like a deer caught in the headlights of a car. Masooda, who like many Afghans has only one name, doesn't know how old she is, but she does know she is in trouble. Her burka is folded back over her face, revealing big brown eyes that are red from crying. She picks nervously at her fingers and fidgets with her clothing, her face is a mask of red blotches over pale skin, and she dabs at her nose incessantly with a tissue that is balled up in her hand. She is nervous and watchful, seemingly caught between the urge to bolt and helpless submission. Sultani puts in a call to Jamila Ghairat at the women's shelter, assures Masooda that she is safe, and recounts the girl's story.

Masooda grew up next door to Mohamed Rafi, a young man who is now twenty-two and is on his way to the commission office. Both are from dirt-poor families. They played together with the other kids in the neighbourhood and suffered together through the Taliban years when Masooda had to watch boys such as Rafi go to school while she had to stay at home. Eventually the friendship between them developed into love. They were inseparable. Everyone in the neighbourhood knew that—everyone, that is, except Masooda's family, and in particular her grandfather, a harsh man who rules the family roost. The young lovers wanted to get married. They knew Masooda's conservative family would never allow a daughter to choose her own husband, so they decided to run away to Pakistan and have the wedding ceremony performed there, a safe distance from Masooda's grandfather and the dysfunctional jurisprudence of Afghanistan.

They were married and lived in Pakistan for eight months. But, as happens in many love stories, the besotted pair made a grave error. They missed their families with an ache that grew by the day. After three-quarters of a year had passed, they decided that it was safe to return, that their families would be so glad to see them that their indiscretion would be forgiven. One more thing: Masooda was six months pregnant.

There was no joyful reunion. Instead, the lovers were struck by a devastating triple whammy. Firstly, Masooda's family accused Rafi of having kidnapped Masooda. Secondly, Rafi's family made it clear they wanted nothing to do with his bride. Thirdly, Masooda's life was threatened because she had brought shame to her family. She was quite likely to become the victim of an honour killing.

Masooda's furious grandfather sent Rafi packing. His family had been so frightened by the rage of their new in-laws after the pair had escaped to Pakistan that they had moved to another neighbourhood. Masooda was kept in the house while her grandfather decided her fate. Not a girl to be easily intimidated, Masooda fled at the first opportunity. Out on the street, she asked for directions to the human rights commission and wound up in Homa Sultani's office. At which point, this human drama came to epitomize women's lives in Afghanistan.

While the constitution grants equal rights to women, tribal law denies such rights, dismissing them as the product of foolish Western thinking. Civil law says a girl must be sixteen to marry. Tribal law says a girl is married when, and to whom, the male members in her family decide. Homa Sultani knows she needs to find a solution that embraces both civil and tribal law to make sure all parties will abide by the ruling. The negotiations began this morning with a meeting in a judge's court at the police station. "The grandfather was screaming in the court, demanding revenge, begging God to kill the girl who played with his dignity, saying he would never forgive her, and that she had sinned against Islam," says Sultani. But this shrieking demand for revenge, although it sounds terrifying, is just the usual starting point, she says. The truth is that if Rafi gives him one hundred thousand afghanis (about two thousand dollars), the case will be closed. So for all the allusions to tribal law and religious piety, it's really about cash. The giving of a dowry is not allowed by either civil or sharia law, but the custom of *mahar*—the groom giving money to the bride—is allowed as long as the price is not fixed, and so that is the route Sultani decides to take to save Masooda from certain death. "I don't agree with it, but I'll do it to get peace," she says. "The mediation will begin now. I think I can get the grandfather's price down to twenty-five hundred afghanis [about $500]. We'll give Rafi the money, and after a very long time, he'll pay us back. It's the way we're managing these cases now. Masooda will stay at the shelter, away from her husband, until we get this solved. We'll arrange for him to visit her here at the commission."

Jamila arrives from the women's shelter to fetch her new resident. She is a pretty woman, dressed in a fashionable beige suede jacket, black straight-leg pants, and high-heeled boots. Her makeup has been carefully applied and a small silk scarf barely conceals her beautifully coiffed hair. Rafi has arrived as well, wearing a black leather jacket, and with a Burberry-like scarf flung waggishly around his neck. He sits outside the office waiting to see Masooda. Jamila offers a sympathetic shoulder-pat to the girl, tries to convince her that this is the best solution, and picks up the paperwork from Homa Sultani. It is time for Masooda to say goodbye to Rafi.

Outside in the waiting area, they sit side by side in two oversized chairs, the armrests coming between them like parents still barring the way. They whisper to each other and shyly touch each other's hands. Rafi looks as forlorn as Masooda. I ask her what she wants. "To be at home with Rafi," she says. Why did you marry him? She casts her eyes down. "Because I love him." Rafi adds unbidden, "I love her too." My next question: Are you afraid? She starts to tremble. "Yes ... from my family." Big, watery tears are falling down her cheeks, wetting her entire face. "They will beat me, kill me." When I ask Rafi what he will do, wondering if he will abandon the marriage and leave the girl to her fate, he says, "She has to stay in the shelter so we can solve this problem. My family isn't angry with me now. They were before, but not now. They won't let Masooda stay with us because her family will make trouble for us, or with the police, or they'll come and grab Masooda and take her away. But when the problem is solved, we can be together again."

He knows the stakes are high. The judge at the court said Masooda has to have a test to determine her age. A bone X-ray will be arranged by the commission. "We can only hope she's sixteen or more," says Sultani. "Otherwise she'll go to jail." The family may have their revenge after all. Six months pregnant, still a child really, Masooda faces the unknown in a women's shelter, caught between her love for Rafi and her fear of being killed by her family.

It is time to go. Masooda is crying so hard and trembling so much she can hardly get out of the chair. She takes one more look at Rafi, stares at his face as though to record it with her eyes, struggles to her feet, and then, in one swift move, brings the burka down over her head and is invisible. Masooda follows Jamila to the stairs. Rafi hangs his head, covers his face with his hands, and tries to hide his own tears. The only sound is the clicking of Masooda's heels as she descends the stairs, and the choking noise coming from her throat as she attempts in vain to stifle her crying. Then they are gone: out the door, into a van, and off to the shelter.

Sultani comforts Rafi. She reminds him they will arrange times to visit here at the commission office and assures him that Masooda will be safe because no one is allowed to know the address of the shelter. He thanks her and, with his head still drooping like that of an old man, shuffles to the stairs and leaves. A woman in the commission sniffs furiously. "You see, we don't even have the right to love in this country."

It is a significant observation. While the rest of the world can't claim victory on love marriages versus arranged marriages—the statistics on the success of one against the other are a draw—there are issues among women who are controlled by so-called religious men the world over that need to be addressed. Although cloaked by piety, these issues invariably are about sex and ownership. Indeed, the Madonna/whore designation is part of the lives of women wherever fundamentalists are in power. Falling in love is interpreted as seeking illicit sex. And by tradition, sex is the domain of men: Men use sex to fulfill their own needs and to control, punish, and isolate women. What is worse, men are not held accountable for their sexual behaviour, the suggestion being that a man's sexual desires cannot, and should not, be restrained as they are the fault of women. But if a man cannot govern himself, how is it that he has the right to govern women?

A fundamentalist will tell you it is about righteousness, that a woman is the centre of the family honour and she must be protected at all costs. If she strays from the coveted position she holds, gives up the status of fragile creature that requires protection, she is by default taking on the role of an evil Jezebel. In which case, the accepted tradition says, she must be cast aside, even killed, so the stain she has spattered on the family is removed. Or, in a slightly less extreme version, the woman who strays is seen as someone who deserves to be raped, so she can be taught a lesson about who is in charge. The protection bestowed upon a woman includes keeping her out of public life, confining her behind a purdah wall, and denying her an education or the right to participate in civil society. While those restrictions have been modified recently in some parts of Afghanistan, where education is seen as having value, and the right to run for public office is even encouraged in several provinces, the fact remains that even the most emancipated woman is still seen as the vessel of blame for a man's sexual urges. So she must cover herself, keep her eyes cast downward, and refuse the company of a man who is not a husband, brother, or son.

These bizarre restrictions are not imposed on the women of Afghanistan alone, nor are they found only in Islamic countries. History is littered with stories of women who are denied ownership over their own lives. From Hecuba in ancient Greece to the Cherokee in America, women and girls have been traded like bounty. There was a time when the Catholic Church said women didn't have souls. In Canada, women were not considered persons under the law until 1928. Prior to that, they were designated by the British North America Act as persons in matters of "pains and penalties" but not in matters of rights and privileges. And rape was not considered a war crime until the International Criminal Tribunal for the Former Yugoslavia declared it to be against international law in 2001.

The same issues bearing on the status of women are deeply rooted in almost every religion and in every part of the world. Although they are more prevalent in Asia and Africa, they are also evident in Europe, Britain, the United States, and Canada. Those who hijack religion, and issue decrees and punishments in the name of God, are rarely challenged by governments or international bodies that opt instead for the politically correct excuse of cultural relativism—as if religious tradition justifies criminal assault.

THESE BITTER ROOTS HAVE GROWN FROM the centuries-old impunity bestowed upon men who usurp women and girls as property and impeach them for their own sexual indiscretions. To be female in much of the world means bearing sons, being forbidden to voice an opinion, and being subjected to the fancies and furies of men. The suggestion that women should be held responsible for a man's lack of sexual control is preposterous, and yet, until the recent past, it has gone unquestioned. It has been taboo even to raise the subject in the village, the centre of worship, the town hall, or legislature. If women are ever to take their place in society—within the community, in the corporate hierarchy, or in positions of political power—these outdated notions need to be addressed.

Afghanistan and a dozen other countries cannot prosper until they alter the status of women. We know this to be true because studies done by the World Bank, the North-South Institute, the Grameen Bank (a community development bank specializing in microfinance for women), and even the International Monetary Fund have demonstrated unequivocally that if the women are treated fairly, the village will prosper. But all the laws in the world (the U.N. Charter, the Universal Declaration of Human Rights, the Convention on the Elimination of All Forms of Discrimination Against Women) are not going to change the status of women until and unless the international community condemns misogyny and puts teeth into its vow to protect citizens.

But first, many countries need to look to their own laws and their ingrained attitudes towards women. For example:

2002, PAKISTAN: A tribal council of adult men in Meerwala ordered an eighteen-year-old girl to be gang-raped because her eleven-year-old brother had been seen walking with a girl from a higher-class tribe. During the six subsequent years, the men who raped her have been charged, found guilty, sentenced, sent to jail, acquitted, released, charged again, and set free once more. The victim, Mukhtar Mai, was invited by a human rights group to address an audience in the United States, but the government of Pakistan barred her from travelling abroad. The travel ban has been lifted, but the case is still in the courts; the perpetrators still have not been made accountable for their crime.

2002, SAUDI ARABIA: On July 15, fifteen school girls died in a fire in Mecca when the religious police refused to let them out of the burning building because they weren't wearing correct Islamic dress—head scarves and *abayas* (black robes). One witness reported that the police were actually beating the girls back while they tried to escape the flames. The police came from the Commission for the Promotion of Virtue and the Prevention of Vice. (This is the same mob that cruised the streets of Afghanistan during the Taliban regime, whipping women whose hands slipped out from under a burka, or who dared to wear white socks, which was considered a sign of sexual promiscuity.) These guardians of morality also turned away parents and local residents who came to assist the girls. Even the reporters who arrived to cover the story knew they were risking arrest by criticizing the barbarity of the action of the vice-and-virtue squad. The crown prince, seeing a brewing storm in his tightly controlled kingdom, quickly issued a press release calling for an inquiry and saying "the deaths were unacceptable, the work of negligent, incompetent, careless officials."

2003, ONTARIO: It was late afternoon when the phone rang. Ten-year-old Tara was doing her math homework—her favourite subject—when she picked up the receiver in the Mississauga apartment where she lived with her mother. It was her father on the line from Iran, and the words she heard would shatter the sense of safety both mother and daughter had found in Canada: "I know where you are. I am coming to get you. You belong to me."

Tara knew this was not an empty threat. A year earlier, in Iran, nine-year-old Tara had been forced to stay with her father when her mother, Minoo Homily, fled to a friend's house after being beaten to a bloody pulp for the umpteenth time in their ten-year marriage. Minoo was allowed to see Tara for two hours on Fridays during supervised visits at the courthouse. Her friends encouraged her to escape from Iran, and during one Friday visit, even the guard at the courthouse whispered to her: "Take your child and get out of here. Your husband is not to be trusted." After a harrowing getaway over the mountains into Turkey, the terrified mother and daughter found their way to Canada in 2002. They thought they were out of the reach of Iran's sharia laws.

They weren't. Not only did Tara's father discover their Toronto phone number and the address of her school, he also knew that, in a stunning turn of events, the government of Ontario had agreed to allow the application of sharia law in settling family disputes. According to the rules of sharia law, Tara would be returned to her father. The very law they had escaped in Iran had now followed them to Canada.

The news that sharia law was being used in Ontario hit like a thunderbolt. Women activists were outraged. Most Muslim women were shocked. "Removing family disputes from the public court is a loss for women," said Andrée Côté from the National Association of Women and the Law. "By accepting sharia law, we're renouncing thirty years of reform." It was two long years before the size of the protest persuaded the premier to overturn his decision.

2004, BRITISH COLUMBIA: Polygamy is practised in the small town of Bountiful, even though it is against the Criminal Code of Canada. Inside the colony, there used to be a collection of nine rocks that spelled out the words *Keep Sweet*, the mantra for the women and girls who live here with their husbands and sons, in a sect called the Fundamentalist Church of Jesus Christ of Latter Day Saints. Recently, someone flipped the rocks over to spell *Fuck you!* The long-held secrets of Bountiful have been exposed by the media. They tell a story about polygamy, incest, and brainwashing, about convictions for sexual abuse, and accusations of cross-border trafficking in brides. Some reports accuse the men of the community of breeding young girls like cattle, of committing tax fraud, and of promoting a white supremacist agenda. Not your average Canadian tale.

The fine print on the ticket to paradise sold in Bountiful says the only way to get to heaven is through plural marriage. It is illegal to practise polygamy in Canada. The Criminal Code and Charter of Rights and Freedoms outlaw underage marriage and cite impregnating a child as abuse. Cross-border trafficking in girls is also illegal.

Various attorneys general in British Columbia have claimed their hands are tied because, under the Charter of Rights and Freedoms, the men who run the colony are protected by freedom of religion. Despite this claim, one of the authors of the charter, lawyer Marilou McPhedran, says, "In the Bountiful case, the excuse that women and girls have consented to their treatment would likely collapse when measured with the Criminal Code prohibition of polygamy and equality rights of women and girls in sections 15 and 28 of the Charter." But so far, there's been no action from the attorney general.

2006, SWAZILAND: In Swaziland, a woman does not have the right to refuse sex with her husband, even when he is HIV-positive. Swazi women have no rights when it comes to sex: Polygamy, a practice that denigrates women and spreads the virus, is the norm. A woman can't demand that the man wear a condom. She can't even go to the hospital without her husband's permission. What's more, a widow is expected and, in fact, often forced to marry her husband's brother. Women are considered minors with no legal status. Life expectancy has dropped to a stunning thirty-one years due to the AIDS epidemic. It is expected to drop to twenty-nine by 2010.

Siphiwe Hlophe and four other women formed Swaziland Positive Living and began the task of changing the cultural mores of one million people. "Our objective is to teach our partners and families about HIV and AIDS so that they have knowledge, so we can live positively, and prolong our lives." The challenge involves nothing less than taking on the myths, superstitions, and ancient male-dominated laws of the entire country. Even King Mswati keeps a harem. The women who are leading the protest against these deadly traditions say, "We have to do this or we'll all be dead."

2007, ISRAEL: Ultra-orthodox Haredi Jews in Israel demand that women ride in the back of the bus and stay out of the universities, so as not to tempt the men among them. Mariam Shear, a fifty-year-old Toronto woman, was in Jerusalem for religious studies when she was told to move to the back of the bus. She refused, was slapped, pushed out of her seat and onto the floor, beaten, and kicked. News reports said her cheek was bruised and her head scarf flew off in the altercation, further embarrassing the observant woman. The same Haredi group has been accused of throwing bleach on women who were not modestly dressed, and setting fire to shops that sell clothing considered inappropriate. They also announced that post-secondary education was anathema for women, and in the process earned the nickname the "Israeli Taliban."

2007, QUEBEC: A Montreal mosque posted a warning on its website that said if young girls took off their hijab (head scarf), they could end up "getting raped and having illegitimate children." The posting also warned that failure to wear a hijab could lead to "stresses, insecurity, and suspicion in the minds of husbands," and "instigating young people to deviate towards the path of lust."

2007, SAUDI ARABIA: A judge in Saudi Arabia ordered a victim of gang rape to receive ninety lashes because she had been alone in a car with a man who was not her husband, brother, or son when the attack occurred, so it must be her own fault that seven men raped her. The nineteen-year-old girl had the temerity to protest this unjust verdict. Her reward for speaking up was a six-month jail sentence and two hundred lashes. Her lawyer's comeuppance for taking on this human rights case was the threat of losing the right to practise law. When human rights organizations and women around the world protested the case, the Saudi king made headlines by "pardoning the victim"—an oxymoron if ever there was one—in his annual year-end list of exculpations.

2008, AFGHANISTAN: In the Afghanistan province of Sar-e Pol, a well-known judge handed over a nine-year-old girl to a fifty-year-old man in marriage. The decision contravened the constitution, civil law, and even sharia law. Why did he do it? Because he can—and no one would dare to stop him. This is just one example of the abuse of women selected from the dozens of cases recorded by the women's project at the Afghanistan Independent Human Rights Commission. Among the others are cases of women brutally beaten by their husbands, of women forced into unsuitable marriage, of death threats and humiliations. Every week, more such cases are added to the list.

To murder your own daughter and call it honour. To give your blameless child to a man knowing she will be sexually assaulted. To send your girl back to her husband when she comes pleading to you with her broken arms and blackened eyes. To shroud her in black garments that absorb the blazing heat, so she will avert the eyes of men who strut about in white robes that deflect the heat. To ask her how she was dressed—was it modest enough?—when the rapist defiled her. To suggest that her loss of chastity is her own fault, that a man can't help himself. These are the norms in the lives of women who are controlled by so-called religious men. While the concept of human rights has entered the lexicon of common discourse, when it comes to the treatment of women and girls and their sexuality, most of the world is silent. It leads one to wonder how we can sell ourselves so cheaply.

This indifference prevails especially in zones of conflict. Women have been brutalized in war at least since Hannibal crossed the Alps. Nowadays, we are told they are victims of the "culture of war," as if that somehow justifies the savagery. Until a few brave women from Bosnia and Rwanda who had been gang-raped by soldiers took their case to The Hague, women were seen as the spoils of war. But even now, in the Democratic Republic of Congo, Afghanistan, and Iraq, and wherever civil strife boils over, women are raped, humiliated, mutilated, kept as sex slaves, and traded as bounty. The level of violence the victims endure is almost unspeakable. Women have been paraded naked in town squares, assaulted vaginally with broken beer bottles, and plucked from villages to be raped repeatedly by soldiers. Some of the victims are no more than eight years old; some are eighty. The world invariably tut-tuts at the barbarity and then looks the other way.

These crimes against women can have long-lasting effects. For example, in Congo, crop production went down 70 percent in 2004 because the planters are women and they had been so traumatized by sexual violence they could not work in the fields. When the workers and caregivers are down, the paralyzing effects of war continue.

Unless these wrongs are addressed, experts claim the debilitating effects of war will continue. A Canadian-led team of women from six continents drafted the Nairobi Declaration to correct the systemic flaws of national truth-and-reconciliation initiatives and existing reparation schemes. They came from Peru, Colombia, Chili, Guatemala, South Africa, Congo, Rwanda, Burundi, Kenya, Sierra Leone, Sudan, India, Belgium, and Canada to write the report that calls for a comprehensive response that courts would be bound by. Led by the Montreal-based Coalition on Women's Human Rights in Conflict Situations, and in collaboration with Rights and Democracy and the Urgent Action Fund, the Nairobi Declaration was written as an instrument to establish basic principles that legislators can use to right the wrongs visited on victims of violence.

Says Ariane Brunet, coordinator of the coalition: "The right to reparation is not only about restitution, compensation, and access to judicial redress, it's about women playing an active role in repairing the social fabric and building a just and equal society."

Hundreds of millions of women have been the victims of sexual violence. From the comfort women defiled by the Japanese army during the Second World War, to the twenty thousand women gang-raped by Serbian belligerents in Bosnia in the early nineties, to the sex slaves of Sierra Leone and Rwanda during the civil wars in those countries, to the female Aboriginal students of the residential schools in Canada, all have been forced to endure the stigma, prejudice, and exclusion that victims of sex crimes have to live with. The consequences affect everyone.

The point of the Nairobi Declaration is this: Condemning the perpetrator is not enough. Jailing the rapist will not restore a girl's dignity. A mere apology will not regain her trust. Reparation is essential to empower women and girls and support them in rebuilding their lives. Without it, as decades of evidence shows, the reconstruction of society will fail.

The Nairobi Declaration has been endorsed by Amnesty International, Human Rights Watch, and dozens of non-governmental organizations, as well as by leaders such as Stephen Lewis, Charlotte Bunch (Centre for Women's Global Leadership), Dr. Sima Samar (Afghanistan Independent Human Rights Commission), jurists such as Claire L'Heureaux Dubé of

Canada and Carmen Argibay of Argentina, scholars such as Janice Stein, and legislators such as Carolyn Bennett, MP.

The challenge the reformers face is to overcome the long history of neglect and failure. The Truth and Justice Commission in Afghanistan has been shelved. The Truth and Reconciliation Commission in South Africa interviewed twenty-two thousand victims, 70 percent of them women, but only sixteen victims of sexual assault were heard in court. In Rwanda, human rights groups threw the government reparation report in the garbage because it ignored the crimes against women. Not a single covenant or convention of the United Nations requires adherents to be fully accountable; they depend instead on the politics of embarrassment. What the authors of the Nairobi Declaration want is a document that is enforceable. If governments accept the declaration and its recommendations, they will have an instrument to right the wrongs for women and girls.

In an unprecedented move, the United States presented a resolution to the United Nations Security Council on June 19, 2008, that called the sexual abuse of women a security issue because it prolongs civil war. Rape was referred to as a weapon of war, a strategy for continued destabilization. Humanitarian Stephen Lewis said, "If all the peacekeepers were women, and the men of a country were under pervasive sexual assault, do you think the women would simply observe the carnage? Not a chance. And they wouldn't need a Security Council Resolution to tell them what to do."

I once asked Louise Arbour, the retired high commissioner of the United Nations Human Rights Commission, why it is that women are always on the short end of the stick when it comes to human rights. In typical Arbour fashion, she replied, "Well, there are lots of theories, but one I prefer—being an optimist— is the desire and need of men to rein in the obvious, natural superior power of women. Women give birth. In a very immediate way, we are immensely powerful. We literally, individually and collectively—if we decided to do that—hold and can control absolutely the future of the planet. That's just speculation. But it's not that we are easily dominated because we are naturally weak. That has no plausibility whatsoever. I don't see any examples of that anywhere. Half of humanity has every reason to be worried because the other half has the upper hand in controlling the future."

ONE THOUSAND YEARS HAVE PASSED since the young poet Rabbia Balkhi was murdered for falling in love with Baktash. Today, the fact that an uneducated girl such as Masooda even knew there was help available at the human rights commission, the very fact that the commission exists, and the gumption that girl demonstrated when she escaped her home to find safety signal a tidal change. It comes down to this: If you can't talk about it, you can't change it. The conversation in Afghanistan has begun.

CHAPTER 2

AFTER THE TALIBAN

Afghanistan can't move ahead without the women.

—Christopher Alexander, Interview with author, June 2006

AFGHANISTAN IS A COUNTRY THAT most Canadians would not have been able to find on a map seven years ago. Now we can't get it out of the news, off our minds, away from our tax dollars. It is creating controversy, challenging patriotism, and putting military men and women at risk. Many Canadians are asking what we think we are doing in quite a primitive country half a world away that seems to be bent on self-destruction.

The simple answer is this: We are helping them to rebuild, as we promised we would in the Bonn Agreement, signed in December 2001. And we are protecting ourselves as we discovered we must in the traumatized aftermath of 9/11.

The rhetoric in the debate needs to address the facts. Firstly, Canada did not invade Afghanistan. The military was invited by the Afghan government to help them establish security. Secondly, Canada is not occupying Afghanistan. The mandate is to secure a village and turn it over to the chiefs and elders. Thirdly, in my experience, you would be hard-pressed to find a single Afghan, apart from the extremists, who wants Canada to leave. Most are terrified they will be abandoned again, as they were at the end of the Cold War. Everyone I have spoken to believes that if the international community pulls out, the fighting will start within twenty-four hours, and Afghanistan will resume its pariah-state status within a week.

Beating the Taliban is not the issue. That would be like saying you can defeat the Mafia. What NATO can do is drive them back into their caves and keep them there until the Afghan government gets on its feet and its national army can be trained to contain them. These are not overnight tasks.

The international community's intervention has produced some excellent results, including an elected government and an independent human rights commission, but six years of combined effort from forty-four countries has not significantly altered the lives of Afghans. This is likely because the investment in Afghanistan has been relatively modest. The number of foreign troops in the country is only one-twenty-fifth the number sent into Kosovo and Bosnia. The aid to Afghanistan is just one-fiftieth the amount invested in the Balkans.

The Taliban insurgency is mostly confined to the four southern provinces of the country. While the other thirty provinces have confounding challenges to overcome—out-of-control warlords and drug barons, brutal tribal customs, and a dysfunctional justice system—it is fair to say, that apart from the insurgency in the south, the rest of the country is marginally better off now that it has an elected government and an infrastructure that is starting to improve. The scale of the problems Afghanistan faces is immense, but they are being addressed.

There is no doubt that the Taliban and al Qaeda are yoked together through their fanaticism and the financial support they receive from Saudi Arabia and Pakistan, among others, but they are not bound to the same ideology. The Taliban, a mostly illiterate band of thugs, want to impose a medieval theocracy on Afghanistan. Al Qaeda, an international network of extremists seeking power, wants to take jihad to the rest of the world. Both groups have hijacked their religion for political opportunism. Both claim to act in the name of God and use misconstrued religious dogma to distort the facts and feed fanaticism. What's more, both confuse modernity with Westernization, so that everything that is seen as modern is denounced as Western. This includes human rights, particularly the rights of women. But human rights aren't Western or Eastern—they're human.

This campaign to make politics sacred isn't new. Historian Charles Allen examines the jihadist movement in his book, *God's Terrorists: The Wahhabi Cult and the Hidden Roots of Modern Jihad*. He traces its beginnings to 1827 in British-controlled India and what the British referred to as the Hindustani or fanatic camp, a secret organization bent on getting rid of the British and restoring the glory days of Islam that had been in decline since about 1200.

That movement remained in precarious existence until 1989, when the Soviet Union withdrew from Afghanistan and world events brought players from Egypt, Saudi Arabia, Pakistan, and Jordan together to foment revolution. With the Cold War over, the international community that had made its presence felt along the border of Afghanistan and Pakistan for ten years took off like a school of minnows, suddenly and altogether, and left a vacuum that was filled by seven rival mujahedeen factions, each seeking control. By 1994, Allen says, three leaders had emerged: Mullah Mohammed Omar, the one-eyed leader of the Taliban; Osama bin Laden, the exiled Saudi who sees violence, oppression, and fear as the path to worldwide jihad and Muslim domination; and Ayman al-Zawahri, a disgraced Egyptian doctor and radical Islamist, who founded al Qaeda. Allen explains how their jihad was bolstered by thirty years of *madrassa* (Islamic religious school) mania in Pakistan, through which boys were trained to become the foot soldiers of the movement.

By the time the Taliban defeated the six other mujahedeen leaders in a fratricidal bloodbath in a post–Soviet Afghanistan, the country had become an outcast among nations, ruled by fanatics and drug barons, and financed by people whose goal was to punish the West for every perceived insult since 1200.

While al Qaeda was well organized and highly financed before 9/11, the same cannot be said of the Taliban, which relied on the ravings of uneducated zealots and used the tried-and-true Afghan method of denouncing the opposition by accusing their opponents of heresy. By the winter of 2001, inadequate finances and internal dissension were taking their toll. There was infighting within the Taliban. Rumours were spreading that Mullah Omar did not have control of his troops and that it was only a matter of time before the Taliban fell.

Then September 11 dawned, and the world was forced to pay attention to a country that had become a terrorist training ground. The invasion of Afghanistan began on October 7, 2001, and the Taliban government was toppled in a matter of weeks. The former U.N. eminence grise, Lakhdar Brahimi, admits it was a mistake to assume the Taliban would acknowledge defeat and disappear. Now, he says, the United Nations should have gone after the Taliban when they were disorganized, disillusioned, scattered, and small. But the United Nations ignored them. The Taliban regrouped with al Qaeda and, by 2005, were posing a major threat not only to the people of Afghanistan, but also to any country that has Western values (such as democracy) and a secular government.

According to Charles Allen, the Afghan people hold one ace with which to beat the Taliban. "History teaches that fundamentalist theocracy does not work because people will simply not put up with it," he writes. By the fall of 2007, NATO, the United Nations, and humanitarian organizations such as the Canadian International Development Agency (CIDA) were coming to the realization that the initial plan simply had not worked well enough. They came to the conclusion—five years after the fact—that this is not a post-conflict country; it is war-devastated in ways the international community hasn't seen for sixty years. Today, *change* is the operative word, and revised policies are now at work.

NATO

The answer to two questions will decide the outcome of the insurgency. Firstly, will Afghan villagers put up with the fanatics? And secondly, will the Afghan government build a functioning democracy in time? The task of the Canadian military is to rid Kandahar province of Taliban forces and ease the people into democratic rule. Best known as peacekeepers, the Canadians have been assigned the task of turning around the *Titanic* that Afghanistan has become. But the cost is mighty. Ninety-three Canadian soldiers dead at the time of writing (in the summer of 2008), $2 billion spent in military operations, and $100 million per year pledged until 2011. As a result, hard questions were asked about whether Canadian troops ought to be in Afghanistan in the first place or whether NATO should just let the Afghans fight it out among themselves. The hue and cry was spurred partly by compassion for the men and women who serve in Canada's armed forces and partly by the bizarre silence surrounding the government of Prime Minister Stephen Harper. Put another way, there was an extraordinary reluctance on the part of the government to share information with the citizens of Canada, a fact that was highlighted by the report of the Independent Panel on Canada's Future Role in Afghanistan, best known as the Manley report after its chairman, former Liberal cabinet minister, John Manley. Manley wrote:

> The panel learned early that we must be careful to define our expectations for success. Afghanistan is a deeply divided tribal society. It has been wracked by decades of war and is one of the poorest countries on earth. There should be no thought that after five or even ten years of western military presence and aid, Afghanistan will resemble Europe or North America. But we came to the conviction that with patience, commitment, financial and other forms of assistance, there is a reasonable prospect that its people will be able to live together in relative peace and security, while living standards slowly improve.

In his conclusion, he added: "We like to talk about Canada's role in the world. Well, we have a meaningful one in Afghanistan. As our report states, it should not be faint-hearted, nor should it be open-ended. Above all, we must not abandon it prematurely."

Canada has roughly twenty-three hundred soldiers working under NATO's command in the Kandahar region. One of those killed while serving in 2006 was Captain Nichola Goddard, a courageous woman who was eulogized by her father, Tim Goddard, a professor who teaches post-conflict studies at the University of Calgary. To a hushed congregation and an equally rapt television audience, Professor Goddard recounted a conversation he had had with Nichola. He had told her that education was the only solution for Afghanistan. Nichola agreed but explained that without security, education was impossible. During the four months she had served in

Afghanistan, dozens of girls' schools were fire-bombed, teachers were murdered, and parents were warned in night letters not to send their girls to school. Goddard quoted his daughter as saying, "I do what I do so you can do what you do."

THE UNITED NATIONS

The mood in Afghanistan today is tense, the equivalent of waiting for a summer storm. Threatening clouds are building on the horizon; rumblings of discontent can be heard above the clamour of everyday life. Canadian wunderkind Christopher Alexander, the deputy special representative of the United Nations, is at the centre of the brewing tempest. Named one of Canada's Top Forty Under Forty (an award that recognizes business and community leadership) in 2006, the thirty-nine-year-old Alexander is the articulate mandarin charged with the military, governance, and human rights files in Afghanistan. His job is to stay in touch with the principal players and set an agenda everyone can live with. It is a tricky assignment given the characters he has to contend with: President Hamid Karzai in his Persian lamb cap and tribal cape; the macho NATO generals; the Canadian soldiers who have the toughest job and the most dangerous assignment; and the swaggering Americans who are the biggest donors with the most powerful military forces. While one general boasts that they're winning the war against the insurgency, Alexander puts it another way: "We aren't losing." The key paradox of this new-millennium conflict is that the Taliban won't quit, and yet they can't possibly win. On one topic, Alexander is adamant: "Without the success of women, there's no success for Afghanistan."

In June 2006, his assessment was ominous. The Taliban insurgency in the south was growing increasingly bold. The poppy harvest had racked up a record U.S.$8 billion. The

United Nations program to disband the warlords' illegally armed militias had stalled. "Failure is definitely an option," Alexander said at the time. "This is a fragile state." But he scoffed at the notion that recent events have made Afghanistan comparable to Iraq. "Those who say that simply haven't read enough history." And the usually affable diplomat was affronted by the suggestion that nation building is beyond Afghans. "That is, quite frankly, not the case. We need to dispense with these insulting assumptions." He was confident that if the international community stays the course, and does what is necessary to set conditions for peace, "it will emerge, and economic growth will be spectacular by the standards of the last half century."

Stickhandling his way through the rogues, citizens, and representatives of the international community is Alexander's forte. "Despite what you see on TV, things are happening here, there is an appetite for change, and change is possible. Afghans have come to that conclusion after trying so many other options, most of them violent."

In 2008, when I asked him why it was taking so long to knock off a ragtag collection of twenty-something thugs who had dragged the country into the dark ages in the mid-nineties, he said, "We need a much bigger footprint in Afghanistan than we thought we needed at the beginning." He admits that two of the critical assessments made at the beginning turned out to be wrong. "It was thought that development and reconstruction would be automatic, and that small investments would have big payoffs and put the country back on its feet. But we began to realize that the country was war-devastated by thirty years of continuous conflict to an extent we had not considered. The infrastructure, the irrigation systems, power lines, agriculture, human capital—everything was degraded to a shocking degree." The second challenge was state building— literally bringing Afghans together in one set of institutions that had legitimacy. "The Bonn process was successful in restoring legitimacy, but didn't guarantee the systems would work." For the most part, they didn't work. While Alexander won't name names, everyone else invariably points to the corruption in the Ministry of the Interior, as well as the ministries dealing with transportation, power, and water.

At the outset, the ministries were controlled by various mujahedeen leaders who refused to give them up. The charges of corruption started flowing as early as 2002. It was said that jihadi figures were running the ministries and the police department because of who they knew or what they did during the conflict. Literally hundreds of men were said to be getting non-merit-based appointments. Everyone knew there were police officers who were engaged in criminal activity or drug trading, or who were under the influence of those who controlled organized crime and opium production. For example, the Ministry of the Interior (meaning the police) was made up essentially of factional militias; most posts were given to Northern Alliance soldiers who switched their army gear for police uniforms and reported to Minister Qanooni, a warlord. The same was true of the Ministry of Defence until reforms were begun in 2003. Alexander confirms the allegations and says, "If they were told to reform at that stage, they would simply have said 'no.' Now the old commanders don't have the same access to heavy weapons. The National Security Force has about one hundred and forty thousand on the payroll. They weren't there as recently as 2004."

But the Taliban weren't ready in 2004 either. Now they are better organized, have access to technology, and easily make contact anywhere in the world via conference calls. Alexander says he can name one hundred Taliban commanders who strut around the streets of Quetta, Pakistan, with impunity and float in and out of Afghanistan at will. "Part of this story is about suicide bombs and improvised explosive devices, but part of it is a story of safe havens and training camps across the border," he says.

It is also about the way the story is told. He recounts a report about twenty Afghan children who were killed by NATO forces when a village in Kandahar province was bombed. The story made headlines around the world. A NATO investigation conducted in the subsequent days discovered that no children had been killed. The Taliban had written the report within an hour of the bombing and sent it by email to the Middle East–based news agency Al Jazeera, which had no way of verifying the facts but broadcast the report anyway. It took another ten days before the NATO investigation was checked, rechecked, authorized, and finally released to the media. It played on the back pages of newspapers, where it would be seen by only a fraction of the public that read the original story. The point is that the Taliban were winning the public relations war because NATO did not have the means, or the rapid-response capability, to get its own story out. After that incident, NATO decided to employ the necessary resources to get their version of the incidents to the media as quickly as the reports sent by the insurgents.

The confounding reality is that Afghans have a history of staring down their enemies, including the Russians and the British before them (not to mention Alexander the Great, Darius the First, and Genghis Khan). They all entered Afghanistan anticipating an easy conquest and left with their tails barely intact. There is an expression people here still use when they're putting their kids to bed: "Stay under your covers or the British will get you." The historical baggage remains even though there are eight thousand British troops in Helmand province today who are fighting on the side of the government. Although the Taliban command is operating from outside the border, they are Pashtun brothers who have considerable, maybe even increasing, support inside the country. This is one reason why some critics claim the efforts of the international community are doomed to failure.

Alexander begs to differ. "This chapter in the brutal, colourful history of this country is different." And he knows what he is talking about. He spent six years in Russia, the last three in the number-two post at the Canadian Embassy in Moscow. He is fluent in Russian (as well as French and German) and fascinated by the former Soviet Union. He became interested in Afghanistan when he was studying the conflicts in the Caucuses and Central Asia. "The defining showdown of the twentieth century was the confrontation between the Warsaw Pact and those who favour free markets and democracy," he says. "The conflict here in Afghanistan was the final and most violent instalment in that whole story. You can only understand why the Soviet Union is no longer, and Russia has arisen from its ruins, by understanding the history of Afghanistan."

He points out that the population gave a massive vote of confidence to the government in the presidential election. "People who really know the ebb and flow here say confidence has not been withdrawn from the government. People want peace and know they can only get it through these institutions."

That said, if you were to stop one hundred people at the bazaar in Kabul and ask them how they think the country is faring, 80 percent would say, "It's getting worse, the police are corrupt, I don't trust the government, and my life is not getting better despite the promises made to me." Alexander blames this kind of response on fear of the Taliban agenda; even though it was the losing side of the civil war, there is widespread anxiety that the Taliban will return. "The Taliban are about revenge. They never accepted defeat. They're about drugs; their operations are financed by drug barons. What's more, their values have been rejected by Afghans and the international community at every turn. Isolationism—Afghanistan for Afghans—and the reductionist interpretation of Islam is an exclusivist vision of how this country should live. People don't want it, but it's sold to them down the barrel of a gun."

The fragility of the state was tested on May 29, 2006, when Kabul erupted in violence after an American military vehicle careened out of control, killing several bystanders. Rumours swept through the city that U.S. forces were killing Afghans. People took to the streets, among them opportunists and criminals who looted stores, trashed the offices of non-governmental organizations (NGOs), and burned buildings. The police were cowed into paralysis.

The postscript of the Kabul riot is that Karzai is not in control. He is jokingly referred to in some circles as the president of Kabul. Alexander bristles at the suggestion that the United States is running the show. "If you're implying that this is a puppet state run by Americans, that's just not true. Karzai gets a lot of advice, and extreme lobbying that's not always wholesome, from groups within the country as well as the international community, but when the cabinet meets or the parliament is in session, the U.S. is not there. It simply can't work that way in Afghanistan."

There is still discontent and civil unrest in Kabul today. Crime is a bigger problem than terrorism, due to the corrupt, poorly equipped police, the drug trade, and poverty. The situation is compounded by a population that has exploded from seven hundred and fifty thousand to three million. The power supply can cope with only a third of that number, so the electricity is an on-again, off-again nuisance that won't be repaired until 2009. Housing stock is totally unequal to the load. There is high unemployment and there are not enough spaces in the universities. Alexander isolates a single factor that adds up to more than the sum of all the other parts. "Half the population now is under the age of fifteen," he says. "Their hopes and expectations are high, but their disappointment and alienation are acute. They perceive the country to be poorly run by the government or by the international partners."

This is not just a military campaign; the fate of a country is at stake, he says. "Our objective isn't to simply invest well-equipped forces under strong leadership into the eye of the storm that is Kandahar. It's to support a transition from war to long-lasting peace. It's not there yet, but it's within reach if countries like Canada remain. The consequences of leaving the job unfinished would be catastrophic."

He has high praise for Canada. "One thing Canada has done particularly well is to make interventions that are time-sensitive." For example, the electoral process: when people weren't even talking about when elections would happen, Canada launched voter registration projects. It was the first country to put money into the containment of heavy weapons and to start thinking about how ammunition should be dealt with. "These were very early investments that paid off. The micro-finance projects in villages across the country are hugely successful. Canada was the one to say, 'we'll take Kandahar,' when our key allies were focused in Iraq." He says, "Those are leadership positions that help intrinsically to make a difference, but also to set the stage for what others might do."

His third mandate—human rights—is the one that makes him pause and take a deep breath. "This is a tough one," he says. "Human rights abuses were catastrophic during the Taliban [period], particularly for women. There's a huge legacy of repression and disenfranchisement that has to be overcome. This is a country that is in desperate need of reform." Alexander says the single biggest achievement in Afghanistan has been the human rights commission. Under the leadership of Dr. Samar, the AIHRC took on the most intractable file in the country: the rights of women and girls. That meant tackling civil, tribal, and sharia law and a country-wide and millennium-old conviction that women are second class and not part of civil society. Says Samar: "It was Christopher Alexander, when he was Canadian Ambassador, who helped push the government to make our work happen." She makes it clear that she wants nothing less than reform. Alexander supports her, but adds, "We may never in our lifetime see Afghans meeting international standards of human rights for women."

While the road is tortuous, women are playing a growing role in civil society, and even Karzai recognizes their demands for change. On International Women's Day, March 8, 2008, his message to Afghans was a positive one for women: "I call on all religious leaders, tribal elders, and particularly men: Stop forcing your underaged girls to marry, stop marrying them to old men." There are indications that men, mullahs, and elders are starting to listen.

But listening and acting on change aren't always compatible in a country that is still extremely traumatized. The majority of people here have grown up with war. Many have lost family members to rocket attacks or as "collateral damage" in military engagements. Two million people died in the last thirty years of conflict. That is one in ten Afghans. There is anxiety at every level of society and the legacy of that trauma can't be underestimated. Overcoming it and healing it is a long process. Afghans are suspicious of one another and everyone else. They criticize one another in a way that is practically ritualistic, as if it were a national sport. You could be excused for believing the country is about to tear itself apart.

"There are fault lines and disconnects and different versions of the country," says Alexander, "but they watch the same media, complain about the same government, meet together in the same parliament—sometimes for better or for worse. There are ways that Afghans are coming together that are unprecedented. I don't see the country pulling itself apart. There's a sense of stubborn resilience now—people think there is a chance."

Despite the rising insecurity, there is a feeling that the centre is holding and taking on weight—institutional weight. "I'm not guaranteeing success, but there is an asset base that Afghans want to protect. The alternative is the Taliban, a compromise that is really unacceptable to Afghans. While no one is negotiating with Omar, who is only as good as his welcome in Pakistan—there would be huge political issues and barriers to that—but there are contacts with lower-level [Taliban] people—even with us at the U.N. from people saying, 'Help us get out of this cycle of violence, we don't want to fight any more.' If they're willing to live under the constitution, within the laws, and don't have blood on their hands, they're welcome. Some have come, but the trickle needs to turn into a larger flow."

The insurgency is now fighting on two fronts, in Pakistan as well as Afghanistan. Although that doesn't aid the peace process, it does create a space for Afghanistan to pull itself together because the Taliban now have to split their efforts between the two countries and the institutions they face in Afghanistan are stronger. "I feel more confident now because there's a conceptual clarity—it's exposed. People see where the groups are, who they are, what their agenda is, and how they are operating. Two years ago we didn't know this," says Alexander.

The strongest new kid on the institutional block is the Directorate of Local Governance. Created on August 30, 2007, and led by reformist Jalali Popal, it is tasked with the management of the provincial governors and district managers, and it reports directly to the president. This is seen as a sea change in Afghanistan, as the Ministry of the Interior (a.k.a. the police) has historically been in charge of governance. The new institutional arrangement bypasses the notorious corruption of several ministries.

The year 2007 was so volatile that it shocked the players at the United Nations, as well as the Afghan government, into action. More than seven thousand people were killed in terrorist attacks, and 140 suicide bombers blew up themselves and their surroundings. The new year was hardly started when, on January 14, the terrorists struck the Serena Hotel with stunning efficiency. The swanky hotel had been celebrated as a sign of a prosperous new beginning for Afghanistan. It was to have been a modern and safe haven to show off to visitors. But the double suicide bombing and subsequent murder of foreigners sent the population into a paroxysm of fear. Many felt that if it can happen at the Serena, it can happen anywhere. "This attack had a huge impact," said Alexander. "But these are terrorists. If they put their minds to it, they can make any place unsafe."

The good news is that the International Assistance Force in Afghanistan (ISAF) doubled its numbers in 2007, and the amount of aid delivered through the budget almost tripled. Afghan revenues from national businesses met their targets and are growing at a rate of 30 to 40 percent a year. But there still aren't enough troops or enough money to get the job done.

CIDA

In April 2007, the Canadian International Development Agency created an Afghanistan task force, a mini-CIDA, even taking the trouble to house the eighty-member team in a separate building. Like other aid organizations, CIDA realized that insecurity in Afghanistan means insecurity at home—in Montreal, Vancouver, and Toronto. "Afghanistan is a globalized platform for terrorism, an opium economy with trans-border and cross-border trafficking," says Stephen Wallace, vice-president of the new task force.

Gender is one of the three pillars in CIDA's unprecedented new approach. (The other two are governance and growth). The underlying motivation for it rests on recognition of Afghanistan's dire position on a number of international rankings. The country is second lowest on the world development index (Niger is at the bottom). Eighty-seven percent of women and 80 percent of men are illiterate. Maternal mortality is astronomically high, even higher than it was two hundred years ago. Infant mortality is similarly high. The new thinking is that the country is so fragile, it requires a specific initiative.

CIDA now is spending close to $300 million a year on Afghanistan alone, which makes Canada one of the country's top five donors. The task force also calls for measurable results.

While the deteriorating situation in Afghanistan demanded this kind of innovative thinking, it may also have been sparked by criticism of CIDA's work. The Senlis Council, a think tank that monitors the failures in Afghanistan, has singled out CIDA for especially stinging rebukes. The council charged, for example, that CIDA was not delivering aid in the southern provinces. In its defence, Ellen Wright, senior adviser to the vice-president of the task force, argues that there's a reason their work is not high-profile, saying, "You can't wave a Canadian flag over the work we're doing or the project will be targeted by terrorists." This is a fair point, but why is it that families caught in the insurgency don't have enough food? Surely the aid organization can find a way to deliver it, even if they have to drop it in bundles from planes? Aly-Khan Rajani, senior adviser to the task force, explains, "You can't drop food out of the sky or you'll have a situation like we had in Somalia, when food distribution was controlled by warlords and wound up on the black market." What is working, brilliantly some say, is a work-for-food or food-for-literacy program. Local men are hired to repair village infrastructure and are paid with food. Women who have been denied education by their husbands are encouraged to attend literacy classes and are rewarded with food.

CIDA has also been criticized for the conditions at the Miwais Hospital in Kandahar, even though that mandate is in the hands of the Red Crescent (the Muslim version of the Red Cross). A spokesperson for CIDA replies that there is much that is right about the hospital. An independent study confirmed that medications are being administered correctly, intravenous tubes are functioning properly, prescriptions are monitored suitably, and pharmaceuticals are stored adequately. But anyone who has been in the hospital would agree that the place could use more beds, a coat of paint, some clean linen, and a thorough scrubbing. CIDA argues that if these improvements were made by a Canadian agency, the hospital would be targeted for attack. Not everyone agrees. Norine MacDonald, president and founder of the Senlis Council, accuses CIDA of bad management: "They've never been able to point me to a location I can check—a food distribution project or evidence of medical equipment they've delivered." Her criticism is often echoed by journalists who claim they can't get access to CIDA programs because the Harper government keeps tight control over information. Requests for interviews go unanswered; field visits often are denied.

In the rest of the country, CIDA has received high praise for its micro-credit programs—more than seven hundred thousand of them. Sixty percent of the loans go to households headed by women. The loans are being repaid on time, and the initiative is considered a runaway success. CIDA also runs a program that trains women to be police officers. In the last year, Afghanistan has seen a 22 percent decline in mortality rates in children under five. The number of women giving birth in the presence of midwives or trained attendants has quadrupled. CIDA is also the biggest donor ($80 million a year) in land-mine clearance. They claim the casualty rate for people stepping on land mines has dropped from four to two a day, and they plan to see it drop to one a day by 2010.

But the most innovative of CIDA's programs is the establishment of community development councils: men and women sitting together to decide the direction the village will take. This is unheard of in Afghanistan and, by all accounts, it is changing local reality. The program is time-intensive and requires enormous patience on the part of advisers to bring people around to a new way of thinking, but even the president of Afghanistan is presenting these councils as the way forward.

"In Afghanistan, it's about taking the best Canada has to offer, mobilizing it, and focusing it on a problem," says Wallace. "There have been some hard-won lessons: You can't do development without security and you can't do security without development."

IT WOULD BE EASY TO DISMISS the criticism of the treatment of women in Afghanistan as the product of Western cultural assumptions. But it wouldn't be correct. The problem isn't Westernization, it is modernization, according to Nasrine Gross, founder of the Roqia Center for Rights, Studies, and Education in Kabul. "Afghanistan has to come up to speed with modernity or it will die of obsolescence," she says. Her focus is on women's rights because "it is the ingredient for success in Afghanistan. For a very long time, the situation of women has been used to hold us back. It is all because of a lack of understanding and [a lack of] acceptance of modernity."

Gross is not afraid of change. "Change leads to development, literacy, and a mobile society. In Afghanistan this is invariably referred to as the 'demon Westernization' when in fact it's modernization." She feels that women have been the primary victims of this thinking. She says that three hundred years ago the most advanced and powerful countries in the world— England, France, and the states that made up the Ottoman Empire—did not have women in parliament, in business, in careers, or anyplace in the public sphere. Now they do. "No society can move forward, let alone advance, without the full participation of women. In Afghanistan the treatment of women is used as a barrier against modernity." She cites clothing as an example. "Look at history: At the end of the nineteenth century, men and women were wearing what Afghans wear today—baggy body-covering clothing. As other countries moved from an agrarian society to an industrial society, from working in fields to sitting behind a desk, from horse-and-buggy to railways and planes, the people adjusted. Some people here say that if Afghans change [their habits or their dress], they're contributing to a loss of identity and are Westernizing. They aren't; they're modernizing. It's not about the West wanting Afghanistan to Westernize; it's about wanting Afghans to modernize."

Her comments remind me of a conversation I had with a Taliban commander a decade ago. He was telling me not to take photos because they are un-Islamic. He also said, "Your yellow hair must be fully covered, and you're not to smile, and don't say hello with your hand [shake hands]," all while he was surfing the internet.

Gross remembers that when she was a child in Afghanistan fifty years ago, a group of men was assigned to go through the village in the morning calling, "*Naqara!*" This was the village wake-up call, meaning, "Wake up, everyone!" "Now that we use alarm clocks," she says, "it doesn't mean we are less Afghan or less Muslim. There is only one Quran, but it is so deep, it can be interpreted for today."

This anti-modern attitude was attacked during the Soviet era when the secular Russians denounced, and poked fun at, the pious and primitive ways of Afghans. The mujahedeen forces seized on this threat to their culture and religion, accusing the invaders of stripping Afghans of their identity. When the Soviets withdrew, leaving the mujahedeen factions engaged in an internecine battle, they vied with one another to proclaim their greater devotion to Afghan religion and culture in order to gain the support of the people. When the Taliban, with their suffocating interpretation of both religion and culture triumphed, they also inherited the destroyed infrastructure of the country. President Karzai, left with the ruins, treads a fine line between the need to modernize and accusations of being un-Islamic.

Nasrine Gross explains that every society has two states: One is the state of being, the other the state of becoming. "Afghanistan is in a constant state of being, never becoming." Her reasoning is that nobody dares to apply the definition of modernity to the country today. Given the bustling airport, the computers on every government desk, the cellphones and iPods carried by both urban and rural dwellers, the duplicity of leaders who condemn Westernization for Afghanistan's problems approaches the ridiculous.

While many observers claim the anti-Western rhetoric is about controlling the population and diverting attention from the root causes of their troubles, Gross blames it on the lack of education and experience. "Most adult Afghans have never been to school. They don't have electricity. Many have never watched television or gone to a movie. When I was growing up, women were kept inside. I couldn't go to my friend's house after school or during holidays. It just wasn't done. When you are raised with so much restriction, you don't learn decision-making, you aren't confronted with choice. It will take a least a generation—twenty-five years—to change this thinking."

IN THE WINTER OF 2008, when I left Canada to return to Afghanistan, I had mixed messages on my mind. There were the grumbling echoes of protestors who felt Canada ought to leave immediately; the heartfelt concerns of women's organizations that worried about setbacks; and my own optimistic thoughts about finding girls such as Lima, and women such as Sharifa, who had shaped my view of the women of Afghanistan on my previous journeys.

The first thing I noticed when I was driving into the city from the Kabul airport was that the usually chaotic traffic was slightly tamed. The garbage that had been piling up, sometimes in heaps that were several metres high, had mostly been collected. The stinking, overflowing latrines on the streets of Kabul were being cleared out by teams of men dressed in bright orange overalls, which made me ask if they were prisoners. (I was assured they worked for the government—and were glad to have a paying job.) The houses on the mountainsides that border Kabul had been reduced to rubble in the civil war, and had remained that way for year after frustrating year. Now they had been rebuilt, and when the power was on—which is still hit and miss—the warm glow of lights shone from their newly installed windows. What's more, the street lights were working. It was the first time I had seen street lights in Kabul. A woman who runs an NGO reminded me that the last time I saw her she had to carry the organization's entire payroll in her purse, and was terrified that it would be stolen. Now she puts the money in an account in the newly opened bank and writes cheques for the staff.

Change has also come to some of the villages in far-flung districts of Panjshir, the Shomali Plains, Bamiyan, the central highlands, Herat, and Mazar-e Sharif, although not to the same degree.

But there's also a miasma of fear that permeates every corner of this land. People are scared to death—that they will be caught in the next suicide bomb, that an IED will be detonated as they drive by, that their girls will be harmed on the way to school, that their teachers will be beheaded for teaching children to read and write, that the international community will abandon them again.

The problems throughout the country are immense. In the absence of a clear win over the Taliban, warlords who have enjoyed immunity from prosecution, and have even occupied cabinet posts in President Karzai's government, are bolstering their militias, as though standing by for a power grab in case the government collapses. Communiqués are regularly issued from the office of one member of parliament or another proposing stupefying new laws, such as banning the hugely popular Indian soap operas Afghans watch on television or forbidding women from speaking to men outside their homes. Never mind that they can catch the soaps on their computers or that conversation between men and women is required at the workplace. So fear and foolishness both feature in Afghan life. In addition, there is widespread discontent among people who were promised a better life with the arrival of the international community.

Says Sima Samar of the AIHRC: "Human security is a basic requirement for everything else." She wants war crimes—many of them committed by warlords—prosecuted. In 2002, President Karzai suggested that a future government should establish a truth commission to "ensure that the people will have justice." Two years later, the AIHRC filed their report, "A Call for Justice," and a five-step action plan that would address the wrongs of the past. It collected dust on the president's desk for two years. Now, Samar acknowledges that it won't be released mostly because the judiciary in the country is dysfunctional and could not begin to act on war crimes. Furthermore, President Karzai has declared an amnesty. Samar is irked by the suppression of the report, which she sees as another delay on the journey to full accountability. She also resents the slow pace of change, the continued corruption at every level of government, and admits that the rights of women and girls are only marginally better than they were in the past. "Accountability, justice, and security must work together for peace," she says. Acutely aware of the difficult and dangerous role Canada is playing, she says, "Stability here will help security throughout the world. Security here means law enforcement and a decrease in training camps for terrorists, maybe even a decrease in poppy growing. These are problems for everyone in the world, not specifically Afghans." She also sees Canada as the country that can pull off this confounding mission. "Canada doesn't have ambition to control, or rule, or occupy another country. The international community knows that. So do Afghans." And she adds in an ominous warning: "If Afghanistan is not safe, Canada is not safe."

Afghanistan is at a very delicate place in its history. Much has been accomplished, but much more is still to be done. The terrorists are determined to grab the country back. The international community needs to be equally determined to thwart them.

For me, success can be measured by the lives of women and girls: their opportunities for education, their participation in civil society, their treatment by the judiciary. They are the canaries in the mine that is Afghanistan.

CHAPTER 3

THE DAUGHTERS OF AFGHANISTAN

Feminism has fought no wars. It has killed no
opponents. It has set up no concentration camps,
starved no enemies, practised no cruelties. Its battles
have been for education, for the vote, for better
working conditions, for safety on the streets, for child
care, for social welfare, for rape crisis centres, women's
refuges, reforms in the law.

—Dale Spender, *For the Record: The Making
and Meaning of Feminist Knowledge* (1985)

LIKE FLOWERS, THEY BURST OUT OF THEIR CASINGS as soon as they
dared in the promising spring of 2002, gutsy women with the
skills and ambition to lead their sisters out of the enforced
dormancy they had endured for five long years. Some came
back from self-imposed exile in India, Canada, and the United
States; others from refugee camps in Pakistan and Iran; and the

rest from the stifling confines of their own Afghan homes. The women who had dared to challenge the Taliban from behind a veil doffed their burkas and sallied forth to stake a claim for women. While masons were slapping cement on the new Ministry of Women's Affairs building, teachers went back to school, midwives went back to work, human rights activists strode into women's centres, and women found their way to the offices from which they had been banished. When the media started reporting again, some of the bylines in the newspapers, the faces of TV presenters, and the voices of radio broadcasters belonged to women.

Not that all was smooth sailing. While the constitution was being written in 2004, and the first-ever national election was being staged in 2005, there were complications and complaints: The wrong people had found their way into the transitional government. International aid wasn't arriving fast enough. The Afghan habit of criticizing one another, pulling down those who rise, was reasserting itself. Nevertheless, the country was taking tentative steps towards nation building.

After the 2005 election, it was clear that the ever-stronger Taliban insurgency, now joined by discontents from across the country and from Pakistan, was trying to crush not only the democratically elected government, but also the shiny new concept of women's rights. Stories of extremists assassinating female journalists, threatening women members of parliament with death, bombing girls' schools, and beheading teachers made disturbing headlines. What's more, with the blessing of President Karzai, the vice-and-virtue police who had whipped women for showing an ankle under a burka, beaten them for not covering a hand while paying for groceries, and chopped off one girl's fingertips for wearing nail polish was re-established. It felt like another siege could begin.

Despite the turmoil, the tender shoots of a women's movement were starting to emerge. They turned up in every province and at all the national meetings. Some of these activist women were sent in delegations to international meetings where women's issues, theirs included, were discussed. They tapped into the solidarity of sisterhood and brought their deliberations home. Thousands of smart, courageous women were risking the ire of their conservative families, if not their lives, to pave the way forward for women. They included Jamila Afghani, who started an education centre in Kabul; Farida Nekzad, who became the editor-in-chief of a countrywide news agency; and Najia Haneefi, a human rights activist from Mazar-e Sharif. Connected by their bold determination to emancipate women and girls in the face of innumerable obstacles in a country where women's rights barely exist, these thirty-something women are the daughters of the new Afghanistan.

JAMILA AFGHANI, THIRTY-FOUR, is a woman who brings new meaning to the phrase *against all odds*. She was stricken with polio when she was one and walks with one leg in a brace. Untreated scoliosis means she struggles with constant back pain. As if this were not enough to bear, she was shot in the head by the Soviets as a fourteen-year-old and still suffers from pain in her left ear. But it was actually a benign incident that shaped her life. "When I was a child, I couldn't move anywhere unless someone carried me, so I sat all day on the floor, listening to the women who came to visit my mother. They talked about the violence in their homes, the beatings, the restrictions that forbade them from visiting family members. And they would always look at me and pity my mother. They'd say, 'Poor you, Jamila cannot walk. She'll be a burden to you, she will never marry.' I was only about eight years old, but I vowed that one day I would not be a burden, and in fact I'd take their burden away myself." Despite the extraordinary odds, Jamila, a devout woman who covers her head and wears layers of ankle-length, conservative clothing, is leading a movement to enfranchise women at the Noor Education Centre.

She was born in Ghazni in the central highlands of Afghanistan, moved with her family to Kabul as a baby, and went to school in the capital city until grade eight. Then the Soviet Union occupied the country and the family, realizing that her father would be targeted by the invaders, made the decision to beat a quick retreat to Pakistan. On the day they were to leave, her father, a well-known and successful business-man, was arrested by Soviet soldiers and sent to jail. He was released four months later, but the family was being watched, which meant their escape had to be postponed for another year. Even then, the road to Pakistan was blocked, so they went to India before eventually finding their way to Pakistan and settling in Peshawar, a northern city near the eastern border with Afghanistan. It was in this hotbed of religious and cultural conservatism that Jamila began a journey that would ultimately estrange her from her family and put her on the front line of the women's war against stifling societal rules, the rules kept them behind purdah walls, as servants to men.

She graduated from high school, went on to Peshawar University, and graduated with a degree in political science and Islamic education. Then she began working towards a master's degree in international relations and continued her study of Islamic education in private. "My studies opened my eyes about what was going on in my family. They were using religion to punish women." Now she saw in a different light the stories the women had told in her childhood home. She knew she had to take action. "I wanted to become a lawyer, and stand in court to fight for women, but my brothers wouldn't let me do that." Instead, after completing her master's degree, she went to work for the Afghan Women's Network in Peshawar. Two months after 9/11, she returned to Kabul. She had been travelling back and forth to Afghanistan during the Taliban regime, to visit the schools the network supported, so she was acutely aware of the size of the problem the women and girls were facing. "I knew this was the time to begin my work." She started small. A group of eight women—all friends—came together to collect medicine and money for women whose situation was desperate. "But eventually I saw this as a form of begging. What these women needed was education, wellness, and psycho-social therapy to alter their lives." So they opened the Noor Education Center, taking the name from *noor*, which means "light." The funding for the program comes from CW4WAfghan. "I love those women," she says. "They are supporting the category of women that really need help here." She describes some donors as "show-offs" because they show up and take off. The Canadians are different, she says. "The Canadian women have become friends and colleagues, they network for us and stay with us for the long term." Her quarrel with other funders is that they want to dictate terms to her. They demand the money be spent in certain ways that Jamila knows aren't effective. "It's not always beneficial to the women we serve." Some say she can't put boys in the same classes as girls, but she sees that as a missed opportunity. "There's a small window open to us now; what they are suggesting would shut it down. We're going to live with our people forever; the foreign donors will be gone in a few years. We don't consider the needs of the people enough; we tend to only consider the happiness of the donor."

Says Janice Eisenhauer of CW4WAfghan: "We first learned about the work of the Noor Education Centre in mid-2003 and gave our first grant to them six months later." They were drawn to the grassroots, volunteer element of the work and wanted to be part of the early funding because they felt it was crucial for a youth-focused organization to get off the ground. As well, the goals and objectives of the education program were aligned with CW4WAfghan's focus on women and girls. "There was a refreshing sense and awareness of the importance of community about their programming, and unique and innovative methods to involve youth and volunteers, and engage parents in the learning process as well," says Eisenhauer. "They needed to change attitudes about the importance of education and that's obviously happening."

The library is the hub of the place. Colourful, clean, and stacked with a variety of books on history and Islam, as well as storybooks, primary readers, novels in both Dari (one of the two official languages in Afghanistan, the other is Pashto) and English. The library also has computers, educational toys, puzzles, and games. It is more like a community resource centre than a library, as it also offers literacy and English-as-a-second-language classes, skills-development workshops, community and maternal health classes, and operates a mobile library. The library encourages young people to write articles for a newsletter, *Baz Tab e Noor* (reflection of light), and has an internet café that is a welcome resource for women and youth throughout the region. "It's an interactive process," says Eisenhauer, "that ensures the participants take ownership, and that the success of the library depends on their efforts. This kind of community work is the foundation of peace-building in Afghanistan."

This group of eight women started with a grant of $10,000. To date the Noor Education Centre has received $163,205 from Canadian women.

Jamila and I sit with the ubiquitous green tea and almonds while she describes the situation she faced when the centre first opened. "The women were in terrible condition. They had no homes, no jobs, were suffering post-war trauma, domestic violence, and harassment," she says. Not everyone agreed with Jamila's plans to emancipate the women, but she's as wily as those who would shut her down. The library, for example, was used at the beginning as a magnet to draw women to the centre. "At first the women were too afraid to come. They feared the Taliban weren't really gone, so the women would send their sons to our library to get books. When I realized it was mostly boys coming to the centre, I told them for every five girls they brought with them, they'd get a present. Soon enough we had lots of girls." But more than that, she started discussion groups, an opportunity for the women to share their stories—which was therapy in itself—and find out what else they needed in their lives. "These were the seeds that started the program." The topic they talked about most was the violence they all experienced at home, so Jamila went to the human rights commission and got a manual for conflict resolution and a trainer to talk to the groups.

Jamila knows about conflict. A single mother of five adopted children (three because her sister-in-law died, and her brother didn't want the kids when he found a new wife; and two others because a woman was left with eight daughters and couldn't take care of all of them), she hired a widow who badly needed work to care for the kids while she went to her office. Her decision sent shock waves through her family, which was already furious because of her insistence on being a career woman.

She pours another cup of tea, adjusts her scarf on this blisteringly hot June day in 2006, and tells me she added fuel to the family fire a week ago when she announced her engagement to—horrors!—a man of her choice and now must suffer the wrath of her mother and father as well as her siblings. "They say: 'We knew it would happen. We said she should not leave the house, go to school, become a working woman. Now look at what has happened! She's selecting someone for herself.'" Her family called her a whore and a prostitute when she decided to go to university in Peshawar. Now that she's engaged to a man they didn't choose, they are barely speaking to her. "They have never spoken of my career or my accomplishments, and always tried to restrict my movements. 'Don't go here!'

'Never go there!' They wanted me to marry and become a housekeeper, but my life is more than that. I wanted a man who could understand me, who knew I had a soul, someone with a spiritual personality." The man she plans to marry, Fazal Dhani Kakr, was her teacher in Peshawar. He sent a proposal of marriage to Jamila's parents two years ago. "At first I said 'no,' I wasn't prepared to lose the work I do for a man." But she began an email exchange with him, got to know him better, enjoyed the messages he was sending, decided this was the man she wanted to marry, and eventually said "yes" to his proposal. Her parents, who had studiously ignored Fazal's initial letter, were apoplectic. Even her sisters in Germany and Australia wrote to tell her it was her duty to stay at home and take care of their parents.

Her uncle, a man she describes as the family member who carries the most weight, acted as their intermediary. Fazal made contact with him, had a meeting, and got the result he and Jamila had hoped for. "He told my father, 'Fazal is a good man. Jamila is not only your daughter; she is the daughter of all Afghans. I want this marriage to happen.'" Although the engagement is not blessed, it is at least permitted. Together with Fazal, a widower with five children of his own, they will have a combined family of ten children. The engagement is only one week old. She is still living under her father's roof and says, "The best thing for me is to get out of the house early in the morning." The last thing they told her this morning was that she was an insult to Islam.

Although the chastisement hurts, Jamila says she sees herself as the way forward for women. "I am educated, a strong social activist. I have the same problems with my family as others do, and I stand on my own two feet." Her family feels she is too open-minded, but she claims it is her open mind and her studies in Islamic education that qualify her to speak out. "They use Islam as a tool against women, and the culture as an excuse for the violence. It's because they are uneducated and don't understand wrong from right." She says those who don't want change accuse women of adopting Western values.

She admitted, while sitting in her peaceful office, that the situation had become precarious. "Everything came to Afghanistan with high speed," she said. The massive SUVs driving around the cities and villages, the huge foreign presence, and the rapid changes they brought with them, were unsettling to many. "People weren't ready for it. After a time, people began to say, 'These changes don't suit us,' so it started to lose its appeal. Now it's going down. Restrictions are increasing again, schools are being burned, some families in rural areas are stopping their daughters from going to school. I've heard of three cases in the last month of girls being kidnapped and raped—all because they went to school."

While women flocked to the centre in ever-increasing numbers—now twenty-five hundred a month—Jamila said the rumbling distrust and fear spread by the Taliban insurgency, and by the stubborn fundamentalists who were its advance guard, were being felt everywhere. There was an unsettling feeling in Afghanistan that spring, as if everyone were waiting for the other shoe to drop.

Eighteen months later, in January 2008, I met Jamila again. In her arms was her eight-month-old son, Hamza Salahuddin Whab, and at her side was her husband, Fazal, who is now the co-director of the Noor Education Centre. He doesn't shake hands with me but is quick to say that this is part of his faith. Jamila, who is obviously smitten by this man, explains: "When the people converted during the Prophet's time, the men put their hand in his, but when women converted he put his hand on top of the water, and the woman's hand was placed below the water. The Prophet didn't touch women he wasn't married to. Fazal follows that tradition." In other ways, he is entirely untraditional. He carries Jamila's laptop, the baby, and the diaper bag up the long staircase into the office and makes sure she is safely settled into a chair, her crutches by her side, before handing her little Hamza. She says throughout her pregnancy he played the role of mother, father, sister, and brother to her, running the household despite the fact that, traditionally, it is her job to serve the family, whether she is pregnant or not, and whether she works outside of the home or not. The story of her pregnancy and delivery is an interesting combination of the old and new Afghanistan. Her polio afflictions were aggravated by the pregnancy, and her scoliosis created more problems. She was confined to bed for the last two months. A month before her due date, she had an emergency Caesarean section, and her premature son was taken to the intensive-care unit (ICU) weighing a healthy 3.3 kilograms, but his early birth meant he would spend ten days in the ICU. Jamila sat and slept on a chair beside him because there were no facilities in the unit for mothers, but she knows that without the medical care she received, care that isn't available to some women because their husbands refuse it, and to others because it isn't reachable, she would not be holding this child in her arms today.

She sees her husband, her child, and her happiness as her reward for the struggles she has had to overcome for most of her life. She blooms with contentment while the staff in the bustling education centre buzz around her, and Fazal hushes the baby and starts to work on the computer. And then she takes a minute to talk about love. "Love is a power. It gives you strength. When I married Fazal, I thought I was in love with him, but the reality was this: He was a way for me to escape my situation at home." Although she is now in touch with her mother occasionally, the family has basically boycotted her. "When I picture my father and brother, I realize I'm part of them, we have a blood-and-soul relationship. But they were harsh with me, gave me no value, and beat me, slapped my face. I never got the knowledge of love from my family. The longer I lived with Fazal, the more I saw what love is. He respects me; he's a humble, intelligent, patient man." He is also tall, studious, and attractive, a man who is clearly comfortable with their relationship.

"The truth is I fell in love with him after we were married." While she says it is not culturally acceptable for a woman to show her love for a man (even her own husband) lest she be called a whore, Jamila has been transformed. The shy smiles directed at him, the confidence she exudes, the contagious happiness that seeps from her facial expressions give her away. "I know I'm lucky," she says. "It's not common for a woman to be in love. We may have a life with a good person, but being in love is totally different. It's time Afghans talked about this."

Her cellphone rings. She glances at the incoming number and her expression changes abruptly. "Bali," she says as she clicks open the phone, listens with growing intensity, and speaks in rapid Dari. When she disconnects, she tells me she has to leave immediately. A single phone call has reactivated the ancient script of this troubled country, turning a page that connects the brutal past to the realties of today. Jamila's uncle, the one who took her side when Fazal proposed marriage, has been kidnapped. A successful businessman, he is being held for a $1.5-million ransom. Kidnapping wealthy people has become a curse in Kabul, with local thugs looking for quick cash, or extremists in need of funding, plucking hapless men from the street, threatening their families, and almost always receiving the ransom. The police, who sometimes are involved in the kidnappings, are useless when it comes to tracing the kidnappers or rescuing the hostage. Jamila, Fazal, and baby Hamza have to go home. In the few seconds it takes to absorb the news, the curtain falls on the blissfully happy wife and mother, and a new drama begins in the family.

She contacted me by email a month after I left Afghanistan to say her uncle had been released after a $1-million ransom was paid. She was back at work. The baby was fine. She would be in touch again soon.

ACROSS THE CITY FROM THE NOOR EDUCATION CENTRE, Farida Nekzad, the thirty-year-old editor-in-chief of the Pajhwok Afghan News agency, is recovering from the fright of her life. She had taken a taxi to a meeting and carefully fixed the price before leaving, which likely alerted the taxi driver that he had an independent woman in the car. He looked at her through the rear-view mirror and asked, "What do you do?" She didn't answer him. Then he started yelling, "I know who you are. You're a journalist. You write all those things about warlords and mujahedeen. You're going to be killed. You're a woman—you should just go home and stay there." He kept up the tirade, accusing her of being an American spy, telling her she had better quit what she was doing. Farida told him to stop the car. He wouldn't. When he slowed down to go around a corner, she opened the door and jumped out, falling to the ground and cutting her arm and hand. People on the street gathered around her while she was yelling, "Get the plate number of the taxi." Nobody did. She picked herself up, wrapped her bleeding arm in a scarf, went back to her office, and wrote the story. Her colleagues, even the foreign ones, were astounded. The old adage about writers having either to publish or perish takes on new meaning in a country that's grappling with the right of a woman even to be seen outside the house, never mind be editor-in-chief of a news agency. Here the aphorism could be "publish and perish." But Farida is undaunted. She sees journalism as the way forward for Afghanistan. She loves her job and vows the fundamentalists and crackpots will never force her to quit.

She attracts attention. Tall, slim, dressed in a chic, pinstriped pantsuit, with fashionable high-heeled boots, and a jaunty silk scarf barely covering her long wavy brown hair, she has the look of a hunter: huge watchful eyes and long legs that seem ready to spring. She walks me through the newsroom, sharing quips with her colleagues, and checking wire copy on a co-worker's computer. She is every inch a journalist, as interested in the news of the day as she is in investigating the history of the women of Afghanistan. She has been married for three months to Rahimullah Samander, who is director of the Afghan Independent Journalists Association, and unlike Jamila Afghani, she has the support of her family. But she admits bucking an old system is exacting a heavy toll.

She had been threatened before the incident with the taxi, once even when she was returning home from the funeral of her friend and fellow journalist Zakia Zaki, a broadcaster, who had been shot seven times in the face in front of her eight-year-old son. Zaki was killed not only for being a woman journalist, but also for daring to expose the truth about the religious fanatics and corruption in government. That message came via Farida's cellphone, the caller saying, "You are a bitch, the daughter of America. We'll kill you as soon as possible, just like Zakia." The Committee to Protect Journalists in New York offered her a scholarship so she could get out of the country, but she refused. While we sit in her office, huddled by a stove to stay warm on a January day when the temperature is minus twenty degrees, she says, "No one in Afghanistan is secure. If I leave, they'll go after the next one, then she'll leave, and soon enough they'll have silenced the women."

In 2005, a popular music-show host, Shaima Rezayee, was shot to death. In 2006, three journalists were murdered. In 2007, the murder of Zakia Zaki, the director of Radio Peace in Parwan province, and Shokiba Sanga Amaaj, a news presenter in Kabul, sent a shudder through the media community. Dozens of threats came to Farida. They were vile and frightening, hooking her work as a journalist to so-called sexual impropriety and accusing her of being anti-Islam—a crime punishable by death in Afghanistan. One caller said, "At least your friend Zakia could be recognized by one side of her face. We'll shoot your face so that nobody will recognize you."

Soon after, Bob Dietz, the Asian program director of the Committee to Protect Journalists, nominated Farida for the 2007 International Press Freedom Award given by the Canadian Journalists for Free Expression. In his nomination letter he wrote: "The award would send a message that the rest of the world is paying attention to the case of this valiant editor, and that the crimes committed against individual journalists will not go unnoticed." The jury easily selected Farida Nekzad. When she stood before a capacity crowd at the Toronto gala, she accepted the award on behalf of all female Afghan journalists.

Back in Kabul, she had to face a new onslaught by fundamentalist critics who accused her of speaking out of turn to the Canadian media. "Are you Talib or American? You are not Afghan." The messages continue to arrive by email and phone, incessantly. "I pray they won't kill me because it would be very difficult for my family, my husband, and for the women," she says matter-of-factly.

Farida was born in Kabul but left during the Taliban regime and vowed she would never return after seeing people hanged from lampposts and dead bodies on the street. But when the hated Taliban were ousted, the draw to the land she grew up in was stronger than the urge to continue the good life she was living in India as a freelance reporter. "We need to show the people that women can work freely, and someone needs to tell the truth about what happened here," she says of her decision to return. She started writing profiles, beginning with a woman who opened a beauty salon and a man who had served time in prison. Her reports were considered both groundbreaking and outrageous because going behind the scenes to find out how people feel or how they actually live their lives had not been done before. When people suggested this personal style of journalism was out of line, she felt she had to make excuses. "It's not my voice, it's the people who are telling their stories," she explained. She admits now that she was scared because it brought attention to her (never a wise move in Afghanistan) but says, "These were the voices of others who need to be heard." Her reputation grew. She took on radio as well as print assignments and ventured into the provinces, which women journalists rarely did, to report everything from snowstorms and accidents to corruption and women's rights. "I did it because how else would the government or the international community know the needs of the people, if the media didn't report them?"

Then she met Jane McElhone, the Canadian woman who came to Afghanistan to train women broadcasters for the Institute for Media, Policy, and Civil Society (IMPACS). Started in Canada in 1997, IMPACS has an international program designed to foster the development of free, critical, and effective communication to enhance the media's role in the process of democratic development, good governance, accountability, and transparency. Unfortunately, the institute closed in late 2007 due to lack of funds. But, while it operated in Afghanistan, McElhone and her colleagues trained dozens of women journalists. The newly minted reporters also began broadcasting information to women. In the run-up to the election, it was these radio broadcasts that walked civil society through the process, explained the need to vote, the rules of an election, and the right of women to cast ballots. McElhone explains:

> When I first travelled to Afghanistan as a radio trainer in January 2003 for IMPACS, I had already worked for many years as a radio producer and journalist, and more recently, as an international media trainer, press freedom activist, and media developer. They asked me to take this job and I didn't hesitate. As a Canadian woman and

journalist, I had had so many professional opportunities, including working for Canada's internationally respected public broadcaster, and the idea of sharing those experiences with Afghan women, and assisting them with their efforts to become good journalists, producers, and managers was irresistible, as was the thought of experiencing first-hand the rebuilding of Afghanistan, and of sitting down face-to-face with Afghan women.

That first training stint was meant to last several weeks, but it turned into two and a half years, and six years later, her work has expanded in scope, just as her relationship with Afghan women journalists who inspire her continues to grow.

In 2003, Farida was hunting for a new challenge and a salary that would allow her to support her family when McElhone hired her for a job-share working both with IMPACS and the Institute of War and Peace Reporting, producing radio stories about and for women and writing articles about post-war recovery. "When some friends and colleagues began setting up Afghanistan's first independent news agency, Farida decided she wanted to become editor-in-chief, so we happily released her from her previous commitments and gave her our full blessing to prosper and grow in her new challenge," says McElhone.

But she stayed close to the budding journalist because she had identified Farida as a "leader in the field of media, freedom of the press, and journalists' protection." Throughout the years they collaborated, McElhone says, Farida worked tirelessly to establish the first independent journalists association in Afghanistan and the first independent news agency. She played a leading role in the coverage of the constitutional Loya Jirga (general assembly) in 2003 and of the first presidential election in 2004. When she became editor-in-chief of Pajhwok News, a job that she continues to hold today, she joined the ranks of a very small group of Afghan women media managers.

Farida has a reputation as a strong leader of Afghan women who speaks publicly and tirelessly on their behalf. When a young friend took her own life, Farida gathered women and men together for a memorial service and spoke eloquently about the lives of young women and the seemingly inexplicable choices they make. When Zakia Zaki was assassinated, she spoke courageously about the importance of women's role in public life, media, and politics, firmly proclaiming that despite the threats and killings, women were not afraid and would continue working, speaking out, and using the media to tell their stories and to fight for their rights. "It was during this time that she herself received threats and became concerned about her own safety and her family's security," says McElhone.

> Were the threats serious? Was she in real danger? It is always hard to say. Yet one of the things I have learned from working with Afghan women is that you never really know if and when they are in danger. What is even more wrenching is that they often don't seem to know themselves. Given that they are fighting so hard and crossing so many new boundaries, it is all a risk and it is all unpredictable.

When McElhone's career took her to a new post in London, England, to work with the Open Society Institute, she stayed in constant contact with Farida, knowing she was being threatened. "Every morning, I would go into Skype [an internet communications service] and check that she had made it to her office in Kabul and was online. She was the only one who could really decide what to do. People like me, who were far away, could simply let her know there were options, if she wanted them and, more than anything, provide moral support."

They still get together. Last year, at Farida's joyous engagement party at a cavernous wedding hall on the outskirts of

Kabul, Farida and Jane sat among her women friends, colleagues, and family members, with the men hidden away on the other side of wooden dividers, where they were visible to the women only on a large video screen. And recently, at Laurier University in Canada, McElhone proudly introduced her Afghan women journalist colleagues at a photo exhibit and invited them to tell a rapt Canadian audience their stories.

Farida admits it is not easy to run a news agency with seventy reporters and eight bureaus but scoffs at the notion that the editor-in-chief's chair is not a woman's place:

> I'm a journalist, just like a teacher or a social worker; it's my job. Why can't these people understand that I'm not a spy or a promoter of America? I am the bridge. I don't take sides. I don't belong to a political party. I report what I'm witness to. I'm trying to bring peace to Afghanistan.

She is recovering this day from laryngitis and says casually, "Oh it's just from stress." Her family, including her husband, worry about her constantly. "I feel badly that they have to deal with the whispering campaign against me. I told them not to tell people where I am, just say I'm out doing my job." She knows she is sometimes followed, and her car was vandalized only a few weeks ago. The police know about these incidents and have told her to change her route to work often, and to sleep in a different part of her house every night. She says, "There are a lot of marked women in Afghanistan, but I won't show that it bothers me." She admits taking on subjects such as corruption or poppies or warlords is an invitation to be kidnapped or killed. "Warlords are still powerful. They have their militias and publicity and guns." While the government supports the journalists verbally, she says, "They don't ever ask who did that, who's threatening you? And if one of us is killed, there's no investigation, no one is arrested. They just say 'sorry.'"

Recently elected vice-president of media at the South Asia Free Media Association, Farida has gained international recognition and, despite the threats and danger to herself, feels that the rights for women will come eventually and the future will be better. "In the end, those people who want to stop me will see that I'm right." She has made an alliance with other women, including members of parliament, development workers, teachers, and other journalists, who are beginning to see the value of collaborating on women's issues, making their voices known, and lobbying the government for change. One of those women is Najia Haneefi.

A HUMAN RIGHTS ACTIVIST, thirty-year-old Najia Haneefi was born in Mazar-e Sharif. She graduated in journalism studies, which was not of much use to her when the Taliban took over her city. So her adult career actually began with pasta- and bread-making when she managed to get a job working for the United Nations Habitat program. Grateful for an income when women around her were forbidden to work, she soon moved to the communications division, which led to a partnership that the sassy Najia giggles about today. "The Taliban allowed the radio station to operate, but only if it broadcast strictly religious programs. They knew I had a journalism background, and hired me to write those radio shows." She had gone to a religious school, read the Quran, and regularly prayed five times a day. She says:

> They wanted shows that would appeal to women and
> children, so doing the research meant I had to read a lot
> about women's rights in the Quran, and I began to realize
> how disgusting things are from a religious point of view
> for women, not only in Islam, in every religion. So I
> became secular while the Taliban were paying me to write
> their shows.

She laughs now at the memory of the misogynist Taliban compensating her while she changed her mind about religion. She also was running a youth group that was becoming increasingly disgruntled about the rules imposed on women. In the process, she recalls, she almost got busted. "We were celebrating International Women's Day. Someone tipped us off that the Taliban were coming to arrest me, so we quickly tore down the banners, and when they arrived I told them it was a birthday party for one of the women."

The ruse seemed to work, but it didn't prevent a member of the Taliban giving a speech about the place of women. Najia tried to hold her tongue, but when the Taliban representative said, "Women are not complete. They don't have a full brain," Najia spoke up and said, "That's wrong. There's no place in the Quran that says that." She was promptly hauled off to court for her audacity. Unbowed by the reprimand, she argued in court: "If women are not complete, how can it be that the first person to accept Islam was a woman?" The Taliban brought forty women to the court to testify that Najia had committed blasphemy and was encouraging immoral behaviour among women. They stepped forward, one by one, and took her side, vowing that she had done no such thing. Miraculously, the court let her go. She admits, "I was braver then than I am now!"

After the Taliban era, she went back to Balkh University and studied civil engineering. In 2003, she became the gender adviser for the government repatriation committee because, she says, "I wanted to be involved in political decisions." Soon afterwards, her friends introduced her to Jane McElhone, and she joined the growing number of women being trained by IMPACS to take their human rights campaign to the mostly illiterate population by creating radio programs. Najia was in her element. McElhone remembers:

I met her in 2003 in Mazar-e Sharif. She was working for the U.N. high commissioner for refugees and, in her spare time, for Radio Rabbia Balki, a women-managed radio station that I helped establish. One of the very first independent stations operating after the fall of the Taliban, it was named after the famous Afghan woman poet who was killed by her brother. Najia was committed to that station, and to ensuring that the spirit of Rabbia Balki lived on, and that women's stories could be told.

For McElhone, Najia was one of the very first Afghan women who belied the burka-covered stereotype. "She was gutsy, strong, opinionated, and funny, and in constant motion, rushing from the United Nations, to Radio Rabbia Balki, to her cool dark home, where we would seek refuge from the blinding northern sun." There is a photograph taken from that time, at a picnic on the leafy shores of a river outside of her dusty town, that depicts the friendship among the women. "We sat on the grass and ate *pilau* [a rice dish] and barbecued meat," says McElhone, "and then joined her Afghan friends as they jumped into the river fully dressed." But it was after the camera recorded the moment that McElhone saw Najia's real character.

> We were drifting along peacefully, but the current suddenly overcame Najia, and she started struggling, and had to be pulled out. She was scared but, as always, exhilarated. That is the image that I have kept of her; plunging into new challenges with determination, at times without knowing or considering where she was going, but always, always setting new limits and new heights for Afghan women. Given the constant uncertainty, I often think that is the only way Afghan women can move forward.

Soon after that incident, Najia moved to Kabul, where she took a variety of jobs and established a reputation as one of the rising women leaders of Afghan civil society. "She kept a poster of Afghan women refugees above her desk in Mazar-e Sharif, and when she moved to Kabul she gave it to me as a present," says McElhone.

> Then, when I left Kabul, I carted it with me to London. Ripped and worn, the poster is now hanging above my own desk, making me ponder the many women like Najia who have worked so hard to create better lives for their Afghan sisters and to tell their stories and who have had to flee Afghanistan themselves to seek safer and better lives.

Najia's interest in being close to the centre of change made her agree to take the job of director of the Afghan Women's Educational Center, a national organization whose mandate is the promotion of rights, self-sufficiency, empowerment, and understanding among Afghan women and children. The centre includes health services, peace education, trauma and conflict resolution, counselling, psychological services, literacy programs, vocational training, and a wool-spinning facility to teach income-generating skills to women.

It was while working as the director of this centre that Najia made the boldest play of her young life. She took on the government, the mullahs, and the extremists when the vice-and-virtue department was re-established. A natural storyteller, she sits cross-legged on the couch in tight black pants and leans forward like a coach, her round mischievous eyes flashing when she recounts the play-by-play action.

The formidable supreme court chief justice, Fazl Hadi Shinwari, had retired. President Karzai had given him an office to keep the eighty-five-year-old fundamentalist busy.

"Everyone knew he was re-starting the vice-and-virtue squad, even though it wasn't announced officially. The president wasn't doing anything to stop him. I knew we needed to take action," she says. She called all the civil-society networks and they said, "Najia don't touch this. You could be accused of being un-Islamic." She ignored them. "They already have a minister of hajj [having to do with the pilgrimage to Mecca required of Muslims] who has corruption charges against him, and a ministry of mosques to take care of religion. And we have police—they're corrupt, but they are supposed to be handling things like vice, so we don't need another structure." She called moderate religious leaders, but they ignored her. She asked the media to cover it, but they felt the vice-and-virtue department was an Islamic order. So she went to the women. The women parliamentarians supported her. So did Sima Samar, the chair of the human rights commission, and Husah Bano from the Ministry of Women's Affairs. She took her protest to the international community and says, "Canada and Italy helped me the most. The U.S. wouldn't help at all." On July 22, 2006, she issued a statement from the Women's Political Participation Committee, an organization founded two years before with about thirty other women. The statement (excerpted as its English version originally appeared) said in part:

> The Women Political Participation Committee expresses their strong protest against the violation of the Article 24 of The Afghan Constitution through the proclamation on the re-establishment of Vice and Virtue Department.
>
> The formation of such department appears designed to ... interfere ... in the personal domain and is [a] violation of personal dignity of the citizens. This ... is against all democratic values.
>
> The Afghan government ... is revitalizing the very institution which left the marks of abuse, insult and

inhuman behavior on Afghans memory by the dictator regimes of the past....

Also according to Article 6 of the Afghan Constitution "The state is obliged to create a prosperous and progressive society based on social justice, protection of human dignity, protection of human rights, and realization of democracy...."

In respect of all the above mentioned the Women Political Participation Committee rejects the formation of Vice and Virtue and asks for reconsideration as women are always the sacrifice of customs, tradition and partial interpretation.

It took forty-five days from start to finish. The vice-and-virtue department was dismantled. Five months later, on December 5, 2007, Najia won the coveted International Service Award for Women's Human Rights for her work to establish her countrywomen's rights at a ceremony held in the British parliament. The judges commented that Najia showed "immense personal courage" to remain committed to her cause despite threats to her life. They also noted the "sustainable and effective" work of the Afghan Women's Educational Center, and, in particular, its successful combination of practical projects and political campaigning. Sima Samar quips, "Whenever I see Najia in the corridors of the Human Rights Commission, I think there's a revolution going on." Najia also led a campaign to have women appointed to the Supreme Court but hasn't won that one—yet.

THERE IS NO TRANSLATION for *feminism* in Dari, so Najia uses the English word and says, "I describe myself as a feminist without hesitation." This stand is like waving a red flag to a bull in Afghanistan, but she takes the criticism with equanimity.

"Most women are scared to call themselves feminists because Afghan leaders condemn feminism as anti-Islamic, although it's not. But the women in my social circle are feminists, even without knowing it."

She reflects on the Taliban days, when women's lives were very constrained, when she had to wear a burka whenever she left the house, when lessons for girls were organized secretly by networks of women. "Things have changed dramatically since then. The presence of the international community here means that women's rights are kept on the agenda; they were never on the government agenda before." She notes that women now are visible in the cinema and the arts, on television, and in the government. She readily admits that they have not yet achieved what they had expected and hoped for but says, "Considering the tribal values—settling disputes by trading women, selling girls as brides—which are not Islamic values, fundamental changes still have to be made. I am optimistic about the future for Afghan women, but sometimes I find myself wishing I had been born somewhere else."

By the time the hot summer of 2007 began, the worrisome backslide in security was leading to a rise in fundamentalism. Women such as Najia were being watched and threatened. Suddenly, in September, Najia left Afghanistan. She has enrolled in a women's studies program at an undisclosed university in Canada and has applied for asylum. When McElhone read the email saying Najia had been seriously threatened and had to leave the country, she says, "I was saddened. I can't help thinking what a loss it is for Afghanistan to be, once again, losing women like her." She also saw the happy photos of Najia's wedding in Canada. "I know she is building a safe and happy life there. She is now married, settled, and as active as ever, and running an Afghan women's network, already contributing to her new country, but not forgetting her old one."

Najia should not be counted out too soon. When I sat with her in Canada during the Christmas holidays, she said, "I'll go back to my beautiful Afghanistan when warlords cease to have power to threaten human rights activists."

CHAPTER 4

A WOMAN'S PLACE IN TRIBAL LAW

Our cultural traditions bind the hands of women like chains.

—Habiba Surabi, from her acceptance speech when appointed
Governor of Bamiyan, March 7, 2005

ON THE STREETS OF KABUL there is plenty of evidence that women are shrugging off their centuries-old oppression, but the usually untold stories from behind the walled compounds in this and other Afghan cities and villages tell a different tale. One of the worst is depicted at the burn unit at Kabul's Esteqlal Hospital, which is located not far from the lustrous new institutions of equality and democracy, including the human rights commission and parliament. It is eerily quiet in the ward. The paint is peeling and the beds are rusty. Rickety poles hold up opaque intravenous bags containing painkillers and antibiotics. An air of fatal futility fills the room in which a dozen patients writhe in agony. It's like a surreal ward of the damned.

A girl I'll call Annisa startles me the most. Her face is burned as black as charcoal. Her eyes stare out from beneath scorched eyelids, sending a message of unspeakable pain. Her arms, bent at right angles, are wrapped in gauze and suspended like the limbs of a marionette over a charred chest that is rutted like a tire. Her lips are grotesquely swollen, stretching her mouth into a silent scream. It will take this blameless eighteen-year-old five or six days to die.

This is the face of the violence that still plagues the women of Afghanistan. Annisa is a victim of *badal*, a tradition of trading daughters without dowries from one tribe or family to another for marriage. It is, in essence, a sentence of hard labour, abuse, and humiliation. *Badal* is common in this country. What happened to Annisa is not unusual, although such incidents are rarely reported. She disobeyed her mother-in-law, so the woman held her down while her son, Annisa's husband, doused her with gasoline and then struck a match that lit her up as though she were tinder. (A survey done in 2007 by Global Rights, a Washington-based human rights organization, found that 30 percent of reported incidents of violence were perpetrated by female household members, often a mother-in-law.)

Badal is one of dozens of practices accepted under tribal law. While only civil and sharia law are sanctioned by the constitutionally mandated judiciary, it is tribal law (or "traditional practice") that is most commonly administered. In tribal law, women and girls can be bought, traded, or given away like any other property. Child marriages are still the norm—girls as young as four are betrothed to old men—and bride prices still exist, meaning that young girls are sold to the highest bidder. Women are raped to dishonour an enemy tribe and daughters are used to settle scores: If someone is killed in a dispute, the killer's family gives a girl child to the victim's family to make amends. The cases of tribal law recorded at the human rights commission and by the Women and Children Legal Research

Foundation (WCLRF) read like tales out of the Dark Ages, but this is post-Taliban Afghanistan. The country is in the process of nation building. It has a new constitution, a human rights commission, and is stepping forward, full of hope, into the twenty-first century. While the international community wrings its hands over warlords, drug barons, and the insurgency in the south, the women of Afghanistan are demanding reform and an end to the tribal laws that have kept women in bondage for a millennium. The process is slow, complex, and precarious, but by all accounts, the reformers are chipping away at the traditional structure that uses women and girls as plunder.

Historically, the rule of law developed from traditional practices. When Islam emerged almost fourteen hundred years ago, there were a number of practices that were contradictory to the Prophet's teaching. Some of these—for example, the custom of burying a newborn girl alive because girls were considered a shame to the family—were dropped. The customs that were considered acceptable to Islam, called *marrof*, were confirmed in the Quran. The Hadiths (speeches or comments by the Prophet that explain the holy text) contain dozens of anecdotes about changing the mentality of society towards women. These commentaries clearly denounce the traditions that violate women's rights.

In the absence of a formal judiciary, tribal law is meant to be the keeper of peace in the village, the court where disputes are aired, shared, and settled, so that families can forgive and be forgiven. This traditional law is used to settle land claims, water quotas, and personal grievances. But, over time in Afghanistan, it has become brutal, vindictive, and irreversible, and the vast majority of the people harmed are women or, more precisely, young girls. Customs such as *badal*, *bad*, forced marriage, underage marriage, trading women for animals or drugs, and the idea that giving birth to baby girls rather than boys is shameful all are commonplace. There are even names given to exemplify the unwelcome birth of girls. For example, if a baby boy is born, although he is named, he also bears the moniker *Neek Sar*, which means "good person." If a girl is born, she too is named, but is referred to as *Bad Sar*, or "bad person." The nickname for women is *Aajeza*, which means "disabled" or "bad luck" person.

Convincing the perpetrators—the village chiefs, elders, and mullahs—that these traditions constitute crimes against women is an immense challenge. Fledging attempts at changing these entrenched beliefs were made under King Amanullah in the 1920s, and again under King Zahir Shah in the 1950s and 1960s, but they were brief, timid, and short-lived.

The Russian occupation of Afghanistan in the 1980s was a relatively permissive era for women. Photos from that time depict women in miniskirts and jeans meeting their friends at restaurants and discos and walking along the river's edge with their boyfriends. Even during the fratricidal bloodbath fought between the seven factions of mujahedeen when the Russians departed, women played a role in civil society. Seventy percent of the teachers in urban centres were women. They also made up 40 percent of the civil service and half the students at Kabul University. Those public gains were wiped out in 1996, when the Taliban emerged victorious and virtually put women and girls under house arrest.

Now, with women in parliament, and a women's movement starting to take action, the real test of the resolve of Afghans and the international community for women's rights has begun. The hardened underbelly of village life, the heretofore unassailable bedrock of tribal law, is under attack.

At a groundbreaking conference in November 2004, the WCLRF highlighted tribal law as the major cause of violence against women in Afghanistan. Founded in 2003 by a group of women lawyers, the foundation's goal was to provide human rights defenders with reliable evidence and facts so they can begin the long, complicated process of altering the way disputes are dealt with. At that conference, they did what no one had dared to do before: They used documented evidence and statistics to identify the common types of traditional practices, the impact they have on women's lives, and the ways and means to stop them.

They began by examining how and why these practices have passed uncontested from one generation to the next, despite the introduction of civil and sharia law. They explored the power of tradition, particularly in the absence of peace, and in a culture where crimes against women go unpunished. And they pointed out that Afghanistan has solved its disputes through *jirgas* (a gathering of Afghan communities) or *shuras* (a local board of community elders and trustees) since the time of the Bactrian Aryans. From that time to this, the problems within the village were viewed from a male perspective. The customary laws were never codified, and no organization was ever mandated to monitor the lawful implementation of these practices. The researchers also raised the question of the consequences that can result when the decision of the *jirga* or *shura* is not obeyed: Violent punishments, or *nagha*, are applied. The alleged violator's home may be burned to the ground; he or she may be forced out of the community or be subjected to enforced removal and isolation from the tribe and other forms of author- ized revenge. There is no time limit to punishment: the enmity of the tribe towards transgressors can last for generations. With the highest illiteracy rate in the world, and a narrative of more war than peace in the long history of Afghanistan, it is no small wonder that tribal law has not only survived but thrived. The WCLRF delegates then produced the evidential details of each of the practices.

They began with *bad*. Although it is against sharia law, as well as the Universal Declaration of Human Rights, international norms and standards, and indeed the civil law of Afghanistan, it has persisted. Its roots can be traced back to ancient Egypt and the story of "The Bride of the Nile." According to this tale, every year the Egyptians selected a beautiful young girl and threw her to her death in the Nile River to stop the river from overflowing. In Afghanistan, the tradition has taken another form. The family that loses in a conflict gives a girl, or sometimes two or three girls, depending on the size of the harm done, to the offended family to slake the misogynist thirst of the tribe and presumably to stop the inter-family conflict from overflowing. Although it is applied differently in different parts of the country, *bad* never produces amity rather than animosity and always results in misery, if not death for the girl. It is so entrenched that, until the WCLRF study came to light, even the government felt that it didn't have the right to intervene in such cases. And it isn't isolated to the rural villages. More than fifty cases of *bad* were reported in Kabul during the research for the report. The WCLRF also claimed that *bad* affected not just the women and girls, but also entire family systems, which disintegrated in the aftermath of the penalty. The authors of the report concluded: "We are witnessing women's slavery in the twenty-first century."

The 486 cases collected by the WCLRF over a twelve-month period described penalties handed out to toddlers as young as three years old and to mature women of fifty, and painted a horrific picture of women treated as chattels. Girls are exchanged for better livestock, to settle drug debts, and for any manner of goods prized by a man who has a daughter to barter.

For example, a girl I will call Fariba (the names of the victims are protected in the report) was fourteen years old when her brother killed a man during a gambling dispute. Fariba was given in *bad* to the deceased man's family for the crime committed by her brother. A few years later she went missing.

The family said they didn't know where she went. It is presumed they killed her.

Another girl was given in *bad* because her brother killed a man in a dispute about the water quota. After three years of beatings, sexual assault, and near starvation, she escaped but was captured and murdered by the patriarch of the family.

A nineteen-year-old girl was given to a fifty-year-old man in *bad* because her father couldn't repay a debt. He gave his daughter instead of money.

In another case, when several sheep were killed by wolves, the young shepherd who was minding them was forced to give his sister in *bad* to the owner of the sheep. She is now used as a beast of burden. And when a girl ran away from home to escape her forced betrothal to an old man, the local *jirga* gave her ten-year-old sister in *bad* to the boy's family to keep the peace.

When a marriage ceremony is being arranged, tradition dictates that the groom's family kill an animal—a goat, sheep, chicken, or cow—to welcome the bride to the in-laws' home. The report cites a case of a father of the groom who gave one of his daughters to the landlord of the village in exchange for a cow because he didn't have any livestock to kill.

And during a game of *buzkashi* (a traditional polo-like sport that uses a dead goat as the "ball"), the report notes, one player's horse was injured. Rather than missing the rest of the contest, he traded his daughter for a new horse so that he could finish the match.

Even though the tradition is widely accepted, the researchers found that families were reluctant to tell the truth. It is a case in which everybody knows the truth, but nobody is willing to step forward to speak. It is also further proof that girls and women are being punished for crimes their fathers and brothers commit.

Tribal elders told the researchers that while they are aware that this is a terrible way to settle disputes, they feel they are obliged to use it as it is part of their tradition. Their justification is in the belief that *bad* will reduce conflict, repair family relationships, and wipe away the stain of dishonour. But in reality, it doesn't stop the tension between the families: The angst is perpetuated and an innocent girl has her life ruined. And it doesn't end there. By not punishing the actual perpetrator, criminal behaviour within the tribe goes unchecked and leads to a culture of impunity.

The report found that the tradition is followed blindly and irrationally by tribal members who never question the inhumanity of their actions. The results frequently are tragic. Victims who run away often turn to crime and become unreported statistics in the legions of mentally unbalanced citizens in a country that has known too much war. Deprived of growing up in a family with parental guidance, and subjected to uncivilized behaviour, they frequently succumb to a life of crime, drug dependence, and violence. Then the cycle repeats itself, the children become drenched in mistrust, hatred, and disgust for the family and the tribe. Mercilessness, ruthlessness, and animosity replace the amnesty and forgiveness the tribal law pretends to foster.

Forced marriage is another custom that defies civil and sharia law. It is estimated that from 60 to 80 percent of all marriages in Afghanistan are forced. The term covers a wide array of practices, from giving a female in marriage as repayment for a debt or to end a feud to simply determining who a daughter should marry without her consent.

While the practice varies between regions and ethnic groups, it is a common feature throughout all social, ethnic, religious, tribal, and economic divisions of Afghan society. What these practices have in common is the unlawful violation of women's human rights. To see a wide-eyed little girl—sometimes as young as four—standing next to her betrothed—a twenty-, thirty-, or forty-year-old man—is such shocking evidence of child abuse that it is hard to imagine how it can be understood or condoned at any level, much less accepted as tribal law.

The unchallenged presumption in the village, and indeed in many homes in the cities, is that women are a subspecies: chattels for trading, vessels for begetting a son, or a punching bag to relieve rage. Says Sima Samar: "Men beat up women because the dinner isn't ready on time, because it isn't cooked properly, has too much or too little salt, or because the children are fighting amongst themselves. He'll pull her hair, hit her with shoes, electric wires, sticks. He'll beat her until his rage is spent for a reason that has nothing to do with her." She says, "The difference between a bad woman and a good woman in this country is a bad woman won't put up with the violence, she'll leave. A good woman is quiet, bears it all, and says nothing. We have to change that."

WHEN WOMEN ARE DENIED AN EDUCATION and kept away from their friends and family, when they are economically dependent on a man and repeatedly told they are unworthy, it is a tried-and-true formula for subservience. Today the women of Afghanistan want these conditions altered. In one of the cases presented to the WCLRF conference in November 2004, a man had cut off his wife's nose and ears and poured boiling oil on her because she had kissed her son-in-law. As long as such a case is decided by a *jirga* rather than by the judiciary, there is little hope for change.

At the conclusion of the conference, a statement signed by all the participants was released, calling for an end to violence against women and making the following demands:

• Tribal law is the source of violence and should be declared a violation of the law and those who practise it should be punished.

- The judiciary must act on the elimination of tribal law.
- The executive authority—police and judges—must take serious steps to prevent tradition-based violence against women.
- *Jirgas* and *shurahs* must select a different conceptual framework and lawful principles with people committed to the rule of law.
- Religious scholars must explain the rights of women and girls to the people.
- The media need to broadcast the voices of women and girls.
- Access to education must be provided, as it will reduce violence.
- Specific initiatives to reduce poverty must be taken that will give economic independence to women.
- National human rights organizations must continue to be active in releasing women from damaging local traditions.
- Responsible authorities must see that these recommendations are acted on.

As this list of demands suggests, the multiple layers of authority that need to be involved in the reform include tribal elders, families, local commanders, local administrative agencies, provincial governors, judicial bodies, police, and the courts: a labyrinthian task for a country struggling with corruption at every level. The good news is the publication of the report received immediate attention by President Karzai, who called *bad* "a cruelty" in his speech on the occasion of Prophet Muhammad's birthday. Then, on International Women's Day in 2004, he referred to *bad* as "one of the worst non-Islamic and inhumane acts," and called on religious leaders to combat it. The chief justice, the deputy chief justice, the minister of women's affairs, and the chair of the Afghanistan Independent Human Rights Commission signed a statement that read: "*Bad* is a crime against humanity and a clear violation of human rights."

So the people with the power to stop the practice of these traditional laws do also have the will. But extrapolating that blessing from the higher-ups into action is a monumental task that starts with a highly controversial subject: the status of women. In Afghanistan, a wife must consult her husband and ask his permission for everything she does. In the absence of her husband, she must ask her brother-in-law or father-in-law, regardless of his age or hers. If she is not married, she needs permission from her own father or brother for anything she wants to do.

Versions of these societal rules existed for women the world over until women themselves demanded change. Until 1968 in Canada, for instance, a woman was expected to say, "I obey," when she took her marriage vows. A married woman could not open a bank account without her husband's signature. It was conferences held in the 1960s and 1970s, such as the one held in Kabul in 2004, that altered the status of women in Canada. There is every indication that Afghan women have embarked on the same journey.

One woman at the conference told a story about hiring staff for the health education program she was running. She knew a woman who would be suitable for the job, and who badly needed the money to feed her family. But the woman's husband was away and she couldn't accept the job without his permission. She asked her brother-in-law, a nasty man who wished the worst for her, and he refused permission. Most employers would simply have hired someone else, but because she knew of the restrictions that applied in the case, and the consequences that would follow if her preferred applicant was denied the job, the health educator waited them out and finally got the husband's permission for the woman to take the job.

Because women have less access to education and their social lives are limited to their family, most women don't even know their rights in civil law or within the constitution of

Afghanistan. Neither do they have access to law enforcement, so they are unable to seek justice for themselves. Until now, the notion of interfering with traditional customs was seen as a challenge too great for the government to tackle.

The conference was a strong starting point for the reform of family law. It took three more years to get the funding, assign the tasks, and coordinate the organizations that would get the movement off the ground. But while the lawyers and human rights activists struggled with the exceedingly slow process of putting reforms in place, the violence continued.

BACK AT THE BURN UNIT AT ESTEQLAL HOSPITAL, head nurse Shakilla Walizada, a strikingly pretty woman garbed in surgical scrubs, is ticking off the survival rate of the dozen female patients in her care this day. She says, "There's little we can do for these women." She is an efficient, no-nonsense professional but confesses the recent increase in burn cases is getting her down. "It's very hard to work here now. We can't do much. Most of them die because the injuries to their heads and necks are so severe," she says.

The rise in self-immolation cases has taxed the already over-crowded, underequipped hospital. These women have chosen death rather than face a forced marriage or another beating. In the last year alone there have been 230 reported cases, and an untold number of others that go unreported. The victims are usually between twenty and thirty-five, and most suffer burns to 95 percent of their bodies. They almost always die an agonizing death. What's more, their families are ashamed of them.

While the human rights commission's mandate is to look out for all Afghans, on the second floor of a building in Karte-se in western Kabul, ironically situated in the section of the city that suffered the most damage and the worst human rights abuses during the mujahedeen era, a cramped office is dedicated to women's issues. Inside, Homa Sultani, the director of the commission's women's project, keeps a thick log of complaints and intends to hold someone accountable for every one. There are floor-to-ceiling files containing details of unimaginable crimes against women. As if the darkness of their contents is not enough to cast a pall over the office, Sultani no sooner starts her description of the cases she is examining than the power fails. It is a daily nuisance she copes with. The computers go down and the room feels airless. We move our chairs to the window to take advantage of the available light, and an increasingly impatient Sultani sends one of the two women who share the space with her for tea. Pots of green tea are served along with heaping plates of almonds, as if to remind a visitor that there are some dependable customs in this country, despite its turbulent present.

Sultani opens an album that reads like a book of horrors. The cases come from the north, south, east, and west of the country and include rich and poor, urban and rural, women and girls. The first photo is of an eight-year-old girl, covered with scars, who was given as a four-year-old in *bad*. "The girls given in *bad* are treated terribly," Sultani says. "After all, they are the enemy's daughters; they come from the family who killed the son. And in Afghanistan, the families love the sons much more than the daughters."

She explains that now, with the emphasis on education, people know *bad* is wrong. It is against both Islam and civil law. But it still goes on. The hapless child in the photo managed to escape after four years of brutality and now lives in an orphanage. Her abuser has been named by the human rights commission, and an investigation has begun. But getting justice from a still-dysfunctional judiciary, and a police force that is corrupt, is another challenge for Sultani.

She turns the page to a woman who used self-immolation to escape her abusive husband. This woman survived: Her head is lashed to her body with strings of immoveable scar tissue, her hands are stumps, her face fixed in an expression conveying both pain and frustration because of her failure to escape. Sultani is already turning the page, so familiar is she with this history of violence. When I ask her why a woman would choose such a horrible way to commit suicide, she explains:

> Women are watched. They have no access to guns, pills aren't available, they can't hang themselves, because setting up the noose would attract attention, and they don't know about slitting their wrists. Every woman has access to petrol, so setting yourself on fire is seen as a fast way out of an intolerable situation.

Sultani turns another page. This woman had her face slashed by her husband because she was working outside the house. Another is the victim of a money-for-opium marriage. Her father owed money to the drug baron and had to give him his daughter when he couldn't pay the debt. Her arms are broken. This one is Nadia Anjoman, a famous poet bludgeoned to death by her husband on November 5, 2005, because her mother-in-law said she left the house without permission. "He's out of jail now," says Sultani. "He is getting married again." And the photo on the last page, of a woman whose face is beaten black and blue, tells a story of a husband who demanded to have sex the way he had seen it in a pornographic film. She refused. He fisted her vagina until she couldn't walk and pummelled her face with his knuckles.

She has a list of 327 women who miscarried this year due to beatings. "And that's only the reported cases," she says.

The list goes on, but so does the work for change. Sultani's team is spread all over the country, teaching groups of women what their rights are in Islam, and in the laws and constitution of Afghanistan. "We tell them the difference between Islam and tradition, between criminal courts and tribal laws. Most women think that being beaten by a man and bearing many children is the place of an Afghan woman. They think Islam has given all the rights to men. We tell them that is wrong, and that Islam gives equal rights to women."

The teapots are empty, the power surges back on, and the buses that ferry the women in this office to their homes are waiting outside when Sultani closes her book of horrors and calls it a day. The oppression of women in this troubled place won't stop overnight, but the difference today is many more women are part of the growing demand for change because now they know what their rights are.

The case of Annisa, the eighteen-year-old burn victim in Esteqlal Hospital, may be a turning point, a sign of a growing demand for accountability. Her father heard about the fate of his daughter and reported it to the human rights commission. Homa Sultani sent officers to the hospital, gathered evidence, and presented it to the police. Although the sentence for this hideous crime is a scant two years in prison, she knows it will send a message, one that will travel as fast as fire across the country.

THE HUMAN RIGHTS SEED WAS PLANTED in 2002 by a Canadian plan designed to right wrongs for the women of Afghanistan. Human rights was as bizarre a concept to most Afghans then, as terrorist attacks were alien to North Americans prior to 9/11. To women who are not even registered as citizens, to girls who are fed last and least after the men and boys, the notion that they have the right to vote, to an education, and to health care created a buzz all across the country. Now Afghan women are talking the talk with Canadian financial backing.

The brainchild of Ariane Brunet at Rights and Democracy in Montreal, the Women's Rights in Afghanistan Fund started in

September 2002, with a donation of $1.7 million from CIDA over two years, to educate women about the empowering concept of human rights. It has turned out to be one of the most ingenious programs in Afghanistan. Says Brunet:

> A window of opportunity opened when the Taliban fell. If women were ever to get out of the oppressive bind they were in, they had to be part of the emerging civil society. It takes rights to do that. Most women had no idea they had the right to anything at all.

Once she secured the funding, she hired Palwasha Hasan, a thirty-three-year-old woman who spent her young life walking the walk of the disenfranchised, first under the communists and then under the Taliban. "By pushing for a Women's Rights Fund headed by an Afghan woman, you accomplish two things," says Brunet. "You ensure that women are visible and make it clear to funders that this is a long-term project." Soon, Hasan was running nineteen projects from Mazar-e Sharif to the streets of Kabul. No one guessed the program would flourish as quickly as it did—it soon was hailed by the Afghan government as well as the U.N. Security Council. But everyone knew the backlash would be ferocious. The fundamentalists and religious extremists threatened the leaders, looted their offices, and lambasted the plan as un-Islamic.

From literacy training and radio broadcasting, to magazine publishing and family health care, every program uses human rights as its base. For example, on the second floor of a mud-brick building in Baymaro on the outskirts of Kabul, twenty-five women are gathered around the classroom table learning to read and write. The lesson that day was based on the upcoming general election. The concept of democracy, and all that it entails, travels outside the classroom and back to the villages, where the women carry their new-found knowledge to their sisters, mothers, and mothers-in-law. One eighteen-year-old woman, Mary Mohammadi, explained, "I have six brothers who always said I couldn't argue with them because I was illiterate. One brother slapped me on my face for speaking about my rights. Now I know more about the constitution and citizens' rights than they do." But the women all acknowledge the men in their lives are against these upstart ideas. "We tell them it is written in the Quran and the constitution, but it's always a big argument," said Mohammadi.

Hasan is proud of her projects but wary as well. Her office was ransacked by intruders who left the payroll and computer but took the list of people she was working with on the human rights file. She said, "If necessary, I'll hire bodyguards. But I won't quit. The work we are doing is too important for the future."

While I am in her office in 2003, disturbing news arrives from Herat, where Governor Ismail Khan rules: Women have been yanked off the street and subjected to abusive gynecological examinations to prove their virginity. Hasan is trying to get these issues into public discussion. The quickest way, she says, is to get people talking, to train women as advocates, and to raise a generation of activists. But first she has to find ways to reach them, in this country with its 85 percent illiteracy rate. One of the projects she was funding was radio broadcasting. Journalists such as Jane McElhone from Canada were training young women to be radio technicians, to conduct interviews, and to create programming that teaches human rights. The broadcast was reaching two hundred thousand listeners in the northern province of Mazar-e Sharif, where some of the most militant warlords in the country hold power. Radio programs encouraged women to stand for public office, to work on the constitution, and to convey information about human rights to villagers. The newly minted broadcasters took their jobs seriously, while trying to avoid the warlords' henchmen, who lurked around the tiny broadcast centre waiting for an excuse the shut the project down.

For those who can read, she funded a magazine called *Women's Mirror*, a four-page weekly that reaches three thousand readers in sixteen provinces. The editorials are about women's participation in the political life of the country, and the articles are critical of everything from the disarmament program to higher education. In one issue, the editors took on the government for closing schools during the Loya Jirga and depriving students of classes. Editor Shukria Barakzai said, "We were called up in front of the minister of culture and information to explain ourselves. They accused us and judged us as if their office was a court." She knows she publishes at her peril. "Fundamentalists threaten us all the time. We have to be careful about every word we print because they'll use them against us." One lesson she learned is that the term *human rights* may be tolerable, but *women's rights* is a flashpoint that is better avoided.

In Shakardara, west of Kabul, women walk more than an hour from all over the district to get to the human rights classes. More than 650 students had completed the four-day workshop started six months earlier. When the father of one student forbade his daughter from attending the class, the teacher, Nafisa Naseeb, invited him to come and check it out for himself. "I wanted his daughter in my class, but I also knew he had a car, and hoped I could convince him to drive the others who had such a long distance to walk." She won on both counts and says, "If we don't teach the men, we'll never get through to the women."

These women know they are in the early stages of a revolution. And Hasan admits it will take time, perhaps ten or twenty years. "You can't legislate change like this. It has to come from the people requesting it."

Hasan left her post in 2006 to study for a master's degree in England. She was replaced by the able and affable Roya

Rahmani, who had just returned to the country after completing her studies at McGill University in Montreal. The idea for Reform of Family Law had flourished in her absence, and Rahmani saw it as the perfect next step for the Women's Rights Fund. She and Brunet presented the plan to CIDA and in early 2007 received the go-ahead. The announcement outlined the initiative's three main objectives:

- To support Afghan civil society to advocate for the progressive reform of family law;
- To promote respect for women's rights at the community level; and
- To support Afghan civil society organizations to become effective women's rights defenders.

Rahmani joined forces with the Women and Children Legal Research Foundation, the human rights commission, and half a dozen other groups that were working on family law reform. She said, "Women need to come together—urban, rural, poor women, and women from different tribes. They need to talk to each other, establish credibility, and become a voice of authority." She said it is the women who have to push for reform of family law, for standardized marriage contracts, and for trained mullahs and judges who can interpret Islam and the constitution correctly. She called for regional and provincial networking to support the women members of parliament. But this takes funding and planning. "People like funding women's rights, but in reality, there's never enough money to do it. Compare the budget for drug eradication to the one for women's rights, and you'll see how far down the priority list women really are."

She was frankly discouraged when I met her soon after the Kabul riot in 2006. She said:

I was born in 1978; all I know about my country is war.
There is insecurity everywhere. We don't know from day
to day whether we'll have jobs, whether a missile will hit
the house. We have no trust in the government or the
police. And we can't leave because no other country
wants us. People have been living like this for decades.

When Palwasha Hasan returned to her post at the Women's
Rights Fund in the summer of 2007, she had a $5 million
project budget and a four-year time frame to kick-start the
reform of family law. "I know the work, it's dear to my heart,
and I feel I can do something," she told me when I caught up
with her five months later.

She began by collaborating with the leading reform association, Women Living Under Muslim Laws (WLUML), which has
played a vital role in family law reform in countries such as Egypt
and Morocco. Using their methods, Hasan established herself as a
facilitator with the Supreme Court, the mullahs, women's groups,
the women's affairs ministry, and the human rights commission.
"This is about the relationship of men and women within the
family, which is very important in Afghanistan. But it's equally
important that women have a legal space in the relationship."
She is focusing on the constitutional status of women in marriage,
inheritance, child custody, and divorce. And she has a collection
of homegrown strategies for the process. First, talk to the community. "This has to be an Afghan solution. There has to be ownership." Second, use a multi-level approach. "It can't just be the
legal officials who solve the problem; it has to be the women and
men in the community who come up with the ways and means
to reform the law." And finally, timing is everything. "Four years
ago everyone wanted to talk about the constitution. Now, for the
first time, they're ready to talk about reform."

She adamantly points out that the objective is not reconciliation between tribal and civil law. "The objective is to get

people talking about it, finding out where the problems exist. Customary laws are oral, so talking is the way to a solution," she says. *Badal*, for example, was simply an accepted custom. Now even village elders are talking about the fact that, while it may be traditional, the result is never good.

Homa Sultani, who works closely with Hasan, describes the distance they have travelled:

> Three years ago, we had the first meeting with mullahs in Kapisa province, at a workshop to discuss Islamic law and human rights. The mullahs were angry that a woman was present, and were not ready to hear a single word from me. One said, "It's not allowed that a mullah hear the voice of a woman." Three years later, they are helping us. In fact, I saw a mullah solving a woman's problem. He was doing mediation, and telling the husband, "Islam says she is a human being, she's equal to you. If you want her to respect you, you have to respect her."

But the process isn't easy, she admits. Most people still do not know the difference between civil and tribal law. For every man who is willing to deal with change, there is another, maybe two or three others, who see it as unthinkable. Sultani had just had a meeting with an elder and asked him what he would do with a girl who leaves the family to marry. "We'll kill her according to tribal law because she is a shame on us," he said and then went into a tirade about women and family honour. Homa interrupted his murderous ravings and said, "According to the Quran, a woman can get married to who she wishes." His reply? "I don't want to talk to you. The thought of a woman talking about the Quran is impossible."

The organization holds workshops with the mullahs, elders, and tribal leaders who are the protectors of tribal law. One of the problems Sultani is dealing with is that the tribal laws give these religious leaders so much power. It benefits them finan-cially because the mullahs are paid by the tribes, not by the government. They tell her: "We'll solve our problems according to our culture, to the will of the people." So she says her task is to explain civil law in a way that it isn't against tribal law. "It takes skill to do this. You need to be clever like a politician."

The human rights commission uses the media to assist with the program by broadcasting spots on television about tribal law and showing films about its dire consequences. Sultani feels that most mullahs are coming around. But she is aware that this is just the beginning: "This is very new for us. Our grandmothers didn't know about human rights, neither did our mothers. In some ways I'm grateful to the Taliban. They motivated us to become activists."

Reflecting on the changes made for and by women since 2002, Palwasha Hasan says the road has been and will continue to be bumpy, but there have been improvements. There are women in the workplace who have gathered experience. The training programs offered by dozens of non-governmental organizations are bearing fruit. You would be hard-pressed to find a government office refusing a woman a job because of her gender. But Hasan says the challenges still are enormous. "There aren't enough skilled people and professionals to do the jobs we need done. We're running on a single tier." To make her point, she says, "If something happened to Sima Samar, I don't know what would happen to the human rights commission." She knows it takes strong, dedicated women to take on reform. "I was three blocks from a suicide bomb last year. I've had threatening messages, although not lately. The lack of security makes you function in an abnormal way."

The key to this bold reform program is that the women's movement is taking shape. "It's not strong yet," she says. "But we all know each other and we're starting to come together." Life is better, she says. "I'm happy and I love my job." The transformation is visible: Hasan greeted me in a long flowing dress and a hijab that trailed to her mid-thighs when we met in 2003. This time she is wearing jeans and a funky jacket with a bright red scarf that spends more time on her shoulders than covering her hair.

Today the incidence of *bad* is decreasing because people know they will be prosecuted and could spend up to two years in jail. Underage marriage and forced marriage are also beginning to wane, again because of the spread of information. *Badal* stubbornly persists. As for Annisa, she died of her injuries two days after I met her. Her husband offered her father money if he would withdraw the complaint the commission had made to the police. Annisa's father accepted the cash, the charges were dropped. The case is closed.

In Afghanistan today there is law, if not order. There is some justice, if too little and too late.

CHAPTER 5

WITNESSES OF WAR

For every child: health, education, equality, protection.

—UNICEF Canada motto

AS SURELY AS AN INCOMING ROCKET-PROPELLED GRENADE finds its mark, as predictably as land mines litter the fields, and just as certainly as malnutrition and half a dozen opportunistic diseases flourish in war zones, the suffering of children is part of the tapestry of conflict. What children experience during the fracas is mind-searing. A child clings to her mother's skirts, terrified she'll be left behind; another one—lost in the chaos— stands alone, screaming his head off; and still another hides under the bed, eyes squeezed shut, hoping the noise and the terror will go away. In the aftermath, at refugee camps, in the broken remains of their homes, or out on the mean streets of the devastated cities, the children are yoked to the conse- quences of war. Some suffer from the psychological trauma that comes from insecurity; others—the homeless ones, the orphans, the wounded, and the malnourished—suffer no less grievously. They are too small for their age, too wise for their years, too needy for words. They have scars, burns, and body sores that speak of the horrors they have seen. Most are coughing, scratching, and yawning. But they are children all the same: fetching and curious, beguiling and vulnerable, eager to make friends, quick to laugh, hungry for love.

During twenty years of reporting from zones of conflict, I have seen these kids in Africa, Asia, the Middle East, and the Balkans. There is not a lot of difference between a street kid in Kabul and a refugee child in Africa. All of them are paying the price for someone else's grievance and, without help, they grow up and keep the war-kettle boiling, carrying the quarrel to the next generation.

It was during the civil war in Somalia in 1993 when I came to that conclusion, after I met a boy who was on the verge of losing his battle to survive. My assignment was to find out who gets the aid being delivered to war zones. In this case, I was following a shipment of wheat from Canada to the point of delivery. That happened to be Baidoa, the centre of the famine belt. One day, I went to a therapeutic feeding centre—the end of the line for people in a famine. Of those who find their way there, and to the intravenous feeding stations, few survive. The boy I met had arrived a few days earlier. This is his story.

His father had been killed when his village was marked by warlords as one that would be denied food. The thing we all learned after the 1984 Ethiopian famine was that people do not usually die because there is no food. They die because warlords decide certain villages are not going to get the donated food. This child's mother had no choice but to gather up her six starving children and try to find her way to Baidoa. Four of the children died along the way. The mother and one other child died the day after they arrived. Now this boy was alone. He lay like a little bag of bones, still as the air on a straw mat in this dank, damaged building that had been taken over by the non-government organization called Caritas. He looked about three years old. In fact, he was six. This is typical in cases of starvation: A youngster looks half his age while adults look twice their age. After the director of the centre told me this boy's story, I wanted to take a photograph, and I kneeled down at the end of the mat where the boy lay to position my camera for the shot. I also turned on the flash because the room was dark as well as cold, even though the Somali sun was scorching the earth. When I pushed the button and the flash went off, the tiny body on the mat stirred. He seemed to be looking for the source of the light. I thought, my God, he is so sick, but he still has that wondrous childhood curiosity. Well, when he stretched his tiny little head around far enough, he saw me: a giant woman with yellow hair. Poor little guy—he probably thought he had died. We made eye contact. Instinctively, I smiled at him, all the while thinking what hopelessly inappropriate behaviour this was, to be smiling when this child was so terribly ill. But here's the thing. He smiled back at me. I stood in that wretched place thinking, What the heck goes on in the world? Here is a child who is very nearly dead, and yet he still has the curiosity we love in children, and he still wants to make friends with a total stranger. What happens to affable little kids that they grow up to be warlords, insurgents, fundamentalists, rapists, suicide bombers?

British journalist Felicity Arbuthnot, who has reported from Iraq on eighteen different occasions, describes the power of trauma in a report she wrote about a boy called Ali whose father was killed in the 1991 Gulf War. Ali was three years old when he saw his father buried. The cemetery was near his house. Day after day he escaped from home and was found at his father's grave. He would dig into the ground with his bare hands, saying, "It's all right, Daddy, you can come out now. The men who have put you here have gone away."

I met nine-year-old Iskra in 1992 in Zagreb, Croatia. She had been playing on the street in front of her home in Bihac when the bombs started to fall. Her mother grabbed her and shouted to everyone else on the street to get into the stairwell of the apartment building. They escaped the explosions on the street, but then a soldier opened the door to the stairwell where they were hiding and threw a grenade at them. Three of the kids were blown to pieces; seventeen more were badly injured. Iskra's hand was hanging by a thread. Her mother knew her child could bleed to death. She scooped her up and ran down the street to the nearest hospital, telling herself all the way: "Don't cry, you need your breath to run faster." Iskra's hand was amputated. In the hospital in Zagreb, the pretty child mimicked her mother's antics, and even laughed as she recounted the frantic dash to the hospital in Bihac, and the transfer to Zagreb, and all the things that went wrong in the process.

Incredibly, the children of war will smile at a stranger, wink at the pomposity of a power-tripping adult, and hang on to a conversation with the curiosity so precious in young people. They seem to have a sixth sense about survival while coping with the unimaginable. But the scars left by their terrible experiences are hidden from view and need as much attention as the bandages on their physical wounds.

Norwegian child psychologist Magne Raundalen is renowned for the work he has done with children of war. When he visited Bosnia in 1992, he discovered that two-thirds of the refugee children he encountered had developed symptoms of psychiatric disorders, and that mothers and newborn infants were not bonding. An entire generation of children needed treatment.

His work, which began with studies of Scandinavian children who survived the atrocities of the Second World War, made him realize that waiting until the conflict is over would be waiting too long. Those survivors, many of them members of the networking association he founded called the Children and War Foundation, were between the ages of fifty and seventy when he started his work in Bosnia. He said the men and women he treated in Scandinavia have extraordinary common bonds: a higher than normal rate of marriage break-down, emotional instability, and alcoholism. The ghosts of their shattered youth were destroying their adulthood as well. Raundalen feared that a similar destiny was in store for the children of the former Yugoslavia.

He tells teachers and parents that there are things they can do to help. When a teacher reprimands a student for whining about the war by saying, for example, "Forget the past, get on with your life!" Raundalen says it contributes to the isolation the child feels. He says the children need to talk about what has happened to them. He suggests the children start a letter-writing campaign from region to region, and from one ethnic group to another. He says kids need to write about this traumatic period in their lives, to talk about the war.

His wise counsel matches the thinking of Bibi Hajji, a sixty-five-year-old grandmother who runs the Fatema Tul Zahra school in the tough centre of Kabul. Hajji has never heard of Professor Raundalen, but her instinct tells her that it is the children who will lead the country to peace. Her school is like an Afghan version of Oliver Twist's poorhouse: A ragtag collection of kids sits cross-legged on the floor of the classrooms, in an ancient building Hajji has reclaimed. The classes are tucked into every conceivable corner of this building: One seems more like a closet; another, a closed-in balcony. Bibi does not care about the surroundings. Her goal is to make sure the 147 kids in her care get an education. "We collect them from the market. Most have no parents: They live with a grandparent or on the street. If we don't teach them here, they'll grow up to be terrorists or thieves and they'll kill each other."

Teaching isn't all Hajji does. She buys clothes from the bazaar for the children (which is probably why all the boys are wearing identical green shirts on the day I visit) and gives them a hot meal at lunchtime. She also has persuaded a doctor to open a clinic, rent-free, in one of the eight rooms in the building, where he can see his own patients as long as Bibi's kids receive free medical attention too. "At my age, I wake up in the morning with a lot of aches and pains," she says, "but when I see the boys and girls in my school, they are my painkillers."

When she started the school, she noticed the students' drawings were of guns, tanks, and blood. She also noticed they fought with one another at lunchtime. She knew they had to talk about these things, that this was ground zero in her war against terrorism. She encouraged them to tell their stories and to help one another. If a student stumbles with a math problem, or over the pronunciation of a word, the others chime in with the answer. They clap after one reads aloud from a text. Noor, who is fourteen, says, "One day, I'll build schools and help the poor. And I'll help the people who helped me."

There is a long way to go for these kids, with no family names and husky, street-smart voices. They work at the market after school selling water, polishing boots, wiping car windshields, or peddling phone cards. But every single one of them can read. Like most kids here, they want to be doctors, pilots, teachers, or the president of Afghanistan. One twelve-year-old girl called Tamanna (which means "hope") tells me she likes math class best. But then she says, "Lunchtime is good too."

Bibi Hajji, whose work is funded by Canadian Women for Women in Afghanistan, has not had the benefit of a world-famous psychologist to guide her curriculum. But the work she is doing takes a page from the teachers in Sarajevo, who dealt with post-conflict trauma when their classrooms reopened after four years of forced closure in the nineties. Ninety percent of the students at the Musa Cazim Catic School saw a family member or friend killed during the horrific siege of Sarajevo and in the battles fought in the surrounding villages of Bosnia.

They were two years old when the war started, six when it ended. By the time they staggered out of the cellars they had been hiding in, they were shell-shocked, malnourished, and knew more about dying than living.

It was in 2001, half a dozen years after the ceasefire in Bosnia, just a month after 9/11, while bombs were dropping all over Afghanistan, when I visited the classroom in Sarajevo. An eleven-year-old boy called Amar was telling his story to his classmates. By the time he got to the end, he was weeping. While the kids on either side of him reached out to console him, their teacher, Edina Zvizdic, jumped into the discussion. "Remember the first class we had together? Remember half of you were crying. You'd lost your fathers, your relatives, your homes; many of you were refugees. You didn't know what a banana was, or a streetlight, because you'd been hiding in the cellar and had never seen fresh fruit or played outside with a friend. Now we know how important we are to each other."

The innovative program they were taking part in is called Building Bridges. It began half a world away, in Toronto in the early nineties, when teachers noticed that refugee kids from places such as the former Yugoslavia, Afghanistan, Sri Lanka, and Somalia were having behavioural problems that were disrupting their ability to learn. The program was developed and implemented in Canada with immigrant and refugee children and then taken to Croatia, Bosnia, Albania, and Kosovo to children affected by war. Building Bridges uses story-telling, art, physical activity, and a buddy system to help kids deal with trauma. They tell their own stories, discuss their feelings, and develop an understanding of someone else's culture, someone else's life experience, someone else's pain. This getting-to-know-each-other breeds the tolerance that has eluded the population in places such as the Balkans, the Middle East, much of Asia and Africa, and is threatening to become an issue in Europe and North America.

After only a few months in the program, these Sarajevo students who lived and watched their friends die in a place that came to be known as the terrorist capital of the world want to talk about kids in America and Afghanistan. They know what happens when intolerance leads to hate, when one group wants to kill another simply because they are different. They feel solidarity with other kids in places such as New York and Kabul. They are wise for their years, but their wisdom has come with a heavy price: It cost them their childhood. On this mid-October afternoon they think about the children in the United States who got up on a sunny morning in September 2001 and said goodbye to their mothers and fathers, not realizing they would never see them again. And they wonder what will become of the kids in Afghanistan who are hungry and cold and have to hide from the guns as they did in Sarajevo.

Dr. Ismet Ceric, head of the department of psychiatry at the Clinical Centre in Sarajevo, says the catastrophe of 9/11 created a flashback effect for the people of Sarajevo, where ten thousand citizens were slaughtered, twelve hundred of them children. Ceric watched the horror in New York City unfold on television. When he saw the looks on the faces of the teenagers who were being hustled from their schools across the East River by the police and their teachers to escape the exploding Twin Towers, he saw the same symptoms as he has been diagnosing in Sarajevo. "I saw those kids, I saw the trauma in their faces, and I knew."

Post-traumatic stress disorder is a fairly recent phenomenon in the therapy business. Ceric says he actually dismissed the claim by Vietnam War veterans that they were suffering from a war-related stress disorder as a political argument when he read about it. But then it began to happen all around him: depression, anxiety, nightmares, illusions, and increased rates of suicide. "We learned something new every day of the war," he says.

It was that missing information about the psychological effects of violence that drove a marketing dynamo, the late Madeline-Ann Aksich, a Montrealer of Croatian descent, to find a way to help the war-affected children of Dubrovnik, the Croatian city where she spent her childhood summers. She discovered that although there were emergency services for children, there was nothing available to deal with the lingering trauma in their lives. "I found out that the more often the Vietnam vets retold their stories, the less impact it had on their cardiovascular systems. If they could rebuild their shattered lives by retelling their stories, why wouldn't it work for the children?" Self-expression is the key to resiliency, she discovered. "It's the process that rebuilds your assumptions about yourself and your self-esteem." A serendipitous meeting with Toronto business consultant Allan Pearson put her in touch with the Toronto teachers, and Aksich recognized the paradigm shift that was needed to deal with the refugee kids in the Toronto classrooms, as well as the children in the war-torn Balkans. If children were going to grow up to be stable, tolerant adults, someone had to deal with the trauma they had suffered along the way. She put together a blue-ribbon team of experts, including social and emotional health experts, teachers, school administrators, and community leaders, as well as Allan Pearson. In 1992, they launched the International Children's Institute (ICI), a non-profit humanitarian organization whose mandate was to help children throughout the world to overcome psychological trauma resulting from natural and human-created disasters. Dr. Ester Cole, the Toronto psychologist on the team, said, "In view of the events since September 11, and the effect those events have had on children, it's a program that's needed in schools all over the world today." Unfortunately, ICI closed its doors in 2005 due to lack of financial support, but the program it funded continues its work with war-traumatized children.

Building Bridges is not a paint-by-numbers solution, says Cole. "We needed to simplify the research and make it user-friendly and capitalize on best practices that teachers do anyway." Its genius is that it fits the normal classroom and works with the current curriculum. "For the most part, what children face all over the world in times of stress is they are scared," she says. "The adults in their lives think they have the answers. But all the kids want is to be listened to." For example, she says, when a teacher looks at a child's painting and says, "Tell me about that. Why is there blood? What are those tanks doing?" the child gets to tell what's on her mind. She says adults mean well when they say to a refugee child: "Now that you're in Canada, you're fine." But Cole says, "That minimizes their fears. It's better to ask questions about their past. What are you proud of? What was your life like there? What did you love?"

Whether in the classrooms of Toronto or elsewhere in the world, the rules in the program are straightforward: no put-downs, no hierarchy, and no "my culture is better than your culture." The approach is to focus on the younger children—grades two, three, four, and five—and to rebuild their mental health. Teachers have found the program is also effective with kids suffering from the trauma of domestic violence, family conflict, and even the woe children feel when the family moves across the country and they have to leave their friends and all that's familiar behind. It's about talking to one another, finding out what makes you proud of who you are, and where you came from, as well as what makes you feel afraid.

Although kids preoccupied with trauma have a hard time academically, socially, and emotionally, the good news, says Cole, is that children are wonderfully resilient. "Once you establish a stable life for them, and they believe it isn't going to be taken away, they move ahead. The time it takes to move ahead depends on a number of factors, such as the duration of the conflict, and the magnitude of the loss." Other factors are the developmental stage the child is at: A baby, for example, adjusts more easily than a fifteen-year-old. The level of self-esteem the child has also counts, and people with a good sense of self are better able to cope.

Teachers report the kids respond quickly to these programs. Their writing changes, the stories become less aggressive, a sense of normality develops. John Campey, a Toronto teacher who spent time in the schools of Sarajevo implementing the program, says, "Having someone to listen and validate and support their experiences is very important to children. It's also of immense value to have a chance to deal with their peers and get the sense that they aren't alone."

It is a difficult concept for kids who come from homes where children are meant to be seen and not heard. Belma Hulusic, who works for the program in Sarajevo, says, "Usually nobody asks children for their opinion. The attitude here is, 'Shut up and listen.'" She starts by telling the children: "There are no marks in this program. No bad answers. Say what you think and how you feel." She says the important thing is to get them to open up. Once they tell their stories, the job is half done.

There is scarcely a child or a teenager in Afghanistan who does not need this kind of program. Hajji's school notwithstanding, two-thirds of the children have no school to go to. And too many others are languishing in jail for crimes, such as running away from an enforced marriage, rather than attending school and getting an education. These children of war desperately need to heal. Instead, their wounds are worsened by the intolerance that clings like mould to cultural and religious interpretations.

Dibah, for example, is a pretty seventeen-year-old with long blonde hair and angry blue eyes. I met her in 2003 when I entered the women's wing of the prison in Kabul. Her crime? She was escaping an abusive husband. Dibah had been forced to marry a Taliban man two years before, and now that the war was over, she wanted a divorce. "He said he would kill me. No one would stop him, so I came here." There are twenty other young women sharing the same fate. They live six to a cell, sleep on mats on a concrete floor, and rely on family members to send them food. There is a window in the cell, but no pane of glass. When the snow flies in Kabul, and the temperature drops to minus twenty degrees, the 3-by-5.5-metre cell turns into an icebox. Ninety percent of all the female prisoners in this jail are here for what are called sex crimes: they were seen with their boyfriends, or had sex with someone other than their husband, or were raped—no one knows, and no one seems to care to know the details. If it involves sex, it is the girl's fault, and she is imprisoned. Unless of course someone is trying to kill her: Then she is imprisoned to prevent the man, who is walking around with impunity, from seeing her dead. When I returned to the prison six months later to find out how Dibah was getting along, the warden said indifferently: "She's gone back to her family," which means she now has been imprisoned by her father in another place. Because of her so-called shame, no man will marry her, and to be a single woman in the village is a terrible fate. She dares not leave the village, and no one is prepared to arrest her husband, the man who threatened to kill her. Even the legal department of the Ministry of Women's Affairs was more interested in sending a woman back to an abusive husband than risking a divorce. "We don't want to be like the West," said Faisia Sadiq, a lawyer who works with the jailed women. "We want to help them to get along with each other."

There are girls as young as sixteen in the prison, some for being caught with their boyfriends, others for running away from home. Spiked, dyed hair pokes out from under their hijabs. Like most teenagers, they are scared and defiant at once. Their cases are going to trial, but there is not much evidence to suggest they have been arrested for legitimate offences or that the judge who hears their cases even knows what sharia law says and does not say about women.

To find out what judges know and who instructs them, I sought an audience with Chief Justice Shinwari, which turned out to be a scene reminiscent of a Gilbert and Sullivan satire. Shrouded in a dark scarf, and covered from head to toe in black clothes, I entered his office with as much trepidation as curiosity. With machinegun-toting guards in attendance, the eighty-five-year-old chief justice began by giving me a lecture about justice and piety. Although he is determined to round up the men who murder their wives, he says, he is equally determined to punish women and girls who behave in a way he calls un-Islamic. Was it un-Islamic for a teenager such as Dibah to languish in a prison cell because a man who thinks he owns her wants to kill her? The unvarnished answer is: "She is a woman. She must do as she's told." But the Quran says she can choose whom she marries, I offer. "You don't understand, so your question isn't important," he replies while turning his head to one of the guards with a look on his face that says, "Get this woman out of here." I need to get his attention, so I ask him about the weapon hanging on the wall behind his desk. He warms to the reply as he tells me it's for "the punishment." The long rubber strap, almost eight centimetres wide and half a centimetre thick, is removed from the wall so he can demonstrate its efficacy. Its flexibility makes it more like a whip. He tells me it is administered to every part of the body except the face, as many as sixty lashes at a time. I think of the teenagers in the prison and wince for them. Before leaving, I tell him the chief justice in Canada, Beverley McLachlin, does not have a whip on her wall. He misses the point and says he would like to meet *him*.

Although Shinwari is now retired, the injustice meted out to children and teenagers continues on a dozen different fronts. Says Nigel Fisher, president and CEO of UNICEF Canada:

"There are improvements, many of them, but we need a better coordinated effort." He has decades of experience in dealing with children in conflict zones. When asked why it takes so long to alter the lives of the kids in Afghanistan, he points to India as an example. "We started in India in 1949. Look at that country now." But he adds, "We still have ten offices there, and $100 million in programs. Development and reconstruction take decades. Afghanistan started at close to zero." It is not the answer I am looking for. The children in this country fall into the lowest levels on almost every health index—malnutrition, infant mortality, under-five mortality—that the World Health Organization measures. Surely we have learned something since 1949?

The blame game in Afghanistan is great for providing excuses but does little to help the kids. "Donors have not delivered on their promises." Or: "The Afghans themselves don't want outsiders interfering." Fisher agrees with the first statement and disagrees with the second. "Afghans are independent and entrepreneurial. They say: 'We're glad you're here and we'll be happy when we don't need you any more.' They hear all the promises of billions of dollars from donors, but they aren't seeing that."

So what is being done? He produces a three-page document of numbers—the usual U.N. accountability system. This one covers the health status of children in Afghanistan. Fisher, who has spent his adult life trying to find ways to help children, is as disappointed as the next person with the dismally slow progress being made. He knows as well as anyone that a population in which 50 percent are under age fifteen is in trouble if these children's needs are ignored. And he reminds anyone who will listen that new mechanisms need to be put in place to alter the future for the children. He points to a bold new experiment in progress in Afghanistan today that is completely revamping the entire health-care system for children and mothers. He recommends that I visit the Rukha clinic, which is tucked up in the Panjshir valley, northeast of Kabul, to see for myself.

It is the dead of winter—the coldest and snowiest winter in thirty years—when I set out to the Rukha clinic in January 2008. Security is an issue because of the recent terrorist attacks in Kabul that targeted foreigners. Accordingly, drivers willing to make the road trip are scarce. A bit of serendipity leads me to Noor, a knowledgeable and pleasant young man who agrees to borrow his brother's taxi, remove the "for hire" sign, and become my driver for the trip. We set out early in the morning before the chaotic Kabul traffic is underway.

The panorama that is the awesomely beautiful Panjshir valley shows itself in the distance an hour out of Kabul. It is like going through a gateway to a *National Geographic* tour. Also known as the Valley of the Five Lions, its rich history includes legends of Alexander the Great (who left his genetic blueprint visible in some of the blond, blue-eyed Tajiks who now live here) and the infamous Ahmad Shah Masood, also known as the Lion of Panjshir, the martyred mujahedeen leader who kept the Taliban at bay. The Panjshiries kept the Russians out as well, and today they claim that the International Security Assistance Force in Afghanistan will not even venture into the province. Narrow valleys cut through the slopes of the massive Hindu Kush. The craggy peaks of the immense mountains poke out from pillows of snow that blanket the steep fall to the river below. Aquamarine water pools in the eddies before rushing into the fast-flowing river where it creates enormous ice jams and then gurgles around the sharp corners that follow the mountains to the south. The sun glances off the snow and ice, blinding a driver on the hairpin turns of the switchback roads. The scenery is breathtaking. Vignettes of village life flash by, like the canvas of a Bruegel painting: an old man walking with a stick at the river's edge; an overturned truck, its roof smashed in, lying on the riverbed where it met its violent end; women in periwinkle-blue burkas; slaughtered sheep dangling from hooks; little kids darting into the street and back to the stalls because school is closed for the winter. No wonder there is a proud strut in the gait of the Tajiks who have protected this land for centuries.

But the paradox that is Afghanistan soon butts into this landscape of natural wonders and ancient villages when a militia suddenly appears, blocking the road, its leader demanding to know who dares to come to Panjshir. A lot of shouting and gun-waving follows. The leader demands my passport. Noor quickly says, "Don't give it—I'll tell him you don't have one." My attempt to blend in as an Afghan woman in conservative attire (an ankle-length grey winter coat and a scarf covering my head and shoulders that nearly reaches my waist) does not guarantee safe passage with a warlord's militia. Noor gets out of the car to negotiate and tells me he thinks my sunglasses gave me away. What follows are speeches about spies and foreign infidels, followed by more gun-waving. After about ten minutes of begging, explaining, and failing to negotiate a way to proceed to the clinic, the commander of the group announces, "We don't let foreigners into Panjshir unless they come from France—the people in France like Muslims so we let them come to our land. The rest are infidels and aren't welcome here." Noor smiles and says, "Then it isn't a problem, because the lady is from France." The militia steps back, we are waved on (and I want to whistle the "Marseillaise").

Half an hour later, we wind through the bustling town of Rukha and follow the signs to the health clinic where Dr. Sayed Habib Ayobi is waiting for us. The technical adviser from the Ministry of Health responsible for health administration in all of Panjshir, he tells us he has been waiting an hour for our arrival and is horrified to learn that his visitor has been detained on the way to the clinic. And then he leads me, with the pride of a new parent, to the one-storey stucco building perched on a snow-covered hill.

This is the test-case clinic. It is modest and rudimentary, but for the people who have lived in the area all their lives, it is one small miracle in the making. Funded by the World Bank, the plan is to reduce the maternal mortality rate (which was 1,600 per 10,000 pregnant women) by 20 percent in three years and similarly to cut the under-five child mortality rate (which was 257 per 1,000) by 15 percent. For Ayobi, it's all about numbers, needs, and accountability. He and his colleagues have a daunting task. They have the same problems the other provinces in Afghanistan have: the destruction from thirty years of war, pervasive lack of security, and immense gender disparity. There are three priorities: broad access to clinical services; improved quality of patient care; and an efficient clinical operation assessed by monthly tallies that account for success or failure. Access, for example, is measured by patient numbers. If there are two hundred pregnant women in the district of Rukha, the calculation calls for thirty of them to visit the clinic each month. If that number doesn't turn up, Ayobi wants to know why. Is access a problem? If so, they need to send one of the community health-care workers to the patient's house. Is it culture? If that's the case, then a home visit is required to try to change the thinking that doesn't allow women to seek medical help.

There are two levels of service: basic health care, which is delivered by a doctor, nurse, midwife, and two vaccinators at the centre, and more comprehensive care delivered in a larger clinic that has two doctors (one male and one female, since men will not allow their wives to be examined by a male doctor), a midwife, pharmacist, lab technician, two vaccinators, one community health-care worker, and three guards. Ayobi ticks off the jobs and numbers with an obsession for accountability. Of the fifteen thousand people in Rukha, he knows how many are pregnant or of child-bearing age, or less than five years of age. "We make a target for each group," he explains. Although the emphasis on numbers smacks of some totalitarian dystopia, the program is producing excellent results. Cases of measles among children are down; so is polio. In two years, maternal mortality has dropped by almost 20 percent. The under-five mortality rate is down by 12 percent.

The doctor who oversees patient care is Frogh Malalay, a thirty-four-year-old widow whose husband was killed by the Taliban seven years ago. She lives on the site with her eight-year-old son and sees forty patients a day. "It's about changing behaviour," she says. "Men used to tell the women they couldn't come here. They said, 'If she dies, she dies.' It was the attitude. They're more open-minded now. They have learned about things like the value of vaccines." The changes are apparent all over the village. The girls are going to school. Some people have satellite television and access to a series of programs from non-governmental organizations about health care and education. Malalay says some women come to the clinic just to talk about their problems, making excuses at home to have ten minutes with the doctor.

Inside the clinic, a woman called Marzia is sitting on the waiting-room bench, holding her infant son who is snuggled into a bright pink sleeper. She yanks her burka over her face when I approach, but later, she flips it back again and even allows me to take a photo. She explains she has walked for an hour to get here but says, "It's good. I'm happy because here our hundred problems can be solved." She has two other children with her: Aaqila, who is ten, and Subhan, three. Her one-year-old twins are at home with her mother-in-law. This is the first time Marzia has had health care for her children, and the first time a midwife has attended to her. All the kids have been vaccinated. Marzia sees the one-hour walk down the mountain path and into the village as a minor inconvenience.

She says other women walk for two hours to get to the clinic. They know that this clinic, and the new schools in the surrounding villages, as well as the high school in Rukha, are the keys to a better future.

Ayobi says one of their greatest problems is finding women who will stay here to work. "If they're educated, they all want to go to Kabul," he says. But not Malalay, who lives in a two-room house beside the clinic and is on call 24/7. The cement house is heated by a single stove that she stokes with more wood when we sit on the floor mats to talk. She offers one of the huge heavy blankets that are strewn about the place to counter the bitter temperature—it is minus twenty degrees outside. She pays hardly any attention to the frosty air, however, and instead scurries around to prepare a meal and tea, and then settles in to talk about her life. She graduated from medical school in Kabul, and then lived in Mazar-e Sharif until she moved to Panjshir two years ago to run this clinic. "I used to feel very much old during the Taliban time. But now I feel young again." Of the work she is doing here, she says, "The health of the women and children was very poor when we started. But we have made a lot of changes."

As for her own lifestyle, she says she feels safer here as a single woman than she would feel if she were working in Kabul, although the salary—$300 a month—is a little more than half of what she would earn by working for an NGO in the city. She also wears a burka out of respect for, and in solidarity with, the village women she treats, even though most professional women, such as doctors and teachers, stopped wearing it several years ago. She leaves it behind when she travels to Kabul.

She says she is happy here with her son, Ahmad. "He goes to school. I do my work. It's okay." She has received several marriage proposals but says, in her straightforward way: "I don't like any of those men who asked me." She has family nearby: her late husband's mother is from Panjshir, so there is an extended family to help. She is tidying up the lunch dishes, preparing to go back to her patients, when she says, "A lot of the time I help myself. I think it's better that way."

Her reference to the independence of women does not go unnoticed by Marzia, who has joined us for lunch. It is obvious a conversation has started here. It is tentative and cautious, but it's a start. I wonder if the children are part of that conversation. The schools are closed for the winter months because it gets too cold to sit in the unheated classrooms. Just north of Panjshir, more than nine hundred people, mostly children, have died of the cold this winter. Even in Rukha, they don't have winter jackets or boots. The traditional Afghan blankets wrapped around the shoulders can't begin to keep a body warm at minus twenty degrees. Nor can the plastic sandals everyone wears, many without socks. But this little test-case clinic has brought hope to Rukha.

Bringing the lessons developed by Dr. Magne Raundalen to the classrooms of Afghanistan is a pipe dream so far. Even though experts in child health say every child in Afghanistan suffers from post-traumatic stress disorder, the need for security, stable government, and health clinics such as this one is taking precedence over healing the children of war.

September 11 taught most of the world a terrifying lesson, one that the children of Afghanistan, Sarajevo, Somalia, Sierra Leone, Iraq, and a hundred other blood-soaked places on the planet have already learned: They need to know one another better, to share their concerns, to listen to one another's fears, to seek an adulthood that includes tolerance. The child psychologists say the children traumatized by war can't wait for treatment. But the children of Afghanistan have been waiting their entire lives.

Whether a refugee child or an abused one, whether a witness to the evil of hate or an object of it, whether a child of America or a child of Afghanistan, the children of conflict need to rise again—out of the ashes.

CHAPTER 6

LOST AND FOUND

We have no voice. You must ask the women in your country to speak for us.

—Sharifa, Interview with author, Kandahar, January 2001

THEY HAVE BEEN PLAYING ON THE BACK ON MY EYELIDS like old movies, the images of these women and girls I met during the last eleven years in Afghanistan. Their sagas linger after I return home, partly because I am asked to speak at fundraisers all across the country and invariably repeat the desperate details of these women's lives over and over again, but also because it is profoundly difficult to walk away from a human drama knowing there are ways and means of altering the outcome for the better. It has at times felt as much like a crusade as a journalistic assignment, reporting the facts while encouraging others at public events to take action. Whenever there is news of a suicide bombing, a new law trampling the rights of women, or a preposterous suggestion denigrating the status of women as a cultural and religious issue that is no one else's business, I think of the truly vulnerable women and girls I have come to know. Their stories stick in my memory and create inexplicable hope that they will somehow find harmony in the face of despair.

One unforgettable saga belongs to Sharifa, a gentle mother of six children, whose canny survival skills were severely tested in Kandahar under the menacing eye of the Taliban. Another is Lima, a blameless girl, who somehow stayed alive in the sprawling Shomali Plains during the nightmare years of bombing and raiding. And then there's Soghra, a woman of uncommon beauty from Bamiyan, who was forced to tell the biggest lie of her life in order to keep her children from starving to death.

I met these women during the Taliban years and again after the international community arrived with its expansive plans to alter the destiny of this fractious place. I checked in with them once more, when I was writing *Veiled Threat*, and again later, when making a CBC television documentary, *The Daughters of Afghanistan*, with director Robin Benger and cameraman Alister Bell. If an assignment took me anywhere near their villages, I dropped in to visit; if that was impossible, I would ask a foreign aid worker or fellow journalist who was going to the region to carry a parcel for me. Once, Om Bolah, the distinguished consul general for India, even agreed to be my courier when he was going to his office in Kandahar and I was stuck in Kabul. For me, these women and girls were the players on the stage the rest of the world was now watching. How well they progressed would be a measure of the success achieved by the new Afghanistan.

SHARIFA STRUCK ME AS A CAPABLE MANAGER the first time I met her in January 2001. She was working in the basement of the

Orthopaedic Institute in Kandahar, with a team of five women physiotherapy technicians. Just as women at home had to block their windows so that no one could see them, so these women also were forced to work behind windows that had been covered in dark blue paint. They wore the wedge-heeled shoes that the Taliban demanded to avoid the tapping sound of high heels. And they weren't allowed to be seen by the men who built the prostheses in the laboratory upstairs. Regardless of the prison-like environment, Sharifa greeted me profession-ally and gave me a tour of the basement facility. A woman with huge round eyes and a serene, almost angelic face, she intro-duced me to her patients. They included polio victims; stroke patients with withered limbs; children who had lost their legs to land mines and were learning to walk again with artificial limbs; amputees who had had a limb cut off in front of a crowd of braying onlookers as punishment for stealing; and others who had fallen prey to the violence and deprivation of drought-stricken Kandahar. The layers of grim despair as we walked from room to room, and from patient to patient, was as oppressive as the presence of the Taliban guards outside. It wasn't until lunchtime, when we were in an enclosed room, that Sharifa and the other therapists dropped the appearance of obedient compliance and tore off the veil of secrecy surround-ing their lives. The floodgates opened and their horror stories gushed into the room. Sharifa knew they were taking a chance. Speaking against the Taliban was an offence punishable by whipping and imprisonment. But, she said, "Someone has to know what is happening to us. We have no voice. You must ask the women in your country to speak for us."

This was the hardened reality of life with the Taliban. These women had been teachers. Now they were forbidden to teach their daughters to read. But at least they had jobs in a country that banned women from the workplace. The loophole they managed to squeeze through was the need for women therapists to attend to female patients who, of course, could not be seen by men. However, their salaries were so meagre that they were only eking out a living, earning barely enough to put food on the table. But as we sat together, the conversation led from the misery in their lives to stories women always share about their children, their homes, and even the humour they find in their day-to-day lives. I marvelled at how they could laugh and poke fun at their difficulties, and dish the dirt about local goings-on. These were the women who took me to see Osama bin Laden's house in Kandahar. We rode in the van that took them to and from work, and while the vehicle bumped along the rutted roads to bin Laden's showy estate on the outskirts of Kandahar, they told me about the wedding party he had for his son just a few weeks before. They described a lavish reception, and a raucous party where video cameras whined and music blared until five o'clock in the morning, in a city whose citizens would be arrested for being outside after dark, taking photographs, watching television, or listening to music. When we reached our destination, we exited the van to have a better look at the two-storey mansion but hung back from the gate lest we be seen by the patrolling guards. Unlike the crowded, dilapidated huts around it, this property was expansive, surrounded by gardens, and protected from the visual reality of life in Kandahar. When I asked, "What does this man do that he can afford to live like this?" they laughed out loud and said, "Nothing good." In hindsight, I can hardly imagine how they had the nerve even to approach the place that reeked of power and exclusivity. On the way back to the city centre, they regaled me with stories about Canada's Joint Task Force Two, a covert special-operations unit whose activities are never reported. The women said, "Your secret soldiers dress like Rambo. We always know where they are. They're good-looking and pretty daring." Not much escapes the women.

The second-largest city in Afghanistan, Kandahar used to be a major trading centre: Its dried fruits and succulent pomegranates were known as the best in the world. Now, although trade has started again and the famous pomegranates are finding their way to Canadian markets, Kandahar is better known for being the centre of the insurgency. Founded by Alexander the Great in 330 BC, it has always been a target because of its strategic location, linking Asia to the Middle and Far East. Despite its many wars, there are a few historic monuments still standing, including one of Islam's holiest sites, the mausoleum of Ahmad Shah Durrani, which has a shrine containing the Prophet's cloak, and another sanctum that holds a snip of his hair. Kandahar is also the home town of President Karzai.

The hot, dry desert air and the infernal sand stand out in my memory of that first visit to Kandahar. At dusk, it can be the spookiest place on the planet: any available light filtered through dust; the streets emptying except for men who cruise with guns; the broken buildings standing as witness to decades of destruction; the frightened and exhausted inhabitants hiding behind the purdah walls of their mud-brick homes, hoping the night won't bring more trouble from marauding Taliban soldiers looking for an excuse to make an example of a citizen.

When it was time to leave, Sharifa tucked naan and sweet cakes into my pocket for the journey back to the Pakistan border. That she had the grace to give, when they all needed so badly to receive, stays with me still. On the way out of the city, I wondered if I would ever be able to repay her kindness and, in fact, whether I would see her again.

Back in Canada I spoke at the annual breakfast fundraiser held by the Canadian Women's Foundation. I shared Sharifa's story with them and described the lives of the other women. I said that, not knowing how to help other than by getting their story to the outside world, and at the same time feeling their discomfort, I had left them the hand lotion and face cream I had in my backpack—as balm, I hoped, to soothe at least the outside layer of the roughened life they were living.

Immediately after the breakfast, a group of women approached me, saying they would like to help. They represented one of the sponsors of the event, L'Oreal, a cosmetics company that had supported the Canadian Women's Foundation for years. They said if I could find a way to transport a box to Afghanistan, they would fill it with cream and lotion for the women. Their solidarity with women half a world away was heart-warming and typical of the response I got from women in Canada whenever I wrote about the women of Afghanistan. I gave them the address of the NGO in Pakistan that was running the Institute of Orthopaedics and paying the salaries of the women. The L'Oreal team stuffed the box with every product they had—being careful not to include anything that would attract Taliban attention. It was enormously expensive to ship the box to Quetta, Pakistan, but sending the goods directly to Afghanistan was out of the question. It was not until I saw Sharifa eighteen months later that I found out the parcel had never arrived. The goodness of those Canadian businesswomen was lost, and the products that might have brought a sense of solidarity to Sharifa and her friends was likely sold on the black market in Quetta, soon after the box was opened.

THERE WAS MUCH REJOICING in the early post-Taliban days, when I returned to Kandahar and saw the women again, this time with the CBC television crew. However, as the camera rolled and the women told their stories, their initial euphoria melted away. They still wear burkas "because Kandahar people aren't open-minded," says Sharifa. "They'll think on me as a bad woman and maybe attack me on the street."

Sharifa also shared a story about the barbarity they had experienced after my last visit, while the Taliban were still in power. Her son had been waylaid after school and had followed crowds of people to the stadium, curious to see what was happening. That night he woke up screaming and told his mother what he had witnessed. Sharifa remembers his horrifying story:

> There were three women in their burkas on the ground.
> The men were kicking them, firing gun shots at them,
> and hitting their bodies with stones. My son said they
> were being punished for not covering their faces or not
> following Islamic rules. He was upset, afraid to sleep for a
> month after that.

I asked her the fate of the women. "They are all dead," she said, her own face a mask of fear. At first, I thought it was just a hangover from the terrible times they had suffered. After all, the Taliban were gone. But Sharifa's instinct told her the fundamentalist menace was still lurking, waiting in ambush.

Her colleague, Sima Shahnawaz, the comic in the group, was more upbeat. She handed her newborn son to me and said, "See what I did?" Then she added, "I want a life like you. You can go everywhere you want, travel, sit with the other women without asking first a man: 'Should I do this, or not?' That would be a very nice life." Another high-spirited member of the team, Frozan Mahram, was making plans to move to the United States. It seemed to most observers that their liberation was at hand.

It was not until later, under cover of darkness, that I learned from Sharifa that the whole experiment in liberation was in serious doubt, and behind the murky scenes, the Taliban were still in charge. She came to the guest house where I was staying and sent a message for me to meet her at the gate. Huddled in a burka, with her husband and children gathered around her, she said, "We want to leave this place. Please help us." The process of immigrating or applying for refugee status was a daunting one. How would she get to a Canadian embassy (the nearest one was then in Pakistan) to seek help? And even if she found her way there, what about the long list of people in front of her? I knew a Canadian embassy was opening in Kabul and suggested she wait until it was operational and seek help there.

In the ensuing years, we had sporadic contact, mostly through friends who agreed to carry messages. Then, just before Christmas in 2007, an email message brought Sharifa back into my life. The message was from Sally Goodrich, a school superintendent in Vermont who had accomplished a miracle. Goodrich met Sharifa during a trip she made to Afghanistan to open a girls' school, and she had managed to bring three of Sharifa's children from Kandahar to Vermont to attend school. Sharifa had told Sally about my attempts to get her to Canada, and Sally had attempted, and failed, to get her into the United States. Now Sally wondered if I could try again. I was flabbergasted. I told Sally of course I would help, but I wondered to myself what it was that drove her to be this interested in the women and girls of Afghanistan, and where on earth she was getting the money to educate three Afghan children at some of the best (and most expensive) private schools in America.

Because I hear from a lot of individuals and groups who want to help the women of Afghanistan, I confess that I often reply to their messages in haste. I scan the message, get the data I need, and cut to the chase. That was the case with the email from Sally Goodrich. I replied to her welcome message with questions I needed answered before I could proceed, still wondering what this woman's motivation was. A split second after I hit *send*, I noticed the address of a website at the bottom of her message: **www.goodrichfoundation.org**. To be honest, while I waited for my computer to bring up the web page, I thought this must be a wealthy American family foundation, one that was willing to be generous to the neediest people in the world. The web page popped up and I saw the full title.

The Peter M. Goodrich Memorial Foundation. Aha! I thought, the patriarch. I was wrong. Peter Goodrich is Sally's son. He was a passenger on the second plane that hit the World Trade Center on September 11. I stared at the page, numb with the realization of what this meant for several minutes, before viewing the photos of the handsome Peter Goodrich and reading the story of a remarkable young man who at the age of thirty-four was in the ascension of his sparkling career when he boarded the flight to New York on that fateful day.

Peter's friends wanted to make sure his life would be remembered for the altruism he lived by, and they collected funds for the foundation and asked the Goodrich family to dispense them as they saw fit. So Sally, the educator, decided schooling was the key to change and boarded another plane—this one to Afghanistan. This was her response to the terrible evil that struck her family's life. In the name of her son, and on behalf of his siblings, her husband, Don, and their grandchildren, Sally Goodrich hooked up with like-minded people in Afghanistan and opened a girls' school and a library in Bamiyan and currently has six Afghan students with her in Vermont. The website doesn't mention that she also is fighting a personal battle with ovarian cancer.

A month after receiving Sally's email, I sat down with Sharifa in Afghanistan. For reasons that are not entirely clear, Sharifa, her husband, and the three children still at home had to leave Kandahar, suddenly and without explanation. Today, when I meet her in a location that needs to remain undisclosed, she is the same as ever: a Madonna-like beauty who is as generous as she always was—providing food and tea to a visitor, when it is clear she has little to spare. She asks after my children, when her own small boys are in a new kind of peril. She apologizes for the frigid room they stay in, and keeps insisting the tiny heater be positioned beside a visitor, although she and the kids are shivering in the cold. Her husband is away in Iran visiting his refugee parents. She tells me about her colleagues at the institute. Sima, the comic, is still there, and has had another child, a daughter this time. Frozan has been in the United States for four years now. The others are still working at the clinic. Life in Kandahar is as difficult as it was when I first met them. The threats and fears, the raids and bombings, the assassinations and school burnings have laid their new world to waste.

She is away from the insurgency now, but she is hiding something, something she dares not mention that makes her twitch when she talks. It was obvious when I met her half a dozen years ago that she was a highly skilled therapist and respected manager. What struck me more than her professionalism, however, was her innate intelligence, her ability to think strategically and to act with dispatch. While raising six children and running a very busy clinic, she was able to manage everyone's needs and keep her family out of harm's way, and used her skills and her enormous patience to seek a better future for them all. I knew Sharifa as a calm, kind, wise, and tenacious woman who had to survive under conditions most of us cannot imagine. But now, sitting in the light of a gas lamp, she seems to be consumed by anxiety. I ask her about her state of mind. The gracious hostess pours more tea and changes the subject.

She wants to talk about immigrating to Canada or the United States. It would be relatively easy to pack up her family and bring them to a new life on the other side of the world. There's hardly any doubt she would make a contribution to her new country. But bureaucracy doesn't work that way. To be fair, it can't. There is a waiting list, requirements for immigration that include financial payments she can't even consider. So she waits, she fills in papers, and she hopes. She is far from whatever it was that drove the family away from Kandahar, but near the poverty and pain they have endured for as long as I have known them.

LIMA'S IS ANOTHER UNFINISHED STORY. I met her by chance in the fall of 2002 when Robin Benger, Alister Bell, and I decided drive through the Shomali Plains looking for people who would help us to tell the story of the daughters of Afghanistan. The Shomali Plains, an area roughly thirty kilometres wide and eighty kilometres long, once were known as Kabul's Garden, or the Breadbasket of Afghanistan. But by 2002, the area was more like a desert, ravaged by a five-year drought and thirty years of constant fighting. It was also, according to the U.N. Mine Action Center for Afghanistan, the most contaminated land-mine area in the world. On our drive north from Kabul, we can see that the tides of war have swamped the plains from all sides. The bones of Russian, British, and Taliban warriors lie here, together with the remains of their decaying bombs and tanks.

From the roadside to the horizon, the landscape is a surreal maze of crumbling village walls. Red flags signal the presence of land mines, and millions of sturdy pink dwarf tulips cover the bloodied earth. A huge tank with its gun pointing at the road, and its Northern Alliance soldiers standing guard, suggests we pull over. Commander Yassin, who like many Afghans has only one name, tells us they are guarding their village, Mavi Khatu, one of the few villages not abandoned during the many years of war. He agrees to take us to the hamlet to meet his family. The potholed dirt road with its hairpin turns, and steep hillocks on which are scattered chunks of the crumbling mud-brick walls, is a challenge for the van we are driving in. But, at last, we arrive in the village and realize that it is definitely not on the radar of the international community. Nothing has improved here. Although we are only about two hours away from the brand-new Ministry of Women's Affairs, it is as though we have stepped into another century. Yassin's two wives complain that there are no schools, no health clinics, and certainly no rights for women. Although we had been warned that the Shomali Plains were no place to go searching for signs of the emancipation of women, and that land-mine clearance was about the most the international community could take on, it is still disheartening.

Then a young girl attracts our attention. She is crouched over the riverbank filling a pail with water, a pail so big I wonder how she can manage to haul it, full of water, up the hill to her mud-brick house. Her name is Lima. While filming her repeated trek to the water's edge, we try to converse with her, but she is painfully shy and frightened perhaps to engage in conversation with strangers. However, there is something about her—the girl child performing her tasks like the cog in the village wheel, the apparent piece of the rural puzzle we were after—that makes us keep the camera on her and seek out her story.

The noise from the Black Hawk helicopter, flying so low overhead that conversation has to be stopped, and from Commander Yassin's men "shooting off a few rounds to let each other know where they are," makes me wonder if Mavi Khatu is typical of the villages off the beaten track or an anomaly. Since the vast majority of Afghans live in villages like this one, and because Lima probably represents most Afghan girls, we decide to revisit Mavi Khatu six months later and find out if the aid promised to all Afghans by the international community would reach them eventually.

It was early spring 2003 when I saw Lima again. In many ways, she was typical of girls I had met while reporting from Afghanistan. She was poor, illiterate, and about as vulnerable as a girl can be, in a country that had bowed to political tyranny in the guise of a message from God. She told her story in a flat monotone, without a sign of emotion on her young face. The Taliban had attacked her village, killing her mother, father, and grandmother. She was now the sole supporter of her four younger siblings. Her commitment was to protect them, keep them alive. Her life was so tough, it was unimaginable. She was up at dawn to find food. She cooked it in what was left of the family kitchen, the Taliban having destroyed the roof with rockets. Her future promised more of the same. While she wasn't sure of her age—she guessed she was thirteen or fourteen—she obviously was reaching puberty, which meant she would soon have to wear a burka, get married, and become a mother, although she was still a child herself.

While the rest of the country was taking hesitant but joyful steps into the post-Taliban world full of promise, Lima's stony-eyed response to my questions made me think her emotions were spent, that a luxury such as happiness was simply not available to her. I asked her what she hoped for. She said, "Nothing." When I asked whether she ever got away from her endless chores and did something she wanted to do, she was quick to take me to a path that circled the perimeter of the village, to show me where she goes when she can escape for a few minutes. I had some cockeyed notion that we were going to a field where children play, or to a brook where we could skip rocks. We weren't. She led me to the village cemetery and the place where she sits under a tree, praying for, and talking to, her mom. We sat there together, Lima picking at the bark of the tree, gesturing towards the grave, mumbling monosyllables, looking away. The scene was so heartbreaking, I felt certain her emotionless body language was a cover she was using to survive.

The documentary crew chipped in to leave her some money, but we worried about a girl on her own in possession of cash, enough that someone might hurt her to get it. Robin, the no-nonsense South African director, took the matter to Yassin, informally appointed him Lima's guardian, and told him—in the friendliest but sternest possible way—that we would be back. I wondered if a Northern Alliance commander would take the warning seriously.

When the documentary aired, I always knew in which country it was being broadcast because of the emails that arrived at the CBC from places such as Norway, Australia, Austria, and Denmark, from people who wanted to help Lima. Some wanted to adopt her but worried about what would become of her siblings if she wasn't there to protect them. Others wanted to send money but could not imagine how it would be administered in a village that wasn't on the list of a single agency within the international community. One family in Norway wrote a heartfelt email at Christmas, saying they had explained to their children that instead of Christmas gifts this year, they were going to help a girl in Afghanistan. I put them in touch with a Norwegian aid agency and hoped for the best.

In June 2006, the editor of *Chatelaine* magazine assigned me an article about the status of the women and girls of Afghanistan and said, "What about that kid called Lima who was in the documentary. Whatever became of her?" I jumped at the chance to find out but knew that finding her, a girl with no last name, who can't read, and doesn't know how old she is, would be a challenge. Was she still in the hardscrabble village I found her in three years earlier? Could I find the village again? Would she have been married off to an older man in another village? And the most worrying question of all: Was Lima, this innocent girl who seemed to be the epitome of a war child, alive?

This is what is on my mind as our low-to-the-road jalopy zigzags its way out of the chaotic Kabul traffic, negotiating a route past goat herds and street vendors, to get on the road north to the Shomali Plains. Some things obviously have not changed. The rusted-out carcasses of Russian and Taliban tanks still stain the landscape. But the highway is busy, crowded with the infamous *jingle trucks* (so named because every inch of them is covered with bright designs and dangling paraphernalia) that carry goods across the country. The fields have been planted. At least some of the buildings in the mud-brick villages have been repaired. There are shepherds herding their sheep, and villagers walking the byways. The red flags marking minefields are fewer in number, but the ones that remain serve as a reminder of the past, as well as a warning for the continuing need for caution.

It is almost the fifth anniversary of 9/11. As the car bumps along the road, I am thinking about the women and girls such as Lima who were caught in the gender apartheid created by the Taliban beginning in September 1996. With the huge presence of the international community in the country today, it is jolting to remember that these same diplomats, and the countries they represent, chose silence over action during the five years the Taliban ruled. In the absence of any protest, the Taliban edicts became harsher (and loonier) by the week. Soon they banned radio and TV, singing and dancing; they even banned laughing in public. Makeup, high-heeled shoes, nail polish, and white socks became anathema to the thugs in power because they were seen as a sign of a sexually promiscuous woman.

I was warned before setting out that some villages in the Shomali Plains have become supportive of the Taliban, which means the journey from Kabul to Mavi Khatu, a hamlet of maybe two hundred souls, might be dangerous. It also means that Lima might be forbidden to speak to a Western woman. A sense of dread rides along with my optimism this day.

All of a sudden, I see it: The sign on the roadside says Mavi Khatu, and the car swerves off the highway and bounces precariously onto the walled, rutted road that leads to the village. There is a circus-like atmosphere here as children run from every direction. Some keep pace with the car as it struggles around the blind turns; others race ahead to announce the arrival of strangers. I scan every face for Lima. We are barely out of the car when Yassin, now the village chief, strides over to greet us. Thankfully, he remembers me. (Maybe because, on the last visit, Alister Bell had cleverly taken Polaroid photos of many villagers—the first photos they had ever seen of themselves). My heart is pounding when I ask for Lima. Yassin is smiling, speaking in Dari. The translator is smiling too, when he repeats his words in English: "The children running ahead of you have already told her you're here."

She suddenly appears, coming down towards me on the same grassy hill where I last saw her, a much taller young woman with strikingly high cheekbones, enormous dark eyes, and a shy but dazzling smile.

"I dreamed about you two days ago. In my dream you came back to the village," she says in her raspy, soft voice. It is an emotional reunion. This girl who was thrice victimized—by a medieval theocracy that refused her an education because she is a girl; by "soldiers of God" who made her an orphan; and by the international community that had not found its way to her village—is telling me she is all right. She looks happy and is quick to smile, even to laugh, which was not the case three years ago. We visit the graves, check the grape crop in the field, sit up on a rocky cliff in the shade of a tall, broad-leafed *chanar* tree, drink tea, and share stories. The interpreter struggles to keep up with my questions, her answers, and the running commentary from her rambunctious siblings.

Lima is not wearing a burka—no woman in this village is. She is not married, although I calculate she must be sixteen or seventeen by now—she actually says she thinks she is nineteen. When I ask her about becoming a wife, she laughs out loud and says, "Not me. Not now." She tells me she wants to go to school, to learn to read and to write her own name, and that her grandfather has an apartment in Kabul, where she and her brothers and sisters stay from time to time. She shuffles her feet and moves a little closer, as though she is about to share a secret. She tells me there is a primary school beside the apartment and that she has already asked the supervisor if she may attend classes in the fall, when the grape harvest is finished. I am amazed at the change in her, this girl who would not make eye contact with a stranger three years ago.

Back in the village, Yassin describes developments in the village that are minor but hard-won and significant. A pipe for drinking water is being brought in, though Yassin says they need ten pipes, not one. There is a new school, but it is only for boys, and there is not enough funding to pay the teacher, so classes are hit and miss. There is a health clinic that is more like a first-aid station, he says, but better than nothing.

We talk about the Taliban, and the fact that some people say surrounding villages are harbouring them. "Not here," says Yassin, while Lima and her entourage of siblings shake their heads in agreement. "They broke our houses, hurt our lives, we'll never let them in this village."

No one here can read or write yet. They badly need a proper road into the village, and adequate nourishment clearly is still a problem. But, even though the village still has not come to the attention of the massive international effort going on in Afghanistan today, change has come to Mavi Khatu, as if by osmosis. They simply know there's something better out there for them. Lima tells me she will take her brothers and sisters to school with her. She is nobody's victim today. She even sounds hopeful.

When it is time to leave, everyone crowds around the car shouting their goodbyes. Lima is silent. She extends her hands. Her eyes speak her farewell, and just like the last time, she turns away and walks back up the hill. I wonder if I will ever lay eyes on her again. But this time, I'm not as worried about her future.

On the way back to Kabul, the conversation in the car is about change, for better and for worse. Although Lima has not benefited directly from the international rescue programs, she was also seemingly untouched by the confounding return to extremism in the previous six months, that saw fundamentalists clawing back the position they had lost.

Not surprisingly, I feel a level of déjà vu when I start back up the road to Mavi Khatu in January 2008, and the same mix of anticipation and dread, as though I am daring fate by seeking out this girl one more time. The Shomali Plains are covered in the heaviest snowfall they have seen in thirty years; the distant mountains sparkle in the sun-split white folds; smoke curls from stove pipes, and there is not a tank relic in sight. The roadside markets are bustling. Modern gas stations beckon drivers in with promises of food and the plastic gift items featured by gas stations everywhere. There is one police check to deal with, but it is reasonably orderly. Even the dirt road into Mavi Khatu seems less challenging. But it is very quiet—too quiet. There are no kids darting about to check out strangers coming to the village. It is cold. Maybe they are inside, I think, trying to convince myself that I will find Lima once again. A lone figure is walking in the direction of the highway. We stop to ask him if Yassin is in the village. He says, "No, the chief has gone to Kabul." Then he bends down so he can see past the driver, looks at me, pauses for a second or two, and says, "Lima has gone away." Away? Where? What has happened? I ask too quickly, maybe too forcefully. I realize I am posing questions with the proprietary air of a parent. He suggests we talk to her uncle. I can't get to the house fast enough and, once there, beg to know what has become of Lima.

"She got married one year ago. She lives in Iran," the uncle tells me with no emotion whatsoever. Did she want to get married? I ask him. "In our culture she has no choice," he says. Who did she marry? "Her father's brother's son," he tells me. I do the family math and figure it is one of the young cousins I met before. He confirms my deduction and says they have a baby, whose name and sex he doesn't know. What about her brothers and sisters? "They're in Kabul with the grandfather," he says. Try as I might, I am unable to persuade him to part with more information. I pull the bags of groceries I had brought for Lima from the back seat of the car and give them to him, not hiding my disappointment, and telling him that I wish there was a way to be in touch with Lima. And then he says, "I can give you her cellphone number." A cellphone? Here in Mavi Khatu, a forgotten place that doesn't even have electricity coming in from the road? I feel as though I have just won the lottery, and scribble down the number so I can call her later. I ask him why the village is so quiet. "We are too poor," he says. "It's cold now. People go and stay with family in Kabul." The international agencies have not yet come to Mavi Khatu.

Back in Kabul I ask a friend who speaks Dari to call the cellphone number. Lima answers. In a rather disjointed conversation, through a translator on a cellphone, we reconnect. She tells me she is fine and living in Iran is okay. Her baby is a daughter called Elnos; she is four months old. She hasn't seen her brothers and sisters since she left a year ago. She misses them, and they her, but "that is the life." She has a family name now: she is Lima Amiri. And I have a mailing address for her, as well as a number to call. The journey seems like a triumph after all.

I AM HOPING FOR A DIFFERENT DENOUEMENT when I set out that same month to find Soghra, a woman whose story is about coping with war and its wretched aftermath. I met her first in a women's shelter in Kabul while filming *The Daughters of Afghanistan*. She struck me as the quintessential Afghan village woman. She had beads braided into her hair and luminescent baubles on her traditional Afghan dress, with its puffy sleeves, voluminous skirt, and a tight bodice woven with silver threads. She looked like a doll in a gift shop. Soghra was born and grew up in Bamiyan, the mystical and remote region about 230 kilometres northwest of Kabul. To get to Bamiyan, you have to endure a nine-hour, bone-rattling drive from the capital, but once there it is like entering a Valhalla of shimmering poplar groves, babbling brooks, and majestic stand-alone mountains. This is where the famous stone Buddhas stood watch for fifteen hundred years before the Taliban blew them up. Located on the Silk Road, the caravan route that linked China to western Asia,

Bamiyan is home to the Hazaras, the most persecuted tribe in Afghanistan, who also are Shiite Muslims and seen as outsiders in the majority Sunni country. The physical features depicted in the few remaining frescoes, in the ancient caves that surround the statues in Bamiyan, have led some historians to conclude that the Hazaras are descendants of Indo-European peoples who built the Buddhas and of the conqueror Genghis Khan.

The enormity of what the Taliban did when they destroyed the giant statues is almost overwhelming when you stand in the empty spaces—one of them the height of a twenty-storey building—left behind in the sandstone cliffs. The Taliban claimed that when foreigners wanted to repair the disintegrating statues, Mullah Omar was outraged that anyone would spend money to improve a piece of stone rather than feed the starving people, so he ordered them destroyed. Others in his coterie claimed the destruction was an act of piety because the Buddhas were un-Islamic. In any case, this was not a spontaneous act: It took a full week to demolish this extraordinary work of culture, art, and history. The Taliban first tried to bring the statues down by using anti-aircraft guns and artillery, which damaged but did not obliterate the Buddhas. Then, in a wicked and cowardly act, they lowered Hazara men lashed to ropes down the face of the cliff and ordered them to place explosives into the fissures and punctures in the bodies of the Buddhas. Those final explosions achieved the Taliban's moronic goal.

The entire Bamiyan valley is a UNESCO World Heritage site. It looks like it has been art directed: copper-toned mountains; lush green fields; stubby flowers growing along beaten earthen paths. Herds of highland cattle are led to the fields to feed, and then down to the brooks to drink, and then finally, home again, in a timeless routine. Donkeys bearing heavy packs plod along in front of young boys who stickhandle them to their destination. There is a spiritual rhythm of life here that plays like the sound of a lute. There are no paved roads. The long-awaited power grid has yet to make an appearance, so when the diesel-powered electricity plant shuts down in the afternoon, a quietude takes over that whispers of the enduring past.

But this region has known more than its share of the noise of war. It held off the Taliban until the last, falling just six months before 9/11. That's when Soghra's story of war began.

Human rights investigators have confirmed that thousands of Hazaras were killed. Some were burned to death or shot execution-style; their villages were razed, their homes reduced to rubble. Some took shelter in the caves that dot the sandstone cliffs like honeycomb and where many still live today while Bamiyan is being rebuilt. It was during this reign of terror that Soghra says her husband was taken by the Taliban. When we meet her, she is sitting on the floor at a shelter for single mothers in Kabul, surrounded by her children. She tells us: "I don't think my husband is alive."

She had joined thousands of Hazaras fleeing the massacres in Bamiyan. With little more than the clothes on their backs, they crossed the mountains by foot, mostly at night to avoid the murderous Taliban. They walked much of the way, hitchhiking whenever possible, and arrived in Kabul ten days later. Soghra was pregnant with her seventh child. She says they were cold, hungry, and scared. Once in Kabul, another Hazara directed her to the shelter, where she was promised she could stay for three years. The children would go to school, Soghra would learn a trade, and this desperate family would have the support they need. The day we visit, they are celebrating a *shaweeshash*, the blessing and naming of a newborn child on the sixth day of life. There is singing, dancing, and welcome platters of food. A man is brought in from the kitchen to do the naming and make the blessing because women are not allowed to preside over the ritual. He plucks the baby, so tightly bound she looks like a covered piece of pipe, from Soghra's arms and begins the traditional chant—"Don't be afraid of the voice of the mother or the father or the voice of the cat, the dog, the children, or the voice of water"—and names her Hadia, which means "gift from God." A slip of hair is cut from the baby's head for long life. It is a bittersweet moment for Soghra, a woman alone in the world. But she is safe here, for now.

When the documentary crew returned six months later, to catch up with Soghra and the twelve widows and twenty-six orphans at the shelter, we learned that she had left. We presumed she had taken her kids back to Bamiyan to eke out a bare living closer to her family. In fact, the proprietor of the shelter told us, our presumption was wrong: Soghra had lied to them. Her husband was not dead. This seemingly naive woman, with her doll-like features, had left the shelter and gone someplace to live with him.

We cruised up and down the alleys of the poorest and most dangerous neighbourhood in the outskirts of Kabul to find her. The guilty look on her face when she answered the door, and the sight of this family of nine living in two rooms, told us a lot. Her first words were: "I lied out of desperation. Everything I said was out of desperation, not out of desire." Her husband, Ahmed, tells the story of nearly unspeakable horror that would break the spirit of most.

They had left Bamiyan together, walking through the killing fields to escape the Taliban. He got a job in a soup kitchen in Kabul, but it was patronized by members of the Taliban militia, who spotted him as a Hazara and beat him up, breaking his wrist, smashing his front teeth, and chasing him off the premises. Speaking in a soft voice while holding her husband's arm, Soghra described what happened next. "The youngest child was sick. My pregnancy was full term. We were desperate. My husband said I should take the children to the shelter and say that he was dead, otherwise none of us would survive."

She went back to the shelter later and apologized for lying. She says, "I hoped that people would understand." In the meantime, neither parent can find work and they depend on their children to do carpet-weaving, as it takes a child's tiny hands to manipulate the threads. They earn a meagre living of $2 a month. The three oldest children are standing on benches just inches from the loom while their parents tell us their harrowing tale. Carpet-weaving has been denounced by children's rights experts such as Craig Kielburger, not only because it deprives kids of the opportunity to go to school, but also because it damages their health. The proof is before me. Their fingernails are broken and split; the skin beside the nails is torn from threading the tough wool fibres through the apparatus. Most children in the carpet business are confined to a closed room, often working in tiers that are stacked on top of one another. They inhale the fluff from the wool and develop chronic lung disorders. They get few breaks, often fall asleep at the loom, and are forbidden to make conversation lest it distract them from the pattern. The silence inside these sweat-shops is broken only by the sound of children coughing. Soghra's kids work outside, but like the others, they need to do their jobs at a rapid pace, in order to earn the pittance the carpet company doles out at the end of the month.

I had hoped Soghra and her family would find their way back to Bamiyan because it is the province showing the most promise in Afghanistan today. The villages that were pulverized during the war are being rebuilt. There are new schools, a library, and university classes in session. But all is not peaceful in Bamiyan. It is the transit route for the drug trade from northern Afghanistan to Pakistan. Warlords and extremists abound. With no paved roads and no electricity, its citizens are becoming frustrated with the broken promises of the govern-ment. The no-nonsense governor, the former minister of women's affairs, Habiba Surabi, is taking some of the heat. She has proposed rebuilding of one of the Buddhist statues from the tons of rubble collected at the base, knowing that the tourist dollars the statues could generate would help the area. However, some locals feel the estimated $30 million to do the repairs is extravagant and would be better spent bringing the province into the twenty-first century.

For the Hazara women here, life is full of contradictory messages. They made up 48 percent of the Bamiyan people who voted in the national election, a far greater proportion than in any other province, and have always enjoyed relatively more freedom than other Afghan women. Yet they are still sold like cattle here, and tribal law still confuses religious and cultural demands. Surabi often settles the quarrels herself, just as she did at the Ministry of Women's Affairs, where she once shackled a man to a radiator in the bathroom and kept him locked in the room until he confessed to beating his wife, and promised her he would reform what she called his "beastly" behaviour.

But still, betting on Bamiyan as an eventual winner is wise. The longer the schools run, the better chance the women have of ending the plague of violence in their lives. Soghra's daughters would do better here than sweating over the carpet looms where they toil today. When I check in with them in February 2008, Ahmed has found a job teaching in a local school, and they have another child, but the older children are still standing at carpet looms, and the family is still struggling to make ends meet.

There is something enduring about Afghans, their struggles and hopes, their stoic acceptance of loss, and their inexplicable belief that tomorrow will be better. They pepper their conversations with the phrase *inshallah*, which means "God willing." Heaven knows, there is scarce evidence in this country that help will come from another source any time soon.

CHAPTER 7

THE CHANGE-MAKERS

The failure of state institutions to protect women's human rights, to ensure abusers are brought to justice and provide redress, points to official apathy towards, and at times blatant sanctioning of, violence against women.

—Amnesty International, *Afghanistan: Women Still Under Attack—A Systematic Failure to Protect*, 2005

IT WAS SOMEHOW EASIER to blame all the ills of Afghanistan on the Taliban. While they did take the oppression of women to new, almost-unimaginable heights, they had an advantageous start in the long, misogynistic history of Afghanistan.

Today the change-makers—the lawyers, women parliamentarians, and human rights activists—are cutting their ties to the politics of yesteryear and trying to establish a new era for women. They are asking the questions that have been on most people's minds for years. They are raising their voices on issues such as women's rights, the practice of polygamy, and entrenched violence against women—topics that have long been strictly taboo in public. Now these issues are on the floor in the Wolesi Jirga, promulgated by the human rights commission, published in newspapers, and broadcast on the radio. The women change-makers are the new challengers of the status quo.

They have a daunting task on their hands: altering the way an entire country considers 50 percent of its population. Many say reform in Afghanistan needs to start in parliament. If there is a single common complaint in the country, it is the number of warlords and war criminals who sit in the Wolesi Jirga, some of them in cabinet posts. Many male MPs see human rights as a Western notion that should be dismissed and are appalled at the suggestion that the status of women needs to be changed. Most think their own rights have been compromised because of the number of seats reserved for women. Although they make up the majority of parliament, people who follow the legislature say the men are taking a backseat to the women when it comes to making parliament work. The U.N.'s deputy special representative, Christopher Alexander, says the women members of the house are the best reformers. "They talk sense on the issues, and are the salvation of the government. They want the country to change and lives to improve. They want people to know their history and their rights." He points to MPs such as Sabrina Sagheb, Safia Sadiqi, and Fawzia Koofi, women who have been attacked both verbally and physically but are the driving force behind the reformist agenda. "They're networking, working long, hard hours; without them, I don't think we'd have the legislative achievement that we have so far."

In 2006, the women MPs voted together against the reappointment of Chief Justice Shinwari, the eighty-five-year-old fundamentalist who keeps a rubber strap on his wall, even

Jamila Afghani, a devout woman who covers her head and wears layers of ankle-length clothing, is leading a movement to enfranchise women at the Noor Education Centre in Kabul.

(Unless otherwise indicated, all photos are by Sally Armstrong.)

Palwasha Hasan, the director of a Canadian-funded women's rights project in Afghanistan, says the key to reform is that a women's movement is taking shape. "It's not strong yet. But we all know each other and we're starting to come together."

Dr. Sima Samar, the chair of the Afghanistan Independent Human Rights Commission, has paid a heavy price for thumbing her nose at the Taliban and criticizing the fundamentalists. She has not been able to leave her home or office without bodyguards for six long years.

Hamida Omid, the most optimistic woman in Afghanistan, is the principal of the women's high school in Kabul. She vows her students' lives will improve.

On the road to Rukha, in the rugged but beautiful Panjshir Valley. Rukha is home to a test-case health clinic where the highest infant- and maternal-mortality rates in the world are starting to fall.

A pint-sized patient at the Rukha clinic in Panjshir waits for treatment. His mother, Marzia, says she walks one hour to the clinic because "here our one hundred problems can be solved."

Children are yoked to the consequences of war. They are too small for their age, too wise for their years, too needy for words. But they are fetching and curious, beguiling and vulnerable, quick to laugh and hungry for love.

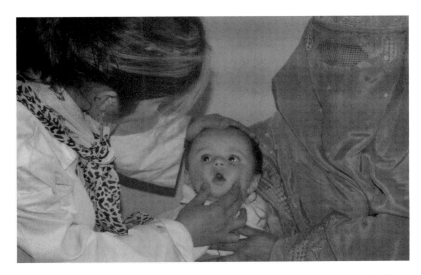

Dr. Frogh Malalay, a widow whose husband was killed by the Taliban, brings medical care to the Rukha clinic. "Men used to tell women they couldn't come here. They said, 'If she dies, she dies.' They're more open-minded now."

Keeping the home fires burning at minus twenty degrees Celcius in Dr. Malalay's house beside the clinic where she lives with her eight-year-old son.

Sharifa with two of her six children in January 2008. She managed to keep her family out of harm's way during the Taliban regime, but still fears for the future.

Tamanna Naveed, seventeen, whose name means "hope," is the inspiration for tomorrow. She can make mouth-watering kabuli, recite the long history of her country, and stand strong for the rights of women.

Twenty-six little girls live in the orphanage funded by the Afghan Women's Association in Canada. Soldiers from the Canadian military dropped off teddy bears that became the prize possession of each of the children.

These children of war will smile at a stranger, wink at the pomposity of power-tripping adults, and hang onto a conversation with the curiosity so precious in young people.

Fatima Gailani, president of the Afghanistan Red Crescent Society, treads a fine line between a life of privilege as the daughter of the spiritual leader of the Sunni Muslims and a job that requires her to be 100 percent neutral. She says, "The Taliban is the enemy, but their children aren't."

Shegofa Mehri with her father, Engineer Akram Mehri, is the example the girls from Jaghori want to follow. She was the first to graduate from high school and is presently a second-year student at Bolzano University in Italy.

Wearing the required black school frocks and white head scarves, the students come in droves over the hills and down the valleys, along the furrowed paths and dusty byways, to their school in faraway Jaghori.

Wahida says she wants to be an astronaut. The teachers' salaries at the school she attends in Jaghori are paid by Canadian Women for Women in Afghanistan. Wahida missed five years of school when the Taliban denied girls an education, but says nothing can stop her now.

There are only eleven girls in this senior class, as opposed to sixty per class in the junior grades. Most girls leave school when they are fifteen to get married. Four of these girls are already engaged, but claim they will not marry until they have graduated from high school.

Turquoise Mountain Foundation: In the reception room of Peacock House in Murad Khane, Kabul, where the work has been completed (see bottom photo), you could be forgiven for thinking you had stumbled into another century. The delicate woven carpets and magnificent wooden carvings of peacocks and flowers, the intricate jali patterns and brilliant coloured threads in the cushions that surround the room, speak of a finer time, a time of self-admiration and self-confidence. (Courtesy of Turquoise Mountain Foundation)

BBC journalist Lyse Doucet, Dr. Sima Samar, and I stand outside the office of the Afghanistan Independent Human Rights Commission in Kabul in 2004. (Photo: Alister Bell)

though the president wanted him to stay on the job. They also boycotted parliament in October 2007, when the house refused a position for women in the Ministry of Finance. Showing a new-found solidarity, they walked out en masse because they felt that gender issues had to be part of every ministry or the women in this country would never go forward. And they worked with the minister of justice to draft a law making it a crime to commit violence against women, deprive education to girls, force a child into marriage, and refuse a woman a job based on her gender. The minister was given three months to send the law to parliament. Then the lower house would have to review it and send it to the upper house, which sends it to the president for signing. With luck, the law will have been legislated by fall 2008.

Sabrina Sagheb is the youngest female member of parliament. Just twenty-eight years old, she represents Kabul and brings a feminist view to the Wolesi Jirga. "I believe that the only two groups who can change the future of Afghanistan are the youth and the women," she says. Her personal life reflects that change. Although women her age are often married with several children, she remains single because, she quips, "I haven't found the ideal gentleman." She plays volleyball with students at the university three times a week and serves on the Asian Olympic committee. She is pragmatic but tenacious about the opportunities women have in parliament. "We are here to change things for the better, and we try hard for that; in some cases we succeed, and in some not." She explains the Afghan parliament is working in two areas. Firstly, they are responding to the urgent short-term needs of the people: building roads, clinics, schools, and establishing clean drinking water and providing electricity. The second task is to draft legislation that will affect people's lives in the long term, a process that is vital but harder to explain to the public. For example, she says, "Last year we were discussing the juvenile code of

Afghanistan and the definition of the child. According to article twenty-two of the constitution, all Afghan citizens have equal rights and no discrimination is allowed." But Sagheb's experience shows that the letter of the law is often meaningless, even in parliament:

> If the child makes a crime, we believe that both the boy
> and the girl should be eighteen years old before being
> held responsible, which is according to the constitution,
> human rights conventions, the child convention, and lots
> of other documents the Afghan government has signed.
> But in the parliament, we faced a problem with the
> extremists and fundamentalists—those who have the
> wrong interpretation of Quran and sharia. They divided
> the child [in]to two categories, boys and girls, and
> insisted that according to Islam we can punish girls of
> nine years old, and the boys of thirteen. After lots of
> fighting and arguing and discussing, we got them to
> change it to seventeen for girls, and eighteen for boys.
> But we aren't finished arguing about it yet. We want the
> age to be the same for the girls as the boys.

Although they lost the argument in the lower house, she says:

> We felt there was still room to campaign, so we talked
> with our friends and colleagues in the upper house, to ask
> them to change it to eighteen years old for both boys and
> girls. We succeeded, and then talked to the president
> himself. It was a difficult process because it has a link
> with Islam and sharia, and in the past the women didn't
> talk about such risky issues, but now we can do that and
> we can succeed because we stayed together.

In fact, the president supported the women MPs and sent the law back to parliament. At the time of writing, it sits with the joint committee for both houses. Sagheb is confident the juvenile code will be amended to age eighteen for both boys and girls, and they will have scored an important victory.

Hangama Anwari, a lawyer from the human rights commission who works closely with the women parliamentarians, isn't holding her breath for change even if the law is passed. "The truth is, as soon as a girl has breasts, even if she's as young as ten years old, she's considered mature and the law is ignored," says Anwari. "Everyone still wants more restrictions for girls than for boys. We need to make people understand that the law is not only to punish people, but to protect them as well." She knows the reform has to start in parliament but says they need the support of the mosque, the minister of health, and the entire judiciary to make these unprecedented changes.

Recent polls have shown that Afghans are happier with the performance of the women MPs than they are with the men. The assumption is that the men take care of their own business and political interests, while the women take care of the people. "It's difficult being a woman in a male-dominated country, and it is more difficult when it comes to the politics," says Sagheb. "There are lots of pressures from the families, elders, and leaders. We have to work three times harder than the male MPs to prove that we are able to do things, even when we don't have political and economical support." Another survey shows that the women in parliament are better educated than the men: 50 percent hold a university degree as opposed to 40 percent of the men. There are no illiterate female MPs but several illiterate men. And 30 percent of the women won their seats outright, without recourse to the rule reserving seats for women. Many constituents voted for women because they were less likely to have blood on their hands from previous regimes. Still, coming together as a voting force is a relatively new concept for the women of Afghanistan.

Critics of their lack of solidarity include Anna Wordsworth, who conducted a study for the Afghanistan Research and Evaluation Unit and published a report in June 2007, "A Matter of Interests: Gender and the Politics of Presence in Afghanistan's Wolesi Jirga." Her conclusion: "In spite of women's sizeable presence in Afghanistan's Wolesi Jirga, the representation of women's gender interests remains minimal." She readily admits that their political influence had increased during the preceding eighteen months, but "women have generally not used this newfound influence to promote their gendered interests."

Making change is a tall order. Given the issues of geography, ethnicity, political affiliation, and language, it is easy to see why women did not come together as a bloc at the beginning. What's more, male parliamentarians tend to assume that women's issues have already been dealt with, simply because they have reserved seats. So getting them onside has been a struggle from the get-go.

Sagheb, a studious and committed young woman who obtained her bachelor of arts degree in English literature from a university in Iran, says there are several examples of women using their gender as a voting bloc, particularly during the last year. But she admits:

> We still have problems among the women themselves, which will take time to solve. You have to remember that just a couple of years ago, we had war, and warlords in the mountains who didn't want to hear the women's voices, but now they came down and accept to sit beside me, and listen to me even if they don't agree—this is a big step for us.

She sees the challenges ahead as manageable and adds, "We are not alone in this journey now; there are some male MPs who do support and assist us."

Her colleague Safia Sadiqi, forty-four, is a been-there-done-that woman who is willing to take the heat. I first met her in Canada in early December 2001, just three months after 9/11. She was sitting in an auditorium in Toronto, listening to her old friend Sima Samar address the crowd about the needs of the country. Samar had the rapt attention of everyone in the room, especially Safia Sadiqi. Afterwards, Sadiqi approached Sima to welcome her to Canada and catch up on news from Afghanistan. Samar said, "Why don't you come home? We need women like you to fix the country." When I saw her again eight weeks later, at a conference organized by Marilou McPhedran at York University that brought together Afghan women to learn the fine art of lobbying for change, Sadiqi was already packing her bags, subletting her Toronto apartment, and preparing—with exhilarating zeal—to join the legions of Afghans seeking change.

Rather than return to her home province of Nangahar, she moved to Kabul, where she was made director of Planning and Foreign Relations in the Ministry of Women's Affairs. She served in the Loya Jirga (the Grand Council of Afghans) held in December 2003 and then was appointed secretary and assistant to the constitutional Loya Jirga. Politics came easily to her. She grew up in Jalalabad with the infamous *pashtunwali*, the fierce tribal code of the Pashtuns that includes draconian restrictions for women, and the duty to provide asylum for those who seek it, and to welcome a stranger, even when that visitor is Osama bin Laden. When it came time to hold an election, Sadiqi decided to run for office and papered her conservative hometown of Jalalabad with a portrait more in keeping with a rock star's than a politician's.

An ambitious woman who trained as a lawyer and writes poetry, she has had her share of challenges, including an assassination attempt when she travelled to Pul-i-Khumri with her seven-month-old son to tour a sugar factory. Sadiqi was delayed by the inconvenience of a flat tire, which put her two minutes behind the explosion that killed six other Afghan members of parliament who were visiting the factory. At times, she seems like a contradiction in terms. She entered a polygamous marriage as a second wife while campaigning for women's rights. And according to one reporter, she once stood up in front of an audience of mostly men in ultra-conservative Kandahar and read a love poem she had written called "I Am Telling the Truth," which included phrases such as "smother you with kisses; put you in the swing of my lap; and cover you with the wings of my hair."

She was elected to parliament as the member from Nangarhar. Not a woman to brook a cover-up, she told reporters just a year after taking her seat that female members were not able to properly serve their constituents and were struggling to make their presence felt. "Women are not a strong bloc, in fact, they are very, very, very weak," she told reporters. But, at the same time, she told the International Crisis Group that the women were holding fast on the restrictions around political parties. "No group may be formed for the purpose of representing local, professional, linguistic, or private interests, or for reasons of religious sectarianism or tribalism."

Her colleague Fawzia Koofi is a delightfully refreshing change from the usually dour custodians of parliament. She is sassy, made up with red lipstick and black eyeliner, and swishes into the room in a fur coat with a tightly cinched belt. She is outspoken and curious, eager to feel the energy of a hall full of dignitaries, and quick to ask questions others fear to pose. She is one of those women who could be standing in the doorway and still seem to be in the centre of the room. An ethnic Tajik from Badakhshan province, she was raised on politics as her father, Abdul Kahman Koofi, was a member of parliament during the reign of King Zahir Shah. "I was a witness to the communist regime, the civil war, and the Taliban," she says. "As a woman who experienced a lot of injustice and discrimination, I wanted to become an agent of change for the next generation."

It was an incident with the Taliban that cemented her commitment. "They put my husband in jail for three months, just ten days after we were married. When I went to see him, they threw stones at me. What they did was make me stronger and more determined to get rid of their kind." A long-time supporter of women's rights, she embraced the plan proposed by the United Nations Development Fund for Women to create a women's caucus but has taken her share of criticism for throwing her lot in with foreign women. One female MP, relying on the smear tactics Afghans resort to, said, "We don't use the Women's Parliamentary Resource Centre because it will give her credit."

But the high-energy, always sanguine Koofi feels things are getting better. "People who used guns against each other are now using red and green cards to disagree," she says, referring to the coloured cards used to vote in parliament.

Koofi takes on all comers: the Pakistan Inter-Services Intelligence agency, which she says has more power in Afghanistan than the cabinet ministers; officials at the Pul-e-Charkhi prison in Kabul, whom she accuses of drugging and sexually abusing female prisoners; and even her women colleagues in the Wolesi Jirga. In 2005, she admonished the other women MPs for failing to support any of the women who ran for the position of chairperson of parliament and urged them to vote for her as second deputy-chairperson. They did.

When I met with the six women parliamentarians (Koofi, Sadiqi, and Sagheb, among them) who visited Ottawa in February 2008 to mark International Women's Day, they had similar complaints about advancing the cause of women in

Afghanistan, but they now had three years of hard-earned experience and were beginning to understand the power of voting in a bloc. The challenges they face are considerable. Most of the women don't have offices and have to hold meetings in their homes. And their salaries—$400 annually—don't even cover travel to their constituencies. Koofi says most male MPs have outside money to supplement their work, but few of the women have such funds.

Their visit to Canada, sponsored by the Canadian government and the International Development Research Centre, was meant to give the women a chance to see women parliamentarians in action. Although they were hustled from one event to another, and paraded in front of the public at breakneck speed, Sagheb says the experience was invaluable. "We saw how Canadians practise democracy in their daily life, how they govern themselves and how they are ready to sacrifice for what they believe in." They also went home with a $5-million-cheque for the Responsive Fund for the Advancement of Women from the minister of international cooperation, Bev Oda. At a follow-up meeting at the Canadian Embassy in Kabul, Sagheb says they made plans to use the money to hold meetings to spread the concept of voters' rights and women's rights and to open constituency offices for the women MPs.

The blame game and mudslinging that goes on in all parliaments is practically a national pastime in Afghanistan. One female MP is accused of being a mouthpiece for a warlord, another of not providing food for her constituents, still another for siding with the wrong ethnic group. Several female MPs are second and third wives and are accused of serving their husbands' interests rather than that of their constituents. It is fair to say the women members of parliament have been on a steep learning curve, and like politicians everywhere, some are rising to the challenge, others are not. But if the last year of parliament is any indication, they are putting their hard-earned experience to the test and, according to Christopher Alexander, they are making their presence felt. "They've been strong on the justice agenda, both with regard to commercial law and criminal law. And they've learned to lobby others, and vote as a bloc for those ministers who've been effective, and conversely against those who haven't." Alexander gives the women credit for a new, broad-based, and diverse media law that would advance a free press and allow public debate. "They voted solidly for provisions that the broader community thought would safeguard media freedom," he says. The law had yet to be signed by the president in summer 2008.

The best known among the women, though she left parliamentarians shaking their heads, is Malalai Joya. A highly animated twenty-four-year-old, Joya rode into parliament like a princess on a white stallion. She stood up during the widely broadcast and exhilarating opening ceremony and shouted her condemnation of the men seated around her, calling them "criminal warlords whose hands are stained with the blood of the people." In the middle of a day that was supposed to mark a fresh beginning and a hopeful future, she had dared to speak the unmentionable truth: that half the men sitting in this house of the people were war criminals. She was hailed as a hero and promptly threatened with assassination. In what would become vintage Joya style, she reacted to these threats with a combination of vitriolic denunciation and an almost-romantic nod to martyrdom. She hired her own bodyguards, a mini Malalai militia, and held a press conference to deliver a poetic response. "They will kill me," she said, "but they will not kill my voice because it will be the voice of all Afghan women. You can cut the flower, but you cannot stop the coming of spring." Then she went on a worldwide speaking tour that unfortunately betrayed her inexperience. I met her in Ottawa, at the twenty-fifth anniversary celebration of the inclusion of women in the Canadian constitution. I asked her about her work as a women's rights activist, her life in the remote province of Farah that she was elected to represent, and her rise to fame in parliament. But she didn't want to talk about any of that. She had a message to deliver and would not be sidetracked from her accusations about warlords, NATO soldiers, NGO workers, even women's rights activists, and everyone else involved in the rebuilding of Afghanistan. She repeated the diatribe in a dozen cities, and she contradicted herself: demanding the international community leave the country one minute, and warning that if they left, the place would collapse into civil war the next. She vilified those who would help Afghanistan in one breath, and in the next one, accused the world of abandoning it. Finally, after she had told one foreign audience after another that the Afghan parliamentarians were corrupt cheats, she was disgraced in the very parliament she was elected to and thrown out. Even the usually even-handed Alexander says her rhetoric was inaccurate and demagogic. "Hers is an incredibly irresponsible position to be taking. It feeds into extremist agendas in and around Afghanistan that need to be exposed for what they are."

At the end of the day, Joya's expulsion from the Wolesi Jirga is a loss for women and for Afghanistan. Although the other women MPs claim she has done nothing for women's rights, her youth and commitment to change could have been the fresh face the country needs. Her courage is remarkable. But she wasted that opportunity for herself and for the people she was elected to serve. Her political demise is a harsh lesson about the delicate business of politicking, and the need to exercise wisdom and understanding in dealing with the public.

One of the people hired to guide the women away from misrepresenting themselves, and to assist in the reform they are seeking, is Annie Serrano, a gender mainstreaming specialist with the United Nations Development Program. Her task is to build gender awareness at the local government level in the provinces and to make sure that women and women's issues are part of any money spent by the United Nations on projects, policies, or training. Her immediate goal is to teach her own staff and everyone else that it is not good enough to say, "Culture doesn't allow this." But she caves in when she must. For example, the United Nations was sending a female judge to Sri Lanka for training. The woman said she could not go because she was breastfeeding her baby. The truth was that she would not go because of *maharam*, the tradition that says a woman must be accompanied by her husband, brother, or son. "So we covered the cost of *maharam* and sent her with her baby and her husband. At this point in the process, we need to deal with the constraints." She wants to develop a strategy for women in the far-flung cities and villages that are often missed on the agenda created in Kabul. "We have a human rights officer assigned to every province, but they really end up lawyering for women. The reality is, women continue to face problems of violence and if they report them, they go to jail. The justice system is attuned to keeping the traditions intact: If you speak up, you get punished."

The change-makers are steadfast, but their numbers are small. "There are men and women in parliament who are pro-civil society but not enough of them," says Hangama Anwari. "We need other pressures and workshops to explain these changes."

Anwari and the activists at the human rights commission are following the blueprint of the association of Women Living Under Muslim Laws who have managed to make changes for women in countries such as Egypt, Morocco, and Malaysia.

One of the test cases this generation of reformers has taken on is the long-accepted, religiously blessed practice of polygamy. Since marriages are not registered, Anwari says they don't know the precise percentage involved in polygamy, but their experience in conducting the research tells them the topic is so sensitive, it elicits equal parts stony silence and vociferous discussion. In a groundbreaking, countrywide study done by the Women and Children Legal Research Foundation in 2006, men, women, religious scholars, and judicial authorities were asked where they stood on a practice that affects more than half of the population. A stunning 86.5 percent replied that they favoured having only one wife in a marriage. Only 13.5 percent agreed with polygamy.

The practice of taking multiple wives was once common in every religion but has since been made illegal by most. While it continues to flourish in surprising places (such as Bountiful, British Columbia), it is mostly confined to religious sects. For Islam, Prophet Muhammad said the number of wives must be limited to four, and there were rules attached. The Quran says, "Marry the woman of your choice, two, three or four; but if you fear that you shall not be able to deal justly with them, then marry only one." The justification often offered for the Prophet's words is that there were many widows at that time who were living without the protection of a man, and the Prophet saw marriage as a means to take care of them. Article eighty-six in the civil code of Afghanistan provides further qualifications:

> Polygamy can take place after the following conditions
> are fulfilled: 1.When there is no fear of injustice between
> the wives. 2. When the person has financial sufficiency to
> sustain the wives, that is provide food, clothes, suitable
> housing and medical treatment. 3. When there is legal
> expediency; when the first wife is childless or when she
> suffers from diseases which are hard to be treated.

While both religious and civil law sanction polygamy, the fact is, most women find it humiliating and demeaning. One woman who doesn't want her name used said, "Imagine how it feels to sleep on a mattress in one corner of the room, while your husband is having sex with his new wife in the other corner." It is also well known that the competition between wives is constant and nasty, that children grow up seeing the conflict, and that the majority of second, third, and fourth marriages are bogus in the letter of religious and civil law because they don't meet the legal criteria for polygamy. That means most polygamous marriages are more like a formula for exploitation, inequality, and abuse.

The 2006 study cited ten reasons polygamy is practised in Afghanistan, eight of them illegal. One is competition, which according to the study, accounted for 26.23 percent of polygamous marriages. If one man decides to marry a second wife, often his brother will follow suit, and if a third wife is acquired, the competition continues. A man from Jalalabad told the researcher: "My wife was sick, so I married another woman. My cousin imitated me and married a second wife, as well. When I saw him marrying for the second time, I got married for the third time."

Custom and tradition made up 14.12 percent of respondents' reasons for multiple marriage. Entrenched customs such as childhood marriage, marrying your brother's widow, bad, badal, and forced marriage contribute to polygamy, and are sometimes imposed on men as well as women.

Civil law cites maternal disease as a legitimate reason to take another wife and was quoted by 13.25 percent of respondents. The researchers discovered that the majority of these women had not been seen by a doctor, 60 percent had curable diseases, and 40 percent had incurable diseases. So some lost the exclusivity of their marriage, and others lost their lives, because no treatment was provided. A woman from Mazar-e Sharif said, "I had diabetes, but my husband wouldn't let me have it treated so he could get married for a second time."

Another 11.1 percent blamed childlessness, which is recognized by the civil code as a reason to marry another wife. The study showed that only 1 percent visited a doctor to discuss fertility problems before a second marriage. None of the respondents understood that not being able to produce a child could be the man's problem.

Access to power is very important to Afghan families, and that means having more men and sons in the family. If a man doesn't have brothers or sons, he feels insecure and takes more wives to beget more sons. Insecurity was the reason given for 9.13 percent of polygamous marriages. A man from Maiden said, "I have enmity in my tribe, and I had only two sons from my first and second wives, so I was compelled to get a third wife."

Conversely, wealth was the deciding factor in 7.32 percent of cases, and the research showed that the men with the most money had the most wives. A man from Kabul said, "God blessed me with wealth, so I can marry four wives and provide them with their needs."

Power and status accounted for 6.82 percent: commanders, warlords, and landlords also tend to have four wives. Because they are influential, people are afraid of them, and give their daughters to them in marriage. One man from Jazjan province said, "Now I want to marry a fourth wife since the people in the area are afraid of me and cannot give me 'no' for an answer."

Not having a son was cited by 6 percent, as traditionally, to be without a son is intolerable in Afghanistan. An oft-repeated proverb says, "A family without a son is like a home without light." None of the respondents knew that the Y chromosome, which creates sons, is found only in the male DNA. In fact, the majority of the men who took second, third, and fourth wives to produce a son failed to do so. A man in Jazjan province commented, "I was so embarrassed by not having a son, I was unable to walk in my village freely."

The research proved that when women in rural areas marry men in urban areas, and the reverse, the differences between them in terms of education, tribe, lifestyle, race, and religion leads to conflict and eventually to second marriages. This was a major factor for 4.97 percent of those questioned. The researchers also found that 65 percent of men who take second wives are rural, the rate of a second marriage decreases by 35 percent when the wife is educated, and those men and women who have equal education have the fewest polygamous marriages.

Only 1.11 percent of men argued the importance of location, saying they need a woman in the home, and that if they must stay in another place for any length of time, they must marry a wife for that location. A man from Badakhshan said, "I go to Kabul to earn money. I stay there for a long time, so I had to marry a woman from Kabul City too."

The results of the study illustrate a staggering disregard for women. They also reveal the disturbing persistence of tradition; a litany of excuses, many of them stupid; and the extent of the problem faced by reformers. In his book *The Need for Islam*, self-appointed Islamic scholar Muhammad Ali Alkhuli writes: "In monogamous systems, the husband who falls in love with another woman is forced to divorce his wife or to commit adultery. In Islam, this husband is allowed to marry the woman he loves instead of committing adultery." He also writes: "Polygamy means that the second wife prefers being a second wife to having no husband at all. This proves that polygamy is in the interest of women also." He also argues that a wife who becomes ill would likely be divorced by her husband anyway, and that the woman would prefer to deal with a second wife than cope with being divorced.

It happens all over the world: a husband or wife bails out of a relationship when one partner is sick. But to legislate the event, to say if you're sick, you deserve less status, is a noxious pill for a civilized society to swallow. I can't resist one more quote from Alkhuli's book: "Some men have an excessively strong sexual desire. Such a man cannot wait during the menstrual period of his wife. Polygamy solves the problem of such men, but monogamy pushes such men to adultery." His theory begs the question: Does self-restraint ever enter the argument? Apparently not. In this paradigm, the accepted dictum is that a man's desire is a woman's fault.

Tunisia is the only Islamic country that has prohibited polygamy. Hangama Anwari knew that calling for its prohibition in Afghanistan was a non-starter because polygamy is sanctioned in both the civil code and sharia law, but her report did call for change. It recommended that marriages and divorces be registered; permission for polygamy be granted only by a court; family courts be established at the provincial and district level; clerics be better informed about the legal implications of polygamy and inform their followers; women be better informed about their rights; those whose rights are violated by polygamy be compensated; and research be done on the effects of polygamy on children.

One of the immediate impacts of the study has been increased awareness. The usually censored topic is now on the table for discussion. "We've asked for reform of family law and eventually an end to polygamy," says Anwari. "People said it wasn't possible to speak of these issues. Now there's a level of recognition and awareness. We put our demands in different ways, respecting the current law—there is some change."

Dr. Soraya Rahim Sobhrang, also a commissioner at the Afghanistan Independent Human Rights Commission, says, "This is a man-dependent society with very strong traditions, and tradition is against women's rights. It is our economic, cultural and social system." Now, with the new constitution, she says it is the first time they can try to change the status quo. With sixty-eight women in the lower house of parliament, and twenty-eight in the upper house, a minister of women's affairs, the deputy minister of public health, and their own chairperson, Sima Samar, and with women activists all over the country, Sobhrang feels women have the leverage to take on the toughest file in the country—the rights of women. With the support of the international community, they can also press for the enforcement of U.N. conventions, such as the Convention on the Elimination of All Forms of Discrimination Against Women, that the country has signed.

But she says, "War destroyed more than buildings here, it destroyed minds." A psychologist and gynecologist by training, Sobhrang points out that women in Europe can walk around in skimpy clothing without eliciting an adverse reaction. "Here, if a man sees a tiny opening, even bare ankles, he stares at it." She blames thirty years of conflict for the violent culture and says more than 70 percent of the population has psychological problems. She says:

> People are behaving like animals. Cars don't even
> stop on the street for children. Men are beating their
> wives and children. Neighbours won't open the door
> to help someone. You can reconstruct the buildings
> in Afghanistan. But someone needs to repair the minds
> and that's going to take a long time.

For all the reform she has seen, and all the changes her office is presently directing, Sobhrang is worried about the current state of affairs. "In 2002 and 2003, it was good, but now there's a suicide bombing every day, the Taliban taking over another village, night letters threatening to kill us, bodies on the street. I look over my shoulder all the time now. Every day this fear becomes more than yesterday." She even confesses that she keeps tablets in her car so that if she's kidnapped, she can commit suicide before the extremists kill her.

Despite her outburst about security, she says, "I'm an optimist for the future. If we only talk about insecurity and death, we'll lose hope." Then she describes the plan to empower women by taking awareness about women's rights to the entire population: the mullahs, teachers, shopkeepers. Everyone has to learn, she says. She will use radio and television spots, produce pamphlets, and attend events where she or other activists can speak. She wants nothing less than a nationwide campaign to alter the thinking about women and girls. The campaign includes the ongoing reform of family law, outlawing violence against women, establishing family courts in every province, and opening separate jails for women.

What the campaign can't and won't include is accountability for war crimes. When President Karzai signed an amnesty agreement, he let the perpetrators off the hook, but his action spurred another change-maker to seek justice by way of naming and shaming the guilty and honouring the victims. In a quiet district of western Kabul, Horia Musadiq takes time from her work to talk about Afghanistan's dirty laundry while the setting sun spills into her office bringing the softness that comes with the end-of-day light and welcome warmth on this frigid winter day.

She is the director of the Human Rights Research and Advocacy Consortium, the founder of the first victims' group in Afghanistan, and a recipient of a National Human Rights Day award. She is a thorn in the side of every fundamentalist and extremist in the country. Everyone knows her. If you're looking for details of a human rights case, people will send you to Musadiq. If you are eavesdropping on a conversation about who is rattling the cages in the government, her name comes up.

She was the beacon of light at the Human Rights Day ceremony in December 2007, the one who had not been victimized, the one who dared to stand up to the bullies and demand their names be known. The stories told that day by the two other award recipients are her reason for persevering in the job she does. One, a woman called Marzia, stood in front of the packed auditorium that included President Karzai, Sima Samar, and Christopher Alexander and stilled the air with her words. She was living in western Kabul in 1993 when warlord Abdul Rasul Sayyaf, a member of parliament and ally of Osama bin Laden, sent his soldiers to search the houses of the Hazaras. They beat Marzia's husband senseless and then told her to hand over her gold wedding ring. She tugged at the ring but could not get it off. They told her to hurry up; she licked her finger hoping to release the ring, but the soldiers decided she was keeping them waiting too long. They splayed her fingers on the table and, using a bayonet attached to the end of a gun, hacked off three of her fingers. The ring bounced to the ground and was quickly snatched up by the soldiers, who then shackled her husband, took him away, and held him hostage for three years.

The story doesn't end there. By the time her husband returned, he had lost his mind. And the child who witnessed the atrocity has never recovered. Like most war crimes, the victims continue to pay, even decades after the fact.

The audience was still reeling from Marzia's story when the other recipient, who doesn't want her name used, went to the podium to describe a similar incident that occurred at about the same time. Because their men had left the area to fight, had been killed, or taken hostage, the women had banded together to look after one another. One day, Sayyaf's mujahedeen came to the compound where the women were staying and said they were looking for the men. She told them there were no men in this place, at which point the soldiers yanked her twelve-year-old son from where he stood, said, "This is a warrior," and smashed his head against the floor and shot him. His three-year-old and five-year-old sisters started to scream. The soldiers shot them dead. Her other child opened his mouth to scream and she clapped her hand over it, stifling the sound to save his life. The child has been traumatized ever since.

And the tormentors were never made accountable. Warlord Sayyaf has been accused of scalping Hazara women during the mujahedeen bloodbath, but rather than being tried as a war criminal when it was over, he became a member of parliament. He had the audacity to tell the new regime that "Islam forbids the participation of women in public life."

Musadiq explains: "There has been no justice for the victims. Now the amnesty bill is passed, so there never will be justice." She wonders if the last six years of trying to restore hope to women such as Marzia have been for naught.

> I have two daughters. I was away a lot, in every single province in this country, and always explained my absence by telling the girls, "I'm making a change for your life." Now my eldest daughter is thirteen and is asking me, "Is this the future you were promising us?" I have nothing to tell her except that I'm not ashamed of myself. I have a clear conscience because I did whatever I could for this country.

She says the warlords were scared in 2002. They defended themselves by saying they were pushed into conflict, and hoped for forgiveness. Now they are brazen. Musadiq says:

> Men like Sayyaf are strutting around saying, "What the hell are you doing with these Western human rights? You're against Islam." Seventy percent of the MPs are war criminals; most of the cabinet is, too. The president is influenced by them. The international community is scared of them. How can we hope for change when 2007 is worse than 2006 in terms of security? The warlords have impunity. It's starting to feel like it did before the Russians invaded.

She says the challenges are so huge, it is easy to forget the achievements they have made by regaining the right for women to work, to go to school, to be in parliament. The ace she holds is the ever-increasing number of tenacious activists who have responded to the clarion call for change.

One is Humaira Habib, a journalist who returned to her native Herat in May 2008 after an eight-month stay in Montreal as a Sauvé Scholar. This is the prestigious fellowship provided by the Jeanne Sauvé Foundation at McGill University. It is awarded to highly motivated people under the age of thirty with demonstrated leadership potential. It brings them to Montreal to research, reflect, question, and enlarge upon their understanding of the state of the world and their role in effecting positive change. It was a watershed opportunity for Habib. When I talked to her, she was preparing to leave. She said:

> This has been an amazing time for me. I learned a lot about the Western culture, and costumes, and people, and everything. I now know where in the world we Afghans are. I know the challenges that women have in different countries, and now I can compare it. Before Sauvé, I didn't have any idea about anything, but now I know a lot.

Dressed in traditionally conservative Afghan clothing, with her hijab wrapped around her head covering all of her hair, the soft-spoken Habib said the experience gave her a chance to think about her people, her country, and what she can do for them. "I've found great friends from different parts of the world that could share with me more about themselves and their countries." She says the classes in women's studies and management, and the workshops and seminars she took part in, are valuable tools for the work she will do back in Afghanistan.

Habib is twenty-five years old. She was born in Kabul where, at the tender age of ten, she escaped with her family to Pakistan during the civil war among the mujahedeen factions. She graduated from high school and university in Peshawar, and returned with her family to Herat during the last year of the Taliban because they had relatives there and were fed up with being refugees in Pakistan.

Understanding Habib's views requires an understanding of Herat, a place that has always set itself apart. Like much of Afghanistan, it has its roots in antiquity, but unlike the others, it has always been more cosmopolitan and sophisticated while maintaining a severely conservative attitude towards women. It has been home to famous poets and painters, musicians and philosophers, and to some of the most barbarous fundamentalist warlords, such as Ismail Khan, the governor who infamously hauled young women off the street and forced them to have gynecological examinations to satisfy himself that Herati women were pure.

Herat, once known as Khosasan, is home to the Tajiks. It is situated in the northwest corner of the country, in the valley of the Hari River, and is the third largest city in Afghanistan, with a population of 349,000. Because it is on the historic trade route that hooks the Middle East, India, and China with Europe, Herat is a strategically important city, not least because of its border with Iran. It was an entry point via Turkmenistan for Soviet soldiers during the Russian occupation and one of the first cities to be conquered by the Taliban. Regardless of its long history of war, it is a pretty place with broad avenues, war-ruined shrines, and the famous Friday Mosque, which is beautifully decorated with blue-tile flowers and has stood as the largest building in the city for eight hundred years.

Like so many other centres of turmoil that are referred to by names that conjure images of their former glories—Lebanon, for example, was known as the Jewel of the Middle East;

Somalia as the Emerald of the Indian Ocean; and Sarajevo as the Jewel of the Balkans—Herat was known as the Pearl of Khosasan.

By the time Habib arrived, Ismail Khan had fled, a punishing drought had destroyed Herat's fertile fields, and the Taliban were issuing their bizarre edicts. "It was a very difficult time. Everyone was afraid. There was a secret school for girls, but they only taught the Quran and the Farsi alphabet." When the Taliban were ousted, Khan returned, but Habib, a cheerful, trusting soul, felt certain that change was on the way. She returned to university in Herat to study journalism. "There was always war in my country, always insecurity. I wondered what I could do to change the situation, especially for women, and thought by becoming a journalist I might be able to do something." There were no books, only two professors, and Habib was the only woman in the journalism class. While she was still at the university, she started a radio station called Sahar, which means "dawn." Programming was a balancing act, as Khan didn't want women either working or talking publicly about women's issues. She called her program "The Voice of the People" and cautiously broadcast women's stories while being ever mindful of the censors in Khan's office. When Khan left to join President Karzai's cabinet, she ratcheted up the stakes and started programs about human rights. "It's a new issue here, a new word to Afghans. People think it comes from other countries, so it was important for us to show that human rights are for all people." She had to go slowly at first, with only ninety minutes a day that she filled with local news and social and family programs. Now Sahar broadcasts all day, covering the courts, and reporting on divorce cases and family violence. The station also has a program called "Qusa-e-az-Ghusa ha," meaning "a story of sadness," which allows women and sometimes men to share their own stories. The program was followed with a discussion by a human rights expert who would talk about the content of the story, what the solution to the problem was, or what action the person should take. The station expanded to include music, sports, and a thirty-minute show for children. A recent survey reported six hundred thousand listeners in a region of three million.

The funds and equipment for the programs came from the Institute for Media, Policy and Civil Society, and Internews Europe. The on-the-job training came from Jane McElhone. "I didn't really know anything about working at a radio station before I met Jane," says Habib. "Our training at university was basic, not practical. She taught us how to behave with people, how to be patient, how to manage the station."

Says McElhone of her protégée:

> I first met Humaira in 2003 in a peaceful garden in Herat. She was one of a dozen Herati women who had gathered to discuss the women-managed radio station. At the time, Humaira was a young university student, with a quiet, thoughtful presence, and a determined air that spoke of her potential. Since then, we have been through so much—working together to establish Radio Sahar, doing training to improve her skills as a journalist, broadcaster, mentor, and manager, celebrating when she became a member of the first-ever journalism class to graduate from Herat University, watching as she helped establish Afghanistan's first independent journalists association, assisting when she applied for a Sauvé scholarship at McGill University, and listening to her field questions about Afghan women with intelligence, focus, and ease at a 2007 photo exhibition at the Centre for International Governance Innovation in Waterloo, Ontario.

Humaira's brave commitment to speaking out on women's issues came at a great cost. Herati people are generally better educated and have more disposable income than people in most other provinces. They are influenced by the more advanced Iran and consider themselves better off. But the extremists spawned by the Taliban did not fade into the background, even after Ismail Khan left the governor's post. Habib was constantly being warned to stop promoting human rights. McElhone remembers an incident in 2004 that exemplified the difference between a victim and an activist.

> We were sipping hot green tea together, at a long table in the smoky restaurant at Herat's Marco Polo Hotel; I was listening to Humaira and her father discuss the threats being uttered against her by the local warlord and his entourage. The threats were serious, banning her from ever again working as a journalist in her own province, yet nonetheless Humaira's father maintained a calm presence, offering advice and guidance, and letting her make her own decisions. Humaira has spoken many times about how lucky she is to have a supportive family. It is this fact that has set her apart from so many other Afghan women, and given her the confidence and determination she needs to move forward as a leader and a role model.

When Humaira reflects on the last six years, she says, "I'm happy with the changes we have made even though they are mostly in the cities. You can't achieve everything in five or six years. But social and family problems—underage marriage, forced marriage, violence—those issues have to change faster." She thinks the radio is the tool to do that. "Things aren't a lot better in Afghanistan. They are a little better, and are getting better all the time." She refers to rules that stubbornly cling to women's lives, customs that are passed off as religious doctrine, people who are not educated and don't know the difference. "If a woman takes her case to court and the family decide they don't want her to go to court, they simply go to the judge and make sure her case is not heard." While she feels changing attitudes will take time, she wonders what's taking the international community so long to alter other aspects of Afghan lives, and why they don't build more hospitals and schools, and train more soldiers. "We want the international community here. Without them, we'll have another black era. But we want them to do more." She feels the international community can bring the tribes together—Tajiks, Hazaras, and Pashtuns. "This has to happen; there are problems between Shia and Shiite, between Tajik and Pashtun, even between Heratis and Kabulis."

When I ask her what would happen if the Taliban came back, she looks as though she has been slapped. "I would die," she says almost inaudibly, and then quickly adds, "I wouldn't leave though." She contemplates the horror of the possibility and says, "This is about my country, my city, my people."

After her homecoming in May, she said, "There are a lot of women on the scene now, but it is the government that stops them from making the changes we need to make." She wants the women in parliament to do more:

> Most of them aren't suitable for the position. They don't
> have the skills to take the issues forward. The women
> from Herat were sent to parliament because they're good-
> looking, and the pictures and posters of them are every-
> where. They still censor themselves, and aren't ready to
> take a position on women's rights in their provinces and
> districts.

She readily concedes that the former commanders who are now in power in parliament make it impossible for most women to be active, and there are limitations from their families and from the society. Nevertheless, she plans to probe that file in her journalism.

They all know one another, these change-makers. From Herat and Kandahar, to Mazar-e Sharif and Kabul, they are drawing strength and ideas from one another, starting the fire of change in one region and fanning the flames to another. But divisiveness is still an issue. Finding agreement still eludes them. Understanding that solidarity is the most powerful tool they hold is a skill they have yet to master.

One woman who has personified an upbeat solidarity throughout the past eleven years is Hamida Omid. She was a refugee teaching high school in the Afghan diaspora in Quetta, Pakistan, when I first met her in 1997. Even then, just months after the Taliban had taken over her homeland, she said, "I'll see you next time in Kabul." She lived across the street from the loudspeaker that blared into her neighbourhood, announcing the arrival of the Taliban in Kabul, shrieking out edicts that were unbelievable to her, that women could no longer work, that girls could no longer go to school. She borrowed a burka from a neighbour and went to check on the high school where she had been principal. She saw the bloated, beaten bodies of government leaders hanging from traffic light-posts and was quickly surrounded by Taliban soldiers who told her to go home and never to leave her house again. She thought the world had gone mad.

It was not enough to stay at home. They came to her neighbourhood soon enough, broke through the barred doors, shot her brother to death in front of the family, and trashed the house. Omid and her family packed what they could and left for Quetta, but not before her son, Romin, was struck in the eye with a piece of shrapnel.

Even in Quetta she was determined to return to Kabul and start over again. Five years later, we met again in Sima Samar's brand-new Ministry of Women's Affairs office. There wasn't a stick of proper furniture in the crumbling building, so the team of women hired by Samar sat in a circle on plastic garden chairs and made their plans to jump-start the country. Omid was made principal of the women's high school that would be housed on the property. She took the post with missionary zeal and filled the classrooms with women who wanted to learn to read, train for a trade, and find out about human rights. She was handling a tide of applications and a host of shell-shocked women who came in droves to the school. "I'll make sure every one of these women has a good job when she finishes here," said the ever-optimistic Omid.

A visit to the house she left on that fateful day in 1997 makes one wonder where she gets her can-do attitude. The four-bedroom home is a heap of rubble, wrecked by the Taliban after the family left. She could not afford to have it repaired. Her husband was out of work, and they didn't even have enough money for the medicines Romin needed for his eye injury. But Omid, in the cold winter of 2002, said, "It will be fine. We'll build up the country and our lives will be good."

Like most of the women I met on assignment, I checked in on Omid every time I was back. Her story somehow reflects the country: full of possibilities but mostly marking time. Her house still has not been rebuilt, her husband still is out of work. Romin's eye injury has healed as much as it will without surgical intervention, which is out of the question. Omid is as charming and upbeat as ever when she describes the fight she has had to keep her high school open. "The new minister of women's affairs, Masooda Jalal, wanted the space for her own offices and tried to close my school. But I didn't allow it." While the school was closed during the winter months, she accepted a position from the minister of justice to travel to every province and gather information about the status of women. She visited the villages and the prisons and wrote a scathing report. She tried to run for parliament but was threatened with death and withdrew her nomination. Back at the high school, she has enrolled 150 students and hired ten teachers, and says she can do more for women's rights here, in this education centre, than she could achieve in parliament. While she admits that security is a problem, and even her own boss, the minister of women's affairs, continues to try to shut her down, Omid is relentless. "My life is good, better than any time when you saw me. My children are doing well. I'm happy that they will be in a good situation, so they can get a position and take my name proudly."

She is a rare ray of sunshine in a place that teeters on hope and dwells on sorrow.

CHAPTER 8

RECLAIMING THE PAST

What's past is prologue.

—William Shakespeare, *The Tempest*

FOR ALL THE CULTURAL TURMOIL caused by ancient tribal laws and religious dictates in the lives of the women of Afghanistan, the aesthetic, artistic, and architectural past that has also shaped their history is on the verge of a renaissance in the country today. Affecting men and women together, it may be the antidote to the destructiveness of recent years and could turn this whole weary place around.

Social anthropologists know that when the libraries are empty or burned to the ground, and the historic buildings have been razed, and the artisans have either been dismissed or have died and their work is in ruins, it has an abiding effect on the people.

But you have to dream big when it comes to rebirth in Afghanistan. The ongoing insurgency and the crushing poverty are nightmares in a place that is trying to find itself. Today, along with the soldiers, human rights activists, and policy wonks, whose mantra is "what's past is prologue," there are visionaries on the scene who dare to see in the relics buried in the rubble of the warring past, a rich architecture, literature, and art that have been "scarce heard amidst the guns below."

Many years ago, while on assignment in the Canadian Arctic, I spent time with an Inuit woman who lived in a camp in the woods and provided shelter and back-to-the-land living for about twenty teenagers who were in trouble with the law. They had been convicted of crimes such as stealing, drug dealing, and vandalism. The way to get through to these young people seemed obvious to her, so she arranged with the court officials in Inuvik to have the teenagers sent to her version of boot camp to serve their time. When I asked her why she thought fishing, hunting, chanting, and drum-making could help, she said simply, "You have to know where you came from before you can figure out where you're going."

Preserving the past—the architecture as well as the artifacts— is a way of capturing the identity of those who went before, telling a story about how people lived, learned, worked, and fought. Although some scoff at the notion of investing fortunes to recreate a village or restock a library when people are starving and trying to stay alive in the midst of conflict, social anthropologists claim that failing to do so has a cost of its own.

As Anne of Green Gables' small house in Prince Edward Island, the Vieux Ville in Quebec, Gastown in Vancouver, Black Creek Pioneer Village in Ontario, and the several forts across the prairies demonstrate, the history and culture of the past are part of the present and a map to the future. When we hoard Victorian furniture or pine hutches that had been forgotten in old barns, and linger over Group of Seven exhibits in art galleries, we bear witness to eras and artists that came before us. And that, say the experts, nourishes the soul.

War has a way of colouring a country various shades of grey: the guns, tanks, dust, mud, and rubble blur into a single hue. To most of the world, Afghanistan has been presented during the last decade as nearly colourless, a sepia image of treeless mountains and endless deserts, populated by beige-blanketed, bearded men. The only break in the monotony has been the periwinkle-blue burkas that are more a flashpoint to the Western media than a vibrant addition to the panaorama. Add to that the traditions that favour the ill-treatment of women, corruption, and brutality, and you come to the conclusion that Afghanistan has always been a dreary, oppressive, and dangerous place. We tend to measure the wins in terms of micro-credit programs and paved roads, or judicial reforms and human rights, and accept the losses in terms of looted museums, bombed Buddhas, and empty schools. While rebuilding and reforming Afghanistan is dependent on getting the people back to work and yanking the law into the twenty-first century, like the Inuit woman said, you need to know where you came from to figure out where you're going.

THE TALIBAN WEREN'T THE FIRST to burn books and destroy art. The Nazis did it. So did Henry the Eighth's Cardinal Wolsey. All of them presumed, preposterously, that you can eliminate ideas, turn thoughts into ashes, and wipe out the creative imagination of a people. But for every regime that tries to destroy art and culture, there are artists and philanthropists with an astonishing determination to fight back and to breathe life back into the ruins. In doing so, they fire the art of the possible as surely as potters fire their kilns.

The Canadian government has stepped up to the plate in a bold endeavour to help Afghanistan to reclaim its past with a donation of $1 million a year for three years to the Turquoise

Mountain Foundation in Kabul. And a Canadian citizen has executed an exceptional example of grassroots philanthropy by gathering an altruistic collection of medical students from across Canada to restock Afghanistan's medical libraries.

The Turquoise Mountain Foundation owes its birth to a mix of royalty, politics, and diplomacy. Prince Charles, the Prince of Wales, was hosting President Karzai at a private dinner at the prince's residence in England when the conversation turned to the historic arts and crafts of Afghanistan. Karzai mentioned that the acclaimed woodwork, ceramics, and calligraphy were dying out, as were the craftsmen, the antiques of the cities had been smashed and looted by war, and the old towns were about to be paved over by developers and drug barons who saw the land as source of money and power. If he was asking for help, he was talking to the right person.

A long-time supporter of cultural conservation, the prince had launched the Prince's School of Traditional Arts in London through his own foundation and proposed a similar project to Karzai to breathe new life into what he called "Afghanistan's unique and incomparable art and architecture." They both knew British diplomat Rory Stewart, and together approached him with the idea, requesting that he devise a plan that would restore the historic past in a way that would involve both artisans and citizens.

Stewart, a Scot from Perthshire, had distinguished himself on half a dozen fronts: as the diplomat who was the British representative to Montenegro in the wake of the Kosovo campaign; as the governor of two provinces in Iraq whose frustration with the allied mission there led to his resignation; and as the adventurer who decided to walk across Nepal, Pakistan, India, Iran, and then, when the Taliban fell from power, Afghanistan, and write about his adventures.

It was the Afghanistan portion of the walk that showed him the essence of the country and its people, and spurred him to want to restore the art and artistry of a culture that had been nearly obliterated by war. Starting in Herat in the winter of 2002, armed with a walking stick, and later accompanied by an abused, toothless Mastiff he called Babar in honour of Afghanistan's first Mogul emperor whose footsteps he was following, he walked across the plains, mountains, and valleys to Kabul. His route took him through snow that was sometimes several metres deep and through villages whose inhabitants saw him variously as a spy, an infidel, a crackpot, and friend. Afterwards, he wrote a bestselling book, *The Places in Between*, which chronicled his extraordinary adventures. He dedicated the book to the people he met in all five countries, saying he owed both the journey and his life to them. In the foreword, he wrote:

> They showed me the way, fed me, protected me, housed me and made this walk possible. They were not all saints although some of them were. A number were greedy, idle, stupid, hypocritical, insensitive, mendacious, ignorant and cruel. Some of them had robbed or killed others; many of them threatened me and begged from me. But never in my twenty-one months of travel did they attempt to kidnap or kill me. I was alone and a stranger, walking in very remote areas; I represented a culture that many of them hated, and I was carrying enough money to save or at least transform their lives. In more than five hundred village houses, I was indulged, fed, nursed, and protected by people poorer, hungrier, sicker and more vulnerable than me.

Stewart developed a deep and abiding respect for the rough-hewn country and its stubborn, loyal people. At the end of his four-month excursion, he visited the old city of Murad Khane in Kabul and thought at the time that this ancient place, once the centre of commerce, now almost buried in garbage and home to derelicts and drug dealers, would be lost if someone didn't save it. "It's unique," he says. "It has narrow mud streets, courtyards, geometric designs." It also had crumbling buildings that were falling down at the rate of one a week, no water or sewage, and more than its share of hooligans. Located on the north side of the Kabul River near the old bird market, it has been under attack from mujahedeen, Taliban, and local thugs throughout the upheaval in Afghanistan. It was a sorry sight when Stewart laid eyes on it. But after his time in Iraq, the disillusioned Stewart had developed a feeling for what needs fixing after bombs have destroyed countries. Murad Khane was slated for the wrecking ball. He wondered if the area could be preserved and the loss of traditional craftsmen reversed.

Then Prince Charles called. Launched under the joint patronage of the Prince of Wales and the President of Afghanistan at the end of January 2006, the Turquoise Mountain Foundation is housed in the Royal Fort, an eighteenth-century mud fortress on a mountainside above Kabul, and has plans so ambitious they make your head spin. Its mandate is to revive the traditional Islamic crafts of woodworking, ceramics, and calligraphy and to sustain the historic cities and landscapes in the rest of the country.

There's something exquisitely serendipitous about the instructions Stewart gives me for meeting him at the fort: "Take the road behind the old British Embassy in Karte Parwan." This crumbling building once played a powerful role, and then paid a hefty price, for its two separate invasions of Afghanistan. It stands with a view of the old fort and the country's cultural past that is about to be reincarnated.

At the fort, sitting at a long, narrow table laden with platters of food for staff that hails from a dozen different countries, Stewart shares his plan as well as his frustrations. "If the old city was regenerated, we could create jobs and a sense of national pride," he explains. While the Prince of Wales and President Karzai want to preserve the cultural past of Afghanistan, Stewart sees the Turquoise Mountain Foundation as all of that and something more. He takes a page out of the Inuit elder's book when he says, "For regeneration to be effective, you have to work holistically."

Named for the indigenous capital of Afghanistan during the Middle Ages, Turquoise Mountain was destroyed by Genghis Khan in 1216, and despite decades of archaeological searches that were repeatedly interrupted by war, the precise site has not been rediscovered—except perhaps by Stewart. In the middle of nowhere, during his now-famous walk across the country, he came upon the extraordinarily beautiful Minaret of Jam, which was presumed to have been constructed at Turquoise Mountain. He described what he saw in his book:

> A slim column of intricately carved terra-cotta set with a
> line of turquoise tiles rose two hundred feet.... Pale
> slender bricks formed in a dense chain of pentagons,
> hexagons and diamonds winding around the column. On
> the neck of the tower, Persian blue tiles the colour of an
> Afghan winter sky spelled: GHIYASSUDIN MUHAMMAD INB
> SAM, KING OF KINGS....

No wonder he named the foundation for the treasure he had found in the snow.

In its first year of operation, the foundation established the Centre for Traditional Afghan Arts and Architecture, gathered some of the great masters in Afghanistan, and opened a school to teach students the art of woodworking, calligraphy, and ceramics, arts that were almost lost, their masters dying before teaching the next generation the old techniques. The fort presently houses this school, but it will eventually move to Murad Khane, which is the most ambitious of all the Turquoise

Mountain projects. The foundation plans to turn the oldest city within Kabul into its former self: a thriving bazaar, a centre of artisans, and a living space for locals.

"Initially, a lot of my plan was based on hope and bluff," Stewart says. "I used the royalties from my book and hired two people." He now has fifty buildings and a staff of three hundred. He also says he underestimated the size of the job. "I planned to set it up and move on. But it [has been] two and a half years now." The delay was caused by the formula he devised for regeneration to work. "In a place that's collapsed into a slum, you need to deal first with the basics, make it liveable, if you want it to be the commercial heart of the city." In the first year, they removed the garbage, 560 truckloads, so much rubbish that the foundations of the buildings had been submerged in refuse for more than sixty years; opened schools, or what he calls "literacy centres," for 165 kids; improved the water quality because there was no potable water or sewer system; and organized health care for the people who live there. "That tends to move the undesirables like drug dealers out," says Stewart.

Every penny invested has gender strings tied to it. Stewart is well aware of the women's needs, but he also is practical. For example, he says, "The women are making traditional *bulani* [an often greasy dough that looks like a pizza pocket but is filled with leeks or potatoes]. It's not very good. They need better ingredients and to be taught how to make better *bulani*— then they'll sell more, which is the point, isn't it?" He also wants to see women involved in the famous ceramics trade, "but it's a father-to-son operation so we're having some difficulty." The women are currently immersed in traditional crafts such as carpet-weaving, embroidery, jewellery-making, and textiles, but many of them are also learning the male-dominated crafts such as woodworking and calligraphy.

At the centre, the mingling scents of wood chips, which surround a carpenter's bench, clay whirring into shape at a potter's wheel, and the fresh ink from the pens of calligraphers fills the air. Here a woman is working on a Nuristani carving, a traditional technique using slender pieces of walnut and shallow relief. There a man is *throwing a pot*—the act of putting clay on the kickwheel—the way it has been done for centuries. Young people are making decorative and delicate *jali* screens. Men and women work together making rammed earth, which is mud pounded so hard it is as strong as concrete.

The master ceramicists come from Istalif, about an hour's drive north of the Shomali Plains, the traditional home of the ceramics for which Afghanistan once was known all over the world. They work here with lead-free glazes, using high-temperature kilns, and new designs, hoping to eventually manufacture ceramic tiles for foreign markets. Master calligrapher Mohammed Mahfouz—he is master of all eight calligraphy scripts—is teaching a class how to do illumination, the delicate background behind the letters. This sacred art of the pen has been central to all Afghan crafts, including woodworking and ceramics, for a millennium.

In this centre where women and men work together, creating art, preserving the past, and celebrating beauty, it is hard to imagine the interminable war that has haunted their lives for thirty years or the terrorist attacks that have taken place within a few kilometres of the site as recently as two days ago. Turquoise Mountain is all about possibilities, artistic realities, and pride of place. The sense of possibility here is tangible, as heads bow over a project, a master teacher demonstrates intricate techniques, and the sounds of saws and hammers swirl with the swish of paintbrushes and the whir of the potter's wheel. It is a sunny, airy space whose skylights let the daylight wash over the art that fills the rooms.

At the other site, in the old city of Murad Khane, with its Sufi shrines and blue-tiled minaret, the work proceeds apace with freshly cut two-by-fours slipping into place beside stripped old timbers that have been varnished and secured. It is in the middle of downtown Kabul. Developers wanted to turn it all into flashy malls and garish mansions when Stewart set his own sights it.

When the reconstruction is complete, there will be galleries and a bazaar, with handicrafts for sale, as well as the Centre for Traditional Afghan Arts and Architecture, with its masters and students showing their art and technique to the public. Stewart wants the five-hectare site opened to the public as soon as possible, so people can see the artisans at work, stroll through the reclaimed buildings, and discover what he calls the last real traditional pottery in the world.

The mud streets are crowded when I visit Murad Khane. Crumbling buildings stand as reminders of the tasks yet to be done, but upstairs in the reception room of Peacock House where the work has been completed, you could be forgiven for thinking you had stumbled into another century. The delicate woven carpets and magnificent wooden carvings of peacocks and flowers, the intricate *jali* patterns and brilliant coloured threads in the cushions that surround the room, speak of a finer time, a time of self-admiration and self-confidence. This is the Afghanistan Rory Stewart wants to show to the world.

IN WINNIPEG, MANITOBA, AN OFFBEAT academic has plans for another side of Afghanistan he wants to show to the world. I met Dr. Richard Gordon in a bookstore soon after *Veiled Threat* was published. He was genuinely concerned about what he had heard and read about the women of Afghanistan and said, "I want to help. What should I do?" I appreciated his solicitude and, if I remember correctly, replied, "Almost anything you decide to do would be helpful." He seemed mild-mannered, stroking the book he held in his hands while he posed his questions about Afghanistan, his wrinkled brow speaking of his humanitarian concern. I didn't know at that time that he was a radiology professor in the faculty of medicine at the University of Manitoba. Nor did I know how serious he was about taking action for Afghans, or how tenacious he is when he decides to fix something. He reminds me of the late June Callwood's story about people who make a difference. "Moments when a useful contribution can be made by taking action almost never wear a name tag," she said. "Instead they always look like 'someone else's responsibility—not my business.'" She was right, of course. Invariably, when we see that something is amiss, we think, "Someone ought to do something about this." That someone turned out to be Richard Gordon.

He called me a few days later with a fine plan but one so immense I wondered how he would pull it off. "They burned the books," he began. "The Taliban destroyed the libraries, including the medical school library at the University of Kabul." Indeed, the library was in ruins. "They need doctors," he went on. "How can they train doctors without books?" Then he announced, with the confidence of a neophyte, that this would be his contribution to Afghanistan. He would find a way to restock the medical library. This was in January 2002. I watched and listened in amazement over the next two years while the professor conquered the considerable barriers thrown in front of him—finding and storing the books, shipping and assembling a library, and ultimately fulfilling the promise he had made to himself that he would indeed help.

Medical textbooks cost a small fortune, as any struggling medical student can attest. Richard Gordon started with a fundraising plan—"a loonie a book"—thinking he could get donors to toss in a loonie with each book they contributed, and he would use the cash to supplement the collection. It seemed like he had a long way to go. Dean Brian Hennen suggested he approach the medical students. What happened next was a win-win solution.

Three medical students at the University of Manitoba volunteered to spearhead the project. When Kevin Warrian, Magda Kujath, and Jason Tapper set out to collect the 650 medical textbooks considered essential for a medical school library, at an estimated value of $110,000, Gordon made it clear to them that these could not be old, cast-off, out-of-date books that nobody wanted. So the trio stipulated to donors that the books needed to be less than ten years old. The language in the textbooks wasn't a problem, as the medical school classes in Kabul are conducted in English. Twenty more students joined the team, calling it The Kabul Medical Library Project. But even with so many volunteers at work, they soon realized the call for books had to reach beyond Manitoba. They contacted medical students from across the country and were astonished when students from thirteen other medical schools vowed to take the request to university libraries, practising physicians, and everyone else they could tap for a book. The effort was then adopted by the Canadian Federation of Medical Students and eventually the project was dubbed Books with Wings. They began steamrolling towards their goal, creating subcommittees and a website, and soon realized that they needed a place to store the books coming in—now an estimated three thousand kilograms of them—and to somehow find a way to ship them to Kabul. Once there, they would need transport from the airport to the university and staff to stock the books on the shelves.

Maybe it was the shipping issue. It could have been the mention of the word *shelves*. Either way, Gordon soon was back on the phone to me. "What's the postal system like from here to there?" he wanted to know. There isn't one, I told him. "How will we get these books to Afghanistan?" he asked rhetorically. I was starting to think his phone calls and emails were his way of thinking through each stage of this project. The campaign he had set in motion was growing exponentially: Not only were the books coming in, but also awareness of the situation in

Afghanistan was increasing among the student volunteers. He told the students they would have to raise more money to buy shelves in Afghanistan. Then he called the Canadian armed forces.

Only the military had the means to get the books to Kabul. At that time, the Canadians were assigned to ISAF headquarters and charged with securing Kabul and the surrounding areas from the Taliban, al Qaeda, and the warlords so that the transitional government could do its work. Later, their mission would be expanded to the rest of the country, and Canadians would lead the fight against the insurgency, but when Gordon was looking for a carrier to take his library to the university in Kabul, Canadians soldiers were mostly stationed in the city. I knew they did humanitarian shipments from time to time. I had been in a girls' orphanage in Kabul once, and had noticed each child had a teddy bear on her bed. Teddy bears are not typical children's toys in Afghanistan, but these ones had become the much-loved, prized possessions of thirty-two little girls. When I asked the woman in charge where the bears came from, she said, "Soldiers patrol this area. They stop and talk to the kids. One of them asked his family in Canada to send some toys, and a month or so later, all these bears arrived." Thirty-two teddy bears is one thing. But three thousand kilograms of books? I thought it was a long shot. But I had underestimated Richard Gordon.

Gordon is the learned author of papers such as "Diatom Nanotechnology" and "The Fundamental Mechanism of Differentiation as Viewed from the Embryo to the Nucleus." Somehow, between lecturing at the university and attending international conferences about "The Genome as a Discrete State," he also was mastering the not-so-delicate art of shipping and library assembly. He is a scientist, after all, and thinks in formulas; in this case, books plus planes equal doctors trained. Every time I spoke to him on the phone or wrote to him by email, I would shake my head at his audacity and the size of the project he had started.

He is not a man who takes setbacks gently. When barriers were thrown in his way, he assumed the cause was either an inconvenient lack of awareness or irritating obstinacy, depending on the day he encountered them, and he simply went around or straight through them. When people hesitated, he demanded that they get over their indecision and just get on board. The students came up with their own ingenious methods to stock the library. They canvassed the residents in hospitals across Canada—these were doctors who had gone on to train in a medical specialty such as surgery, cardiology, or obstetrics—and suggested they no longer needed the books they had used as students of other disciplines, and to please donate them. They did. Kevin Warrian said at the time: "Medical school is tough at the best of times, most of all in a war-torn country with few resources. We can only struggle to imagine what it's like to learn these subjects without even core textbooks."

In May 2003, the library consisted of seventeen hundred textbooks that had been carried across Canada by post, or in trucks that had donated space, and were now housed in the warehouse of Login Brothers Canada, a medical textbook distributor with headquarters in Winnipeg, that had also donated 430 books to the project. Dozens of medical students at the University of Manitoba turned up to sort, label, and catalogue the books. Hundreds of volunteers had joined them in a cross-country effort: librarians, private citizens, and members of the Winnipeg Afghan community, including University of Manitoba student Mariam Omar and former Kabul Medical Institute professor and refugee Dr. Wassay Niazi.

The library left Winnipeg for Trenton, Ontario, the jumping-off point for the military flight, on May 21, 2004, in a truck donated by Login Brothers and under the supervision of

Canadian Forces Reserve officer Gurinder Kler. It was received and delivered by the Canadian forces staff and Lt.-Col. Carl Walker, a Winnipegger who happened to be the commanding officer of health support services at Camp Julien, the military headquarters in Kabul. Every single book bears a nameplate that reads: "A gift from the medical students of Canada to the medical students of Afghanistan."

I was thrilled to hear of the books' arrival in Kabul and thought the project had come to a wonderfully successful end. Then my phone rang. "They don't have a librarian," a very agitated Richard Gordon explained. "The collection is worthless if they can't get it properly onto the shelves and reshelved when the books come back." Fortunately for about two hundred medical students in Afghanistan, half of them women, a philanthropist in Vancouver who prefers to remain nameless came to the rescue. He sent Gordon a cheque—the same day—that would cover the cost of sending a medical librarian to Kabul for three weeks to train a team of librarians. Janis Rapchuk, a volunteer with CW4WAfghan and a librarian in her working life, took a leave of absence and brought a happy conclusion to the odyssey of Books with Wings.

The dean of the medical school at the University of Kabul, Dr. Cheragh Ali, was overwhelmed by the success of the project. He sent his grateful thanks for the efforts of the students and volunteers and for the goodwill the project had created.

Of course, that wasn't the end of the story. When people get up close to a problem and discover that the seemingly impossible can be accomplished, they almost always find that there is more to do. Gordon and his team of medical students have gone on to stock medical, nursing, and dental libraries at eight other learning institutions in Afghanistan. He is now working on the engineering libraries at Kabul University, Kandahar University, and Kardan University, and has started a worldwide project to halt HIV/AIDS from spreading in Afghanistan. A peek at his website, **www.bookswithwings.ca**, as I write this chapter provides continuing evidence of the ongoing commitment of one man who said, "I want to help."

CHAPTER 9

THE LIONESS

If you see an injustice being committed, you're not an observer, you're a participant.

—June Callwood

"I'LL BE LATE FOR SUPPER as I have a meeting at the Serena Hotel with the Norwegian foreign minister." The casual comment from Sima Samar to her family when she left for work on January 14, 2008, gave no hint of the horrible events that would unfold that day or that she would be caught in the middle of a terrorist attack when the Taliban pulled off a well-planned, carefully executed assault on the famed Serena Hotel, the one place that was supposed to be categorically safe.

When Afghans sat down to dinner that night, shocking headlines led the news in Kabul and around the world, claiming the target of the attack was the Norwegian foreign minister, the man Samar was meeting. The secretary-general of the United Nations issued a statement, claiming that the attack was revenge for Norway's assistance in ousting the Taliban along the border with Pakistan, but no one in Kabul saw it that way. The diplomats and foreign aid workers said the brazen raid was an announcement that foreigners were now the target: foreigners and Afghans who do business with them—such as Samar.

As chair of the Afghanistan Independent Human Rights Commission, Samar is often asked to meet with foreign delegations. But her presence signifies more than the courtesy of international diplomacy. She is the Lioness, the woman who dared to thumb her nose at the Taliban, who took the women's quarrel to the outside world during the five miserable years when they were thrust back into the Dark Ages, a passionate human rights advocate who names and shames the war criminals, a tough-minded broker who steadfastly promotes the need for change in Afghanistan. She won't be cowed: not by religious fanatics, not by warlords, not even by President Karzai. It's a costly position for a woman to take in a country whose citizens disavow gender equality, a country governed by a president whose power hardly extends beyond the city centres, and whose warlords, insurgents, and fundamentalist religious leaders would like to see her dead.

This is a woman who has not been able to go for a walk, go shopping, or meet friends in a tea house for six long years. She leaves the sanctity of her home only to go to work, and never without protection.

Samar was driven to the Serena Hotel, which calls itself "an oasis of luxury in a war-ravaged city," in a bulletproof car with her three bodyguards that January afternoon. They checked in with the guards at the gate and manoeuvred their SUV through the anti-terrorist cement blocks that ring the circular driveway to the main entrance. It was a sunny day, but minus twenty-five degrees, so there was no lingering at the door: Samar went directly into the hotel to her 5:30 P.M. rendezvous, in a room on the lower level, with the seven-member Norwegian delegation. She recalls the meeting as nothing out of the ordinary, at first: "We were discussing security in the country when we heard the first explosion. The sound was dull and, after all, we hear these explosions a lot in our country, so I thought it was far away and wasn't worried." Thirty seconds later, she heard the rat-tat-tat of automatic machine gun fire. "I knew it was close. Then the second explosion shook the room—I thought it was on top of us, maybe the floor above."

In fact, the terrorists, dressed in police uniforms, had stormed the gate of the Serena and shot the guards, and as they made their way to the door, a suicide bomber blew himself up in the driveway, acting as a decoy to give the terrorists time to get inside the hotel. A second suicide bomber detonated his explosives in the lobby of the hotel, while the gunmen followed a hallway downstairs to the exercise room where foreigners were known to work out and began firing as soon as they burst through the door.

Inside the meeting room, a man from the Norwegian Embassy barricaded the door. A waiter assigned to serve at the party, who doubled as a security agent, told everyone to get down on the floor. Then Norwegian bodyguards arrived with their guns drawn and instructed Samar and the delegates to get under the large, long table in the middle of the room.

"We all crouched under the table. I thought it was fighting between the security operators or maybe a terrorist attack." While huddled with the others, she called her driver to find out what he knew. "It's really bad out here," he said. At first, he thought they had been hit by a rocket. The tire was punctured and shrapnel had taken chunks out of the side of the armoured vehicle. It took a few minutes before he realized that the debris on the windshield was body parts and that this had been a suicide bomb. "Stay in there, keep yourself safe," he told Samar.

"There's still a lot of shooting. No one knows where the gunmen are now."

"Everyone under the table was on a cellphone," says Samar. They were moved to the bomb shelter, which turned out to be the hotel kitchen, about fifteen minutes later, and joined about 130 others brought from the lobby, the coffee shop, the sauna. One man was wrapped in a towel. He had been in the sauna when the gunmen opened the door. He literally dove out the window naked, then found his way through the hotel garden to a soldier, who took him to the kitchen and gave him a towel. Another man was crying. He kept lamenting the deteriorating security in the country, saying, "We didn't ask for a palace, just a piece of bread." Samar tried to calm him down. She had also noticed piles of linen in the hallway as they were hustled to the kitchen and had decided they would make a good place to hide if it came to that.

They were kept in the shelter for about four hours while soldiers searched the premises, until they could be sure the attack was over. Seven people died, six more were badly wounded. It was 10 P.M.. when Samar was escorted out of the hotel. She went directly to her car, which was now part of the crime site and could not be moved. A police officer drove her home.

WATCHING THE EXTENDED FAMILY wait for a mother, wife, daughter, or sister to return was like being witness to the trials and ills of the last thirty years in Afghanistan. Samar's daughter Tamanna, seventeen, is trying to be calm but blinking her eyes incessantly and starting at every phone call. Samar's mother, Khorshid, who doesn't know how old she is but guesses she is in her late seventies, is a devout woman who prays five times a day and knows her daughter is the target of extremists. She mumbles her prayers, clutches a scarf to her mouth, and walks silently into the room and out again, hoping for news. Samar's husband, Rauf, a handsome, debonair man who runs Shuhada, the NGO that Samar started in 1989, talks to the men who guard their house and phones contacts, trying to get a handle on the unfolding events. Her half-brother, Ahmed Ali, the son of her father's second wife, who had come to Kabul with her as her chief of staff when she was named to Karzai's cabinet in 2001, acts as command central: He is on the phone with Samar and then her bodyguards, her office staff, and government security, trying to piece the information together. And her brother Wahid fingers his worry beads, sits cross-legged on the floor with the others, and glances up whenever a cellphone rings.

Dinner is served without her, and as everyone gathers around the *dastarkhan* (the plastic cover placed on the floor, around which the family gathers for meals), the only sound to break the silence is that of spoons scraping on bowls and cellphones ringing. This roomful of people, who have seen relatives and friends wiped out by the turmoil of the last three decades, tonight live through the agony of waiting. The dinner platters are cleared away, Samar's plate kept aside, pots of tea filled again and again, until at last the gate opens and the Lioness comes home.

The next day she says, "Somehow I wasn't very afraid. My mouth wasn't dry. I was calm during the whole thing. But then, I didn't sleep all night, and today I think it must be post-trauma stress, as I feel scared." There was no time to process the trauma because she found herself receiving calls from literally hundreds of well-wishers, most of them performing an Afghan custom called *qurbani*. While it is normally an offering of food or money to the poor, during celebrations such as Eid ul Fitr, which marks the end of Ramadan, the Islamic month of fasting, *qurbani* is also performed when someone has been saved from death. All day long, they came to her office at the human rights commission and to her home in Karte-se carrying naan, leading sheep to the door (at last count, five days later, there were eight), and bringing packets of money. "It will be distributed to the poor," she explains. "It's a kind of safety tradition that keeps the evil eye from you, and gives the sheep or the bread in your place." Not a woman to be dewy-eyed over tradition, Samar is nevertheless obviously touched by the outpouring of affection and concern. "Almost every friend has called. So has Vice-President Khalili and most of the cabinet ministers, to say they are happy that I'm safe."

But in the safety of her home, she confides that although the attackers were dressed as policemen, one of them actually was a policeman, and the police who came to rescue them were drunk. "We know these things are happening," she says. "The protection and security of the people is the state's responsibility. But we can't trust the legal system, and no one is accountable so there's no justice." She blames corruption, nepotism, and a lack of commitment from people who benefit from the system the way it is.

> This isn't a post-conflict country. We are in conflict.
> And it's not just the Taliban. It's no longer clear who
> to blame. Imagine how people feel after seeing what
> almost hap-pened to me when I'm so well guarded.
> They think if they just go out to clean the street,
> they'll end up in pieces.

Dr. Sima, as she is known to Afghans, is the ultimate been-there-done-that woman. She bucked the system and fought her own family so she could go to school and become a doctor. Her father had two wives and produced four children with one, eight with the other. Sima grew up witnessing the competitions and consequences of polygamy, as well as the unequal treatment of women and girls, and dedicated her life to changing the status of women in Afghanistan. She fought the Soviets, the mujahedeen, and was the Taliban's most hated woman when she kept her girls' schools and women's health clinics open despite the Taliban threat to kill her.

I have been following her as a journalist for eleven years. Her reputation came before her when I was seeking an interview with someone who would talk about the Taliban during my first assignment in 1997. But I was warned: "She could be killed for talking." Our interview began in the arrivals lounge of the airport in Quetta, but she was due back at her clinic, where she was scheduled to do abdominal surgery, and suggested I join her. Pretty impressive, I thought: a women's rights activist, caught in the calamity of war, scrubbing up to go into the operating room. That wasn't all. She had to dash home after the surgery to get the supper started. Back at the clinic, she filled me in on the consequences of a medieval theocracy taking the reins of power. A lot of those consequences were sitting on benches at the clinic waiting for treatment: Women who had been beaten or worked nearly to death. Women who had been refused medical help because of the Taliban edicts and were now perilously close to being too late to benefit from it. Women who were pregnant with an eighth, tenth, or fourteenth child they were too exhausted to care for. Women who could not get pregnant and risked being relegated to slave status, while their husbands took second, third, and fourth wives to ensure male progeny. It was like a list out of the Middle Ages. But even here, she dealt with the many women's ills with a gentle hand and told stories that made everyone laugh. There was a conspiratorial attitude, solidarity, and a sense of humour that spoke of survival.

After a full day of arguing with the United Nations to get her share of donated wheat for her girls' schools, writing prescriptions, and performing surgery, she went home and made yogurt from scratch, prepared *kabuli*, the traditional Afghan dinner of spiced rice heaped over boiled lamb, and turned a pot of spinach into a delicious paste to serve to her extended family of fifteen. All in a day's work.

One of the survival cards she holds is a razor-sharp sense of humour. My favourite Sima Samar story happened in Jaghori, in the central highlands where she grew up. The Taliban had told her to close her hospital. She refused. Then they stole the generator. Not even Samar can run a hospital in a town without power and no generator, so she had to close it down. A few days later, she was working in a clinic nearby when a Taliban soldier threw open the door and barged in, pushing an elderly woman in front of him. "She's sick," he announced. "Fix her." Clearly even the Taliban knew Samar's reputation as a first-rate doctor. She examined the old lady, realized she had tonsillitis, and told the soldier, "Leave her with me overnight, come back tomorrow." She started a course of antibiotics for the woman, chatted with her, and made sure she had a comfortable place to sleep. When the Taliban soldier returned the next afternoon, she sat him down and said, "We have a problem. You have my generator. As it turns out, I have your mother." They made a trade. She was back in business.

After 9/11, Samar became one of five deputy prime ministers of the interim government, and the first-ever minister of women's affairs. But the fundamentalists who saw her as a threat to the status quo were toiling behind the scenes of the newly appointed government, seeking ways to discredit and dismiss the woman who was demanding reform. She had been interviewed and photographed by an Iranian newspaper while she was in Canada receiving the prestigious John Humphrey Freedom Award from Rights and Democracy in December 2001. In the interview, she criticized the Taliban interpretation of sharia law, a reproof widely agreed on by Islamic scholars, and the accompanying photograph showed her without a head scarf.

The extremists pounced in June when she was elected vice-chair of the Loya Jirga by fifteen hundred delegates who had gathered from all over Afghanistan to prepare the country for a two-year transitional government that would follow the six-month interim government and lead towards a nationwide election. The leading Islamic party, Jamiat-e-Islami, proclaimed that she had criticized sharia and had bared her head in public. They said Samar was the Salman Rushdie of Afghanistan (referring to the novelist who incurred the wrath of Iranian fundamentalists when he published *The Satanic Verses*) and issued a fatwah calling for her execution.

The United Nations took her into protective custody. The reformers, especially the women, held their collective breath. The Lioness had been caged, not by the illiterate Taliban but by educated men, some of them graduates of Harvard and Oxford, some of them members of the government's cabinet who wanted her silenced.

The chief justice at that time—the redoubtable Shinwari—waited for the chips to fall before deciding whether to send the case to trial. Everyone at the assembly, and in the diplomatic community in Kabul, knew the real issue was the progress Samar was making for women and girls. But the anti-women warlords made it clear that they would not cooperate with the government if it didn't back off on women's rights.

When Canada's foreign minister, Bill Graham, heard about the debacle, he had a visa issued for Samar and told the United Nations he would make sure she was welcomed in Canada if they could fly her out of the country. Legions of women from all over the world lined up to support her and offered her safe haven in half a dozen countries. But she knew that leaving during the tumult would be a voyage of no return, so she stayed and fought the charges. With Samar in protective custody and Canada asking questions, the stalemate in Kabul was getting messy. Then, in a deal with the devil, President Karzai caved in to the pressure from extremists. Samar was dropped from the cabinet, the transitional government took office, and the case against her was stayed.

The first time I met her, in March 1997, Samar said, "I have three strikes against me. I'm a woman, I speak out for women, and I'm Hazara, the most persecuted tribe in Afghanistan." Now she was the object of attack because she was demanding and getting change for Afghans and challenging the impunity of powerful men. When she was made chair of the Afghanistan Independent Human Rights Commission, those who saw her as a threat in government may have rued the day they finagled her undoing. As human rights chair, she is tackling everything from women's rights and tribal law to government corruption and transitional justice (that is, justice adapted to societies transforming themselves after a period of pervasive human rights abuse). The commission seeks recognition for victims and promotes peace, reconciliation, and democracy for all Afghans. She treads the rough waters stirred up by warlords and religious extremists, and tacks her way through policy at the United Nations as well as the Karzai government.

From the outset, her mission statement was "no peace without justice." But bringing war criminals to account in Afghanistan is a complicated concept. There is not even a word in the Dari or Pashto languages for *transitional justice*. During the Bonn Conference in November 2001, participants said war criminals, and those guilty of crimes against humanity and gross violations of human rights, should be excluded from the interim government that the conference was mandated to create. There was also a discussion about forbidding the newly formed government from issuing an amnesty to any of the known perpetrators. But the wording never made it to the document that was signed on December 5. The only reference to human rights in the Bonn Agreement was the commitment to establish a human rights commission. Samar says everyone presumed that the mandate of the commission would include examining past crimes, but it wasn't put in writing.

Subsequently, President Karzai himself called for a truth commission "to ensure the people will have justice." Samar doubted he would keep his word but leapt at the opportunity to fling open the doors of the Soviet, mujahedeen, and Taliban past and expose the crimes that everyone in the country knew about but hardly dared mention publicly for fear of reprisal. She consulted with Pakistani jurist Asma Jahingar, who was the United Nations' special rapporteur on extrajudicial killing at that time, and with Louise Arbour when she became the high commissioner of the United Nations Human Rights Commission. Then she sent her team across the country to interview six thousand Afghans about the events of the last twenty-five years. It took eight months to gather the evidence—a difficult and dangerous task in the midst of the ongoing conflict—and in January 2005, the report, "A Call for Justice," was given to President Karzai by Samar and High Commissioner Arbour together. It began with an overview of how Afghans arrived at this place:

> More than a million people lost their lives and almost the same number became disabled in the course of the war, as a result of antipersonnel landmines, indiscriminate bombing and rocket attacks by the former Soviet Union and the regime backed by them, and attacks by armed militia groups, including the Mujahideen and Taliban. Thousands of people were put in jail for their political beliefs and tortured. Thousands of children lost their family members and their fathers. Afghanistan's streets are now full of orphaned children who must beg to survive. More than seven million people were forced to leave their villages and towns and take refuge in Iran and Pakistan.

> The miseries of this period of conflict cannot be
> described in words. One can only feel the pain by listen-
> ing to the cries of widows, orphans and other victims
> around the country.

The report made international headlines with the shocking claim that 69 percent of the population had suffered human rights abuses. These were "staggering statistics in comparison to any other conflict in the world," said Arbour. The report focused on a four-step action plan: firstly, to acknowledge the suffering of the Afghan people; secondly, to ensure credible and accountable state institutions and to purge human rights violators and criminals from state institutions; thirdly, to seek and document the truth of what had happened; fourthly, to promote reconciliation and improve national unity. The conclusion called for: "The promotion of peace, reconciliation, justice and the rule of law in Afghanistan, and the establishment of a culture of accountability and respect for human rights." The timeline for accomplishing the action plan was three years.

Samar knew that the concept itself was unheard-of in Afghanistan and that it needed careful explaining, lest the enemies of the report use it to sway public opinion. The commission prepared a detailed statement explaining transitional justice and made it as widely available as possible, sometimes using radio broadcasts to read it to a mostly illiterate population. Samar wanted the public to understand that transitional justice is a question of more than just criminal responsibility; it also is an important step towards reconciliation and the restoration of peace.

The document stated plainly that a transitional justice strategy should include "truth-seeking, victim recovery, reintegration of the deceived and perpetrators in the society, reparations, the preservation of peace and stability, the

strengthening of democracy and the rule of law and the administration of justice." It says in part:

> Transitional justice is often misunderstood as addressing
> questions of criminal responsibility only. As a first step,
> transitional justice strategy aims to realize peace and
> national reconciliation, to restore co-existence and co-
> operation, to heal the wounds and pains of the victims
> and to re-integrate the citizens into a peaceful life in the
> society. Reparations, healing of the physical and psycho-
> logical suffering and re-integration in the community of
> citizens, whose social relationships have been damaged,
> are all attempts that go beyond concepts such as court,
> prison and revenge and run counter to them. Efforts to
> promote the culture of forgiveness, affection, brother-
> hood and sisterhood and to strengthen the solidarity
> between the country's today and tomorrow generations,
> constitute the principal foundation of the present Action
> Plan. The positive experience of countries that have
> passed bloody crises show that the transitional justice
> strategy should balance a variety of goals including truth-
> seeking, victim recovery, re-integration of the deceived
> and perpetrators in the society, reparations, the preserva-
> tion of peace and stability, the strengthening of democ-
> racy and the rule of law and the administration of
> justice ...

As in the earlier report, "A Call for Justice," the document
on transitional justice called for action in four key areas:
symbolic measures such as acknowledging the suffering of the
victims; institutional reform such as establishing accountability institutions; truth-seeking and documentation by, for
example, recording past events in a historically accurate
manner; and reconciliation, which could include reparations

and working to restore the people's trust in its government and institutions.

The commission also called for bold action against war crimes such as genocide and crimes against humanity, saying that "the commission of such crimes does not fall into the scope of amnesty on the basis of the principles of the sacred religion of Islam and internationally accepted standards" and clearly noted that "special attention must be given to ensuring the active participation of women in the process."

Then Samar waited. The government was silent. The report sat on the president's desk, gathering dust. Rumours circulated about the names in the report—some of them cabinet ministers, others close associates of the president. Ministers Rabbani and Fahim, member of parliament Sayyaf, speaker of the house Qanuni, and the grandson of the king were among those said to be named. Leaked versions of the details in the report started turning up in newspapers. For example, when Amanullah Gozar, a former mujahedeen muscleman and alleged war criminal, was appointed chief of police in Kabul, people whispered that he was on the list of human rights abusers in the transitional justice report. (He was actually fired less than a year after being appointed to the post.) There were suggestions that even if the government wanted to act on the report, they didn't have a functioning judiciary to deal with the cases that would be brought before the court.

Samar continued the wait, steaming with indignation, concerned about the consequences of burying the facts, and wondering whether the government's initially welcoming reception of the report was all smoke and mirrors.

Then in March 2007, President Karzai declared an amnesty to all former combatants and those accused of war crimes and violations of human rights, as long as they agreed to abide by the constitution and the laws of Afghanistan. Six months later, he took tentative steps towards adopting the action plan, but it was mostly by shuffling provincial governors, friends, and relatives of people in power from one post to another.

Samar concedes the judiciary presently in place in Afghanistan could not manage trials of war criminals, and that letting the guilty go free after a botched trial would be worse than not charging them. But she hasn't given up the task, saying she has no other choice but to continue the struggle. "It's six years now [since the government was formed]. We had high expectations, maybe too high, that have not been fulfilled. People are tired of waiting for these promised changes." She has support for her call for accountability. A new initiative, A Platform for Citizen Initiative in Truth and Justice, got off the ground soon after the amnesty announcement, and in Louise Arbour's report on Afghanistan to the United Nations in January 2008, the high commissioner said:

> Human rights and its defenders have come under attack by those who view human rights as a Western-imposed concept, as counter to local religious and cultural traditions, and as a luxury that Afghanistan cannot afford. Yet, insecurity in Afghanistan generally emanates from failure to address ongoing human rights concerns and violations, including to effectively address past violations. During my visit to Afghanistan, I found Afghans from all walks of life claiming their rights to food, shelter, education, livelihood, health, justice and physical security. The creation of new institutions to protect human rights should not be perceived as an attack on traditional systems but should seek to complement and build upon their strengths.

Then she added:

> Regrettably, progress in implementing the Action Plan on Peace, Reconciliation and Justice, adopted by the

Government in December 2005 and slated for completion
by end of 2008, has been extremely limited. Significant
political opposition to transitional justice in Afghanistan,
exemplified by the adoption by Parliament of the
National Reconciliation Charter or amnesty law in March
2007, seriously undermines the Action Plan.

Samar addressed an international conference at the
University of Toronto's Munk Centre six weeks before Arbour's
report and challenged the participants to speak out on the
taboo topics of Afghanistan:

> You can't have a democracy without women. It's good
> that they are in the parliament, but how many women
> can make a decision about how many children they'll
> have? The speaker of the house doesn't believe in human
> rights. Who's talking about that? We have freedom of
> expression, but the media outlets are mostly run by Iran,
> warlords, and jihadists. You have to speak out, be with us.

Back in Afghanistan she addressed the Human Rights Day
event, also known as the National Memorial Day of Victims, a
gathering that included President Karzai, and said in part:

> It has always been that innocent people of this land have
> paid a big price due to the unsafe situation. Their sacri-
> fices are not in vain and have captured the attention of
> the government of the Islamic Republic of Afghanistan.
> For this reason, the government has created this day to
> honour the memory of victims of human rights viola-
> tions. But the celebration of this day cannot reflect the
> will of the people and victims through commemoration
> while there is no commitment for justice and no demand
> for justice.

She called for an end to "the culture of the powerful escaping the laws of the land."

Like a bad odour, the government's inaction wouldn't go away. And Samar reminds her audiences everywhere she goes that there can be no peace without justice. On April 23, 2008, her commission took another step to keep the justice issue on the front burner and called on the government and the international community to extend until December 2009 the period in which human rights violations and war crimes committed in the years prior to 2001 can be addressed. "The action plan has not been implemented effectively and according to its own goals; therefore we want it to be extended at least until December 2009," Farid Hamidi, a commissioner in the AIHRC, told IRIN news in Kabul.

Human Rights Watch picked up the torch by criticizing President Karzai and the international community for doing little to bring war criminals to justice and instead following a policy of "reliance" on powerful warlords allegedly involved in past crimes.

Samar has waited a lifetime for justice in Afghanistan. The finish line continues to elude her.

IT IS STILL DARK WHEN SHE PREPARES to leave for Kunduz, the city in the northeast quadrant of the country that is opening a new human rights centre on January 21, 2008. The centre is seen as a symbol of progress, but coming on the heels of the attack on the Serena Hotel just one week previously, the trip to Kunduz is measured through a sniper's scope, a suicide bomber's vest, an insurgent's preference to wipe the human rights program out. The night before her scheduled departure, she is told that weather conditions have forced a change of plans; the plane they are to take to Kunduz can't land due to heavy snow, so they will take a helicopter instead, which means her bodyguards can't go with her. The three men, who have been her protectors ever since she came to Kabul in 2001 to take her post as minister of women's affairs, are apoplectic. They know the risks: With tips from the United Nations, they have aborted a dozen attempts on her life. They are adamant: she can't go to Kunduz without them. They hatch a plan to leave almost immediately, make the ten-hour drive through the snow to Kunduz, and be there when she arrives. They will stay while she cuts the ribbon to the new human rights centre and makes a speech, and once she is safely in the helicopter, they will make the ten-hour drive back to Kabul. The drama plays out at nine o'clock at night. She is on the phone to the United Nations, begging for a seat on the helicopter for one of her bodyguards, who are awaiting the decision with an eye on the menacing weather and an all-night drive. Finally, a seat is secured for one bodyguard, and they revert to plan A, which is to have her at the airport for an early departure.

A flashlight beams off the wall of the dark upstairs hallway while she rushes to leave before dawn, packing a piece of naan and a bit of cheese in her purse, swallowing a cup of tea, stopping quickly in her sleeping daughter's bedroom. There is no power in the house because the grid for Kabul is only activated four hours a day, from 6 P.M. to 10 P.M., so it is cold; so cold you can see your breath in the house. The windows are thick with frost, so only the blur of red brake lights and the beam of the headlights on the car that waits for her outside are visible as the vehicle pulls away from the walled compound, with three machine gun-toting bodyguards and a woman who won't step back from the forces that threaten her work. Her mother walks like a ghost down the hall, whispering prayers for her safety. The tension is palpable.

There is a siege mentality throughout the country in these post-Serena days. Even the United Nations is in lockdown: Staff cannot be outside their offices or their homes. Evacuation plans have been reviewed, checkpoints established, just in case the place collapses and the international community needs to beat a hasty retreat. The strain is evident everywhere. At dinner in the home of three employees from the international community, the conversation takes the form of comic relief in a discussion about the current state of affairs. While Mozart plays from the computer on the sideboard, a bottle of Beaujolais is passed around, and juicy pomegranates are served for dessert, the conversation switches from the attack at the Serena ("Pass the sugar please") to the difficulty of working during a lockdown ("By the way, did you feel the earthquake last night?") to the revised evacuation plan. It is like watching a movie. Diners explain that the woman among them has a burka to wear, and the men have *salwar kameez* (traditional tunic and pyjama-like pants) and *pakol* hats with which to disguise themselves. They have an old wheelbarrow stashed in the backyard that they would use to carry what they can, their computers, for instance, wrapped in ragged linens. And if the unspeakable happens—an all-out attack—they will simply walk away, knowing the guards who are at their gate this night will have been the first to bolt. They will mix in with masses of people on the street and head to a secret rendezvous, where they can use the ID cards tucked in their pockets to secure safe passage.

There is a lot that is surreal about Afghanistan during the cold snowy winter of 2008. On this same day, the Shiites are observing Aushura, a four-day festival that marks the murder of the grandson of the Prophet fourteen hundred years ago. The mullahs are wailing into their loud-hailers, thousands of men are parading in the street, beating their bare backs with sticks, many of them bleeding, most of them weeping, all of them recreating the angst and revenge of yesteryear. They disrupt the traffic, draw condescending stares from the Sunni Muslims who don't mark Aushura, and weave through the huge, black-draped scaffolds set up along the parade route.

To add to the confusion, the opening of the third session of parliament coincides with the final day of the wailing, chanting, and self-flagellation of Aushura. Security is heightened, if that is possible. And over at the Turquoise Mountain Foundation office, Rory Stewart weighs the consequences of the attack on the Serena Hotel and says, "If there are two or three more coordinated attacks like this one, the international community will leave."

The good news of the day is that Samar has safely returned to her office. The helicopter couldn't land in Kunduz because of the weather, so she is back at her desk, this time planning a trip to Darfur because she is the United Nations' special rapporteur for Sudan, an interesting additional assignment for a woman whose plate is overflowing with human rights atrocities in Afghanistan.

Her report card, six years after the world came to her doorstep to search for Osama bin Laden and promised to get this pariah state back on its feet, is this: Security is worse. It improved for a while, but as the promised changes didn't happen and the insurgency picked up speed, the ranks of thieves, hooligans, and terrorists increased. Employment is better. Women who can find jobs are back at work, although they are poorly paid. The school situation has improved. Notwithstanding the fact that girls' schools have been firebombed, teachers murdered, and night letters dropped to warn parents against sending their girls to school, about one-third of the girls are at school. But now the education system needs fixing. The training of teachers and the methods of teaching have to be improved. It is fair to say that access to health services is a little better in urban areas. But violence in the home is worse, although the increased number of incidents could be due to a newly established reporting mechanism. The observation of human rights is somewhat better, but girls and women are still in jail for the crime of being raped, running away from their abusive families, or having a boyfriend. And the police still can't be trusted by women. Poverty is the same or maybe a little worse. When the international community came to town, prices for everything from food to accommodation rose.

"There's an expression here that says, 'You can't reach Mecca by running,'" says Samar, referring to the hajj, the once-in-a-lifetime pilgrimage to Mecca that Muslims with means should make. "It will take more time to bring change to Afghanistan. There are places here where people have never seen a car, where whole families live in the same room as the animals, where men sell their wives. We need champions for women."

In a style I've come to expect as vintage Sima Samar, she is sewing a jacket while she rattles off the report card for Afghanistan. Actually, she is not exactly sewing: she is ripping apart a beautiful embroidered three-quarter-length coat that she bought in India. I enquire—somewhat flabbergasted as she snips off the sleeves and, using a pair of sewing shears, cuts fabric away—about what on earth she is doing to this exquisite jacket. "It's too big," she says in her so-what? style. "But you don't have a pattern or a measuring tape," I object. "I know what size it needs to be," she says and asks someone to turn on the generator so she can use her sewing machine. She slips the sleeves into place, runs them under the needle, and fifteen minutes later puts on the jacket that indeed fits perfectly.

This is a woman who has given the max to her country, first as a country doctor, treating people who had never had medical help in their lives. She travelled by foot, by donkey, and sometimes on horseback to cure their many ills. Then she defied the Taliban at every turn. When they came to her clinic and threatened to kill her if she didn't close it down, she didn't even glance up from the prescription she was writing and said, "You know where I am. I won't stop what I'm doing. Now get out of my clinic."

Her commitment to the human rights of the people of Afghanistan has come at an enormous cost. Her first husband, Abdul Ghafoori Sultani, a physics professor at Kabul University, the father of her son Ali, the man she married so that she could escape her family home and go to university, was *disappeared* by the Russians. She doesn't know what happened to him after they took him away that dreadful night. Questions still haunt her: What did they do to him? Did he suffer? Was it long? Where are his bones buried? She knows there is a mass grave near where she presumes the Soviet soldiers took him, but so far, permission has not been granted to open the grave, not even for the human rights commissioner.

She is the recipient of fifteen international awards, including the Profile in Courage Award that recognizes displays of courage similar to those John F. Kennedy described in his book *Profiles in Courage*. It is given to individuals who, by acting in accordance with their conscience, risked their careers or lives by pursuing a larger vision of the national, state, or local interest in opposition to popular opinion, pressure from constituents, or other local interests.

A medical doctor, a chef, a seamstress, and the champion of women's rights in a country that has historically denied women their place in society, Samar is as tough as the unforgiving country she grew up in and as loyal as the people she serves. When asked what she is most proud of, she doesn't hesitate: "The girls who are graduating from the schools that I started," she says. "They are the future."

CHAPTER 10

"I'M GOING TO BE SOMEBODY"

One of the best ways of enslaving a people is to keep them from education. The second way of enslaving a people is to suppress the sources of information, not only by burning books but by controlling all the other ways in which ideas are transmitted.

—Eleanor Roosevelt, May 11, 1943

WHILE THE GOVERNMENT FUMBLES, the activists strategize, and the Taliban do their worst, the next generation of Afghan girls is scoring tentative victories. The race for education began almost as soon as the interim government took office: The official back-to-school date was March 23, 2002. But, like everything else in Afghanistan, the celebration was layered with difficulties. The schools were in a dismal state of disrepair and the government did not have enough money to run them. Nevertheless, a contagious thrill of anticipation was sweeping across the country throughout that spring and summer. In the fall of that year, I travelled to the central highlands, to the province of Ghazni and the district of Jaghori, to see whether the enthusiasm had spread to the rural heart of Afghanistan.

It was bone-chillingly cold and barely light when I arrived at the Shuhada School at 7 A.M. The area superintendent had told me the students walk a great distance to get to school, and some turn up well before the 8 A.M. start time. I wanted to be there first, to witness the scene. Would they be "creeping unwillingly to school"? Would they come at all? Was this the start of a new era of enlightenment? As the shadows of dawn started to lift off the mountains, I was scanning the hills and valleys; it seemed like such a long hike for kids to make to get to school. The rugged mountainsides were formidable impediments, hardly an easy path for children; the silent valleys were deserted and seemed immense in their emptiness. Then in the distance I saw movement—two little girls trudging down a rutted track, then three more in the valley below. Soon, the landscape was filled with children.

It was a remarkable sight. They were coming over the hills, down the valleys, in twos, in fours, as far as the eye could see along the furrowed paths and dusty byways in this far-flung place called Sunge-e-Masha in Jaghori. Wearing the required black school frocks and white head scarves, they looked like penguins dotting the earth. They came in droves—little kids, teenagers—the blameless youngsters who bore the brunt of the Taliban's ruthless decree that girls were forbidden to learn. Tucked in their little satchels and souls were the hopes and dreams of a generation.

The teachers in the seventeen-room school they were walking to gathered at the door awaiting their arrival. The old man at the gate of the walled property pulled on the rope attached to the ancient iron disc perched at the top of the entrance: Bong! Bong! Bong! Back to school had never been a more powerful milestone.

I had become so accustomed to faces full of fear and furtive glances during the hateful Taliban period that I fully expected the children to avert their eyes from a stranger and walk past me into the school. Instead, they stopped where I stood on the doorstep and with the solemn earnestness that makes children so appealing asked instead what I was doing there. I flipped the question back to them and right there, on the threshold of the school they see as their chance of a better tomorrow, they shared their aspirations with me.

With her green eyes dancing and her blonde hair peeking out from the head scarf that has gone askew, ten-year-old Wahida said, "I will learn. And then I want to be an astronaut." This is a girl who was forbidden to leave her home for five years during Taliban rule, a girl who knew little of the outside world before September 11, 2001, when the international community came to her with bombs and promises to rid her homeland of the terrorists that had trespassed on their lives. Beside her, sixteen-year-old Fatima Anwary, a dark-haired, brown-eyed beauty in grade twelve, answered, "I'm going to change Afghanistan." Then, with all the pretentious sophistication a teenager can muster, she added, "I'll do it by getting an education. Knowledge makes change." Little six-year-old Parwana pushed her way between the older and taller students to the front of the pack and stood staring at the stranger in the midst of her schoolmates. When I asked her why she was here, she said, "This is my school. When I'm grown up, I'm going to be somebody." "Who might that somebody be?" I inquired. "The president of Afghanistan," she replied matter-of-factly.

They are the blueprint of Afghanistan. Their faces reflect the history of its storied past—the fair hair of conqueror Alexander the Great, the dark Persian features of occupier Darius the First, and the broad cheeks and Oriental eyes of Mongol invader

Genghis Khan. But their plans are for the future. They have barely learned to read and write but say, "It is the time of technology. We want computers. We want to be part of the world and get on the internet."

For the girls arriving at school on this sunny, cold morning in Jaghori, it almost did not happen. When the schools for both boys and girls were opened, not everyone had the chance to attend. Of the damaged schools, Sima Samar, who was one of the deputy prime ministers at the time, said, "If the schools aren't ready, let the children sit under the trees. We'll repair the buildings as fast as we can, but the children have to start learning now." Most of them could not afford the mandatory uniforms. So she used part of the money donated to the Ministry of Women's Affairs to buy sewing machines and fabric and asked hundreds of volunteers to stitch together nearly a million uniforms. But a bigger issue lurked in the background. The government could not afford to pay all of the teachers; they simply didn't have the budget. So a lot of the schools, most of them rural, could not get off the starting block in this sprint to educate the youngsters who had been denied the right to read and write.

That's when a Canadian woman stepped in. The campaign to raise money to pay teachers in Afghanistan was the brainchild of Susan Bellan, who operates a shop called Timbuktu in Toronto. She knew that, without an education, the girls of Afghanistan would never be able to break the merciless ties that bind them to second-class status. In spring 2002, she came up with a plan to have potluck dinners, where ten or twelve friends could get together for a shared meal and raise $750 (about $50 each), which would be enough to pay the salary of one teacher in Afghanistan for one year. Says Bellan:

> I phoned an acquaintance, Marilou McPhedran, a well-known feminist and community activist who, with a

group of other prominent Canadian women, had lobbied Foreign Minister Lloyd Axworthy to speak out for Afghan women during the reign of the Taliban. I told Marilou my idea, expecting her to say, "Thank you so much, we'll do it." Instead, to my surprise, she said, "Great idea, but it won't happen unless you take it on yourself. We are overburdened here with all our existing projects. So—will you do it?" This was not at all what I had anticipated and after a very pregnant pause, I said that I would take it on.

McPhedran suggested she ask her friend Nancy Kroeker to advise her on how to set the project up. Nancy had been executive director of the Writers' Development Trust for eight years and had raised hundreds of thousands of dollars for Canadian authors through fundraising dinners held in people's homes. McPhedran also advised her to get in touch with Janice Eisenhauer, co-founder and full-time volunteer running CW4WAfghan in Calgary. At the meeting with Kroeker, the initiative was named Breaking Bread for Women in Afghanistan. Then they contacted Janice Eisenhauer. Bellan was adamant that she did not want to handle the money and insisted on tax receipts for donors. Eisenhauer loved the idea, and quickly called Ariane Brunet, the women's rights coordinator at Rights and Democracy in Montreal. Together they devised a plan that would see 100 percent of the Breaking Bread money going to reliable people who hire teachers in Afghanistan, and tax receipts going to the donors at the potluck dinners. In May that year, the first Breaking Bread potluck supper was held in Toronto and raised $910. The plan took flight.

Potluck suppers started popping up all over the country, often raising more than the requisite $750. Teachers were hired. Students were going back to school. My editor at *Chatelaine* magazine wondered if this brainchild was really effective. After all, it is a bit of a leap to imagine tuna casseroles translating into girls learning to read. She asked me to check it out. I knew that one of the groups being funded was Shuhada, the NGO started by Samar in 1989 and still under her protective wing even while she chairs the human rights commission. Because Samar's schools are far off the beaten path, away from what was at that time the relative security and progress of Kabul, I decided to test the Breaking Bread initiative there, to see if the concept was working, as it must, in rural Afghanistan.

While I waited for the students to arrive at school that morning, I thought about the gracious way Canadian women had reached out to Afghan girls. The Breaking Bread for Women in Afghanistan initiative had spread across the country from Slave Lake in northern Alberta and Vancouver on the West Coast to Saint John, New Brunswick, in the east. It had already raised $147,000 at 115 dinners, enough to pay almost two hundred teachers. At between forty-five and sixty kids per classroom, that is more than ten thousand students learning to think for themselves in Afghanistan.

I had been a guest speaker at some of the Breaking Bread potluck dinners, and I knew the heartfelt hopes of the women who wrote the cheques for the girls here. The student enrolment at the Shuhada School, 1,950 girls, attends classes in shifts, half in the morning from 8:00 A.M. to 11:30 A.M. and the other half in the afternoon from 1:00 P.M. to 4:30 P.M. Another thousand students do the same at Shuhada Bosaid School, about twenty-five kilometres away, and also funded by the Breaking Bread initiative. The six- to twelve-year-olds have never been to school before. The teenagers had their education halted by the Taliban when they were in primary school. Principal Habiba Yosufi boasts, "It's not enough to read and write. My students will be able to go anywhere with their knowledge." Of the thirty-five teachers who work with her, she says, "We couldn't do this without the money from the Canadian women."

The concept works like this: you invite about a dozen friends, colleagues, or people you need to network with to a potluck dinner at your house. Ask everyone to bring a dish and to write a cheque—the goal being to raise $750. At the end of the evening, collect the money, and invite your guests to host a potluck supper of their own with another group of friends. Bellan's model was to invite ten people and charge $75. But she started hearing from seniors and students who felt $75 was too steep. So she suggested they adapt the idea to their own means: a coffee party for fifty at $15 each, or a book-club potluck at $25. Today they have raised more than $1 million, and fifty thousand little girls are going to school on the potluck ticket. (See their website at **www.breakingbreadforwomen.com**.)

She explains, "I'm after quantity, not quality. I want to see as many girls and women become literate as possible. The women of Afghanistan have been so abandoned, so isolated, I felt if we could create a network they'd know all of us are watching out for them." And that, she feels, would help them to get to the next step as equal citizens on their own.

Their infectious enthusiasm is hard to suppress in the class-room where the students clap every time someone gets the right answer. Although each girl has a notebook and pen or pencil, there is no equipment in the classroom except a black-board and tiny bits of chalk. They sit three to a desk, and some are on the floor because there are not enough chairs to go around. (CW4WAfghan replaced the chairs the Taliban stole, but there are so many more students this year, the shortage of chairs is still a problem.) When I visit in November 2002, they are preparing for winter when the schools are closed because of the cold and the dark. But there are no cheers in anticipation of the three-month holiday. When I ask if they are happy to be having vacation, they respond as one: "No!" They are in a hurry to learn, to become the "somebody" they so often refer to when I ask them about the future.

The problems in running the school are immense. They can't dig a deep enough well to provide drinking water, so the kids have to carry water from home. There are five toilets for the two thousand students and staff. They don't have enough books, and even the buildings are in need of repair, but there is enough will in this place to surmount the multiple and confounding problems they face. For example, the school was not registered in the government office because the teachers are not being paid by the Ministry of Education. Since there is no government money to pay the teachers—which is why the Canadian funds are so badly needed—the officials in the ministry take the view that schools like this one simply do not exist. But if the school isn't registered, the graduates can't go to the university. District Education Director Mohammad Yousaf Naibi barely hides his disregard for the ministry when he says, "We're solving that problem now. The graduates of this school will go to university next year." They did.

The road trip from Kabul to Jaghori at that time was a sharp reminder of the tenuous peace the international community had cobbled together and the perilous path these kids had taken by choosing to be educated. The Taliban had already regrouped with al Qaeda and were making daring raids into the villages. Thirty girls' schools had been fire-bombed during the previous ten months. Leaflets warning parents not to send their girls to school had been circulated by the Taliban. The day before I was to leave for Jaghori, the Taliban had issued a new, menacing edict: "Foreigners will be executed. Afghans helping them will be tortured. American journalists will be captured and held until Taliban prisoners are released." Within hours of the edict being issued, a Turkish engineer working on road reconstruction—on the road to Ghazni province that we were to take the next day—was captured and held for ransom. The Taliban wanted ten of their thugs, who were being held by the Americans, released in exchange for this man's life. Not surprisingly, the people I was travelling with suggested I cover my face, and the driver selected a route that would skirt the Taliban, which meant we were nine hours on the road to Shuhada School, a journey that would normally take six hours.

Little did anyone know at the time that the situation would get worse in the years to come. In 2007, the tally of girls' schools burned to the ground was 150; another 305 schools were closed due to lack of security. But the worst statistic was this: 105 students and teachers were killed, and beside their bodies were found handwritten messages that warned villagers of the consequences of educating girls.

This push-pull conundrum is commonplace in Afghanistan today. While initiatives such as Breaking Bread are moving the girls ahead, the fundamentalists who oppose educating girls have managed to force the government to uphold a law, written in the mid-seventies, that says married women, although many are in their mid-teens, cannot attend school. Religious extremists are up to their old tricks, blaming Islam for their anti-woman doctrines. One said, "Allah says in the holy Quran that women should stay at home and not expose their beauty." That is theocracy-speak that attempts to justify denying fundamental rights to women and girls.

Says Samar, "The most useful way to change the mentality of society is education. If you educate a woman, you educate the family. If you educate a man, you only educate one person." In her view, the Breaking Bread initiative is "excellent and responsible." She says, "It creates solidarity between the women here and the women of Canada. The amount of money spent by a Canadian woman may not seem very big, but it can change the life of a girl in Afghanistan."

This school in Jaghori is the very one that nearly cost Samar her life. In 1998, the Taliban demanded she shut the school and reminded her that girls could only attend schools that taught the Quran, and only for grades one to three. Samar made a sign:

THIS SCHOOL TEACHES THE QURAN TO CLASSES ONE TO THREE. And she went right on teaching science, literature, math, and history to the students she sees as the future of the country. In fear for their daughters' lives, most parents decided to keep their girls at home, but officially Shuhada School stayed open. When the Taliban found out what she had done, they threatened to hang her. She replied, "Go ahead and hang me in a public place and tell the people my crime: I was giving papers and pencils to the girls."

Back in Canada, the women who attend the potluck dinners invariably share their experiences in a letter with the cheque they send to Janice Eisenhauer. Suzanne, from Courtice, Ontario, writes:

> As we sat talking about our families and our lives, I
> noticed that my daughter had slipped into the room.
> With her ever-present book in hand, she quietly curled
> up in a chair half-reading, half-listening to the conversa-
> tion. I tried to imagine what her life would be like, if we
> lived in a country where attending school could be
> forbidden to her, simply because she was a girl. We raised
> $875. It was quite an evening.

The potluck supper in Slave Lake was particularly memorable. I had been invited to speak at the event and expected to find a group of women gathered in someone's home. To my amazement, the organizers had invited the whole town and booked the hockey arena for the event. They raised more than $5,000, and if goodwill and solidarity counted for cash, there would have been enough money to educate everyone in Afghanistan.

The funds have found their way to some unexpected and usually forgotten centres of learning. One donation went to the Kabul Children's Centre, which was started by the Afghan

Women's Organization in Canada. When I dropped in for a visit, it was the pots of purple petunias that caught my attention first. They looked so out of place in this heavily shelled district of Kabul. In fact, the white stucco house with the freshly painted green trim behind the flowerpots looked as though it had been dropped here, like Dorothy's house in *The Wizard of Oz*. This neighbourhood is badly scarred by the twenty-three years of civil war Afghanistan has endured. So are the children inside the tidy little house.

Adeena Niazi, the president of the Afghan Women's Organization in Toronto, travels to Kabul regularly. She knows there are thousands of children who have been abandoned, orphaned, or simply left to their own devices in this city. In spring 2002, she decided to do something about it. She found the house, convinced her friends to help her fix it up, hired staff, gathered up twenty-one little girls in need, and gave them a home. They ranged in age from three to eleven, and although all but the three- and four-year-olds go to school, they all need help catching up with what they missed when turmoil took over their young lives. Niazi asked the Breaking Bread team for money to pay a teacher. Now there is a classroom in the house, and a teacher comes every day after the regular school gets out to help them with their homework and give them the boost they need.

Six years later, the house is home to twenty-six girls whose ages range from two to seventeen. None of them has finished high school yet, but Niazi is optimistic about the future. One has plans to be a police officer, and a few others want to go to university, she says. They are like a family, calling one another sister, the older ones taking care of the younger ones. Niazi says they still have obstacles to deal with, like a drug-addicted father or cousin who turns up to claim ownership of a child, with the intention of selling her as a bride. "We pay bribes to keep the girls," she says. "It's the only way right now."

Another lump sum went to hiring a teacher at the Jaghori hospital so that six young women could become nurses. The extraordinary story is vintage Samar. She knew that Herat's hated warlord, Ismail Khan, was holding thirty "wayward" girls in confinement. Indeed, the girls had broken the rules of Khan's ultra-conservative province by going out alone, looking for men, and attending forbidden parties. Samar heard about their plight through the United Nations when they asked her, as the chair of the human rights commission, to intervene. She did, and packed all thirty of them up and took them to Kabul. Some are at her women's shelter; others were returned to their families. But six had the potential to become nurses, she thought. So she asked Janice Eisenhauer if the Breaking Bread money could be used for this kind of teacher, and when she got it, she drove the girls to Jaghori, found them a place to live, and enrolled them in a six-student nursing school.

Denying girls an education is a trick as old as Methuselah. As the woman in the literacy class said, if you can't read, you may as well be blind because you can't see what is going on, and as a result, the women and girls think their lot in life is predestined. What happens to the girls in these schools will affect the future of the country, and maybe even the entire region, where women have struggled for centuries to be treated fairly. Susan Bellan reflects on their tumultuous past when she recalls her own troubles while she was inventing the Breaking Bread plan. She was going through what seemed to be a relentless combination of assaults affecting her health, her livelihood, her home, and her children. "I really identified with Afghan women who were under much worse siege, and I wanted to give them backup." She feels that no matter how terrible a situation you are facing, "you can get through it, or hope to get through it, if you don't feel isolated, and if you have friends in your corner providing you with moral and material support."

That support has come to Afghanistan by way of dozens of women's groups, philanthropists, and governments that understand absolutely that education is the way forward for Afghanistan. The bad news today is that, as the attacks on the schools increase in both number and ferocity, parents become increasingly reluctant to expose their children to the potential violence. Furthermore, while one in four girls attends primary school, only 9 percent continue to secondary school.

Case in point: at the Shuhada School in Jaghori, there are a scant eleven girls in the senior class, as opposed to sixty per classroom in the junior grades. The staff explains that most girls leave school and get married at fifteen. Four of the eleven girls in this senior class are engaged, but claim they won't marry until they have graduated.

The minister of education, Hanif Atmar, addressed these stubborn issues, as well as the considerable successes his ministry has seen, when he visited Canada in December 2007:

> What is happening in Afghanistan in the area of education is a strategic transformation of our society. Whether some would like to see it or not, whether some would admit or not, this is the most fundamental transformation in our society, which is happening around the shared vision and objective of Afghan people—which is the education of their kids.

The numbers back up his claim. Six years ago, there were nine hundred thousand kids in school—all of them boys. Today there are six million in attendance, two million of them girls. "This is the highest enrolment rate ever in Afghanistan," he says. The country has gone from having no female teachers to having forty thousand; from twenty-five hundred schools to nine thousand; and from ten teacher training colleges to thirty-four, one in each province with special facilities for girls. Atmar said:

> If somebody is to take credit for this, that will be first and
> foremost the Afghan women. Through their sacrifice—had
> it not been for the strength of their resolve, we the men of
> Afghanistan would have succumbed to that Talibani
> pressure a long time ago—it was the strength of their
> resolve that actually gave us the strength to fight back. And
> even these days they are making a tremendous sacrifice.

To explain the 40 to 45 percent of girls who still are not
attending school, he points to a shortage of female teachers
and a lack of proper facilities. At the secondary level, the ratio
of boys to girls is five to one. Eighty percent of the rural districts
do not have girls' high schools, and many families still prefer
that their teenage girls be taught by female teachers in all-girls'
classes. "Since there are not enough female teachers, they don't
go to secondary [school], and when they don't go to secondary,
there will never be enough female teachers. That creates a
vicious circle which needs to be broken," he says.

But he puts most of the blame squarely on the Taliban:

> For the past fourteen months that I am the minister of
> education, 115 of my teachers and kids have been killed
> by the terrorists. Why? The terrorists believe that this
> modern, broad-based Islamic system of education in
> Afghanistan is contrary to their terrorist ideology because
> this system will never allow Afghans to hate others, or to
> become terrorists and suicide bombers. That's exactly the
> reason why they are attacking our teachers, our students,
> and our schools in the most brutal and inhumane way
> that would be unacceptable to any civilized nation. But
> despite this, our families are sending their kids to school.

He lists nine obstacles and impediments that have to be dealt
with: terrorist ideology; criminality that leads to another

impediment, lack of security; teacher supply; distance to schools; inadequate facilities; a poor curriculum; out-of-date teaching methods; and poverty. He says:

> If poverty reduction can be achieved only through economic growth, then that economic growth will have to be inclusive. The inclusiveness of economic growth can never be achieved without education. Give them the most precious and sustainable asset of education, and then they will participate in the growth—which will hopefully lead to poverty reduction. That's the understanding of our nation as to why education is so important for children.

Then he takes a shot at what he calls an ineffective and unaccountable administration. "There are elements in our administration, particularly in education administration, that are abusive. And as long as these abusive elements remain in our administration, they will be an impediment to the girls' enrolment." Although he does not mention specifics, he is referring to corporal punishment, which is used freely by the teachers as well as the hard-line Islamists who don't want girls to be educated, men who wield considerable power in Afghan politics today. "We have to get rid of them," he says. "There will be zero tolerance for abuse and abusive elements in the administration." His plan is to take the power from ministers and place it in the hands of the parents. He wants to organize them, turn them into parent councils, and give them full responsibility for their schools. He claims 90 percent of the operating schools now have a council of parents. Their mandate is to provide security and protection for the students, teachers, and the school, responsibly manage the resources allocated for the schools, supervise and monitor the performance of staff, and develop a relationship among teachers and parents.

Tough talk from a cabinet minister. But those who know him claim Atmar is sincere, a reformer who is close enough to President Karzai to get the action he wants on education.

Atmar also secured a $60-million pledge from Bev Oda, the minister of international cooperation, while he was in Canada that will go into curriculum development, teacher training, building additional schools, and hiring more than two hundred specialists, both inside Afghanistan and outside, including Afghan Canadians, to come back to the country and write the badly needed textbooks.

Atmar wants a people-centred, parent-led governance system, not only in the education sector, but also in other sectors of reconstruction and development. He also wants to address the troublesome madrassa schools that preached hatred and brainwashed boys to become jihadists. "They are not only a security threat, but also the biggest enemy of girls' education," he says. He does not call for their closure, but says:

> We must reform them. We must reform their curriculum. We must broaden their base of education. And we must include them and bring them into the mainstream. The old policy of exclusion led to this disaster. Exclusion breeds fundamentalism and terrorism. It's inclusion and having a broad base that would lead to better understanding and better ways of cooperation and shared values.

If the minister and his department can get the security issue under control and convince parents to send their girls, particularly their teenage girls, to school, there is still another major problem to solve: Most teachers in Afghanistan have little or no professional training. If you finish school yourself, you are eligible to teach. What's more, the methods of teaching are hopelessly outdated. Rote learning is still the norm, memorizing and copying text trumps discussion, and teachers shout at students and hit them for everything from disobedience to wrong answers.

The competence of the teachers has been on the minds of the women at CW4WAfghan for as long as they have been funding their salaries. But what is a grassroots volunteer organization to do about teacher training in another country? Well, if you are part of one of the fourteen chapters now operating across Canada, you decide to fix the problem. I am invariably astonished by the bold projects these women take on. So when I heard about their request for $600,000 to train teachers in Afghanistan, I wasn't exactly surprised. They call it "Excel-erate Education."

Janice Eisenhauer explains:

> Excel-erate Education is a two-year project to provide
> high-quality teacher training and annual salary support
> for female and male teachers in several specific, under-
> resourced communities in Kabul Province. Local commu-
> nity and home schools will be identified in consultation
> with the Afghan Ministry of Education, and with two,
> selected, Afghan, implementing partner-organizations
> with experience in teacher training. Our partners have
> the ability to access the much-needed community
> support within these districts. The teacher training
> ultimately benefits women and girls attending commu-
> nity and home schools in areas where a lack of infrastruc-
> ture and access to resources, or security risks create an
> absence or shortage of schools.

Approximately 350 student teachers will be invited to partic-ipate in the teacher-training sessions taking place over a six-month period in both 2008 and 2009. A total of eight trainers will conduct the training, with support from an education consultant and project management team. Following the successful completion of the training, and with the support from their communities, trainees will have the opportunity to apply for up to nine months of teacher salary support. A Teachers' Resource Fund will be made available to purchase teaching supplies and resources and to assist the teachers with other improvements to their classrooms. A Virtual Teachers' Resource Centre will be established at the project office, to provide access to a collection of resources online (and printed copies where possible), in the Dari and Pashto languages. These additional resources will ensure the newly learned skills acquired by the student trainees are immediately implemented and practised within the classroom setting. Under-resourced communities in need of teachers for girls will have a way to access professionally trained teachers, and schools will be given further resources towards eventual integration within the formal education system.

Janice Eisenhauer and Alaina Podmorow made the trip from their respective homes in Calgary and the Okanagan Valley to attend the lunch Bev Oda was holding in Ottawa to mark International Women's Day and to announce the funding for the teacher-training project. Oda had a surprise for both of them. She pledged her ministry would match donations received from Canadians as part of their Breaking Bread fundraising initiative.

Eisenhauer, an unassuming woman who wears her heart on her sleeve, has been on this file for more than a decade. She was completing a degree in development studies at the University of Calgary when she and fellow student Carolyn Reicher and author Deborah Ellis launched CW4WAfghan.

In the face of such seemingly insurmountable odds—rescuing women from a medieval theocracy—most people would back away, feeling they could not possibly alter the course of events. But some, such as Eisenhauer and Reicher and the women they recruited to the cause, simply do not see the barriers the same way. I remember receiving a call during those early days from a woman in Vancouver who identified herself as Lauryn Oates, asking if I would speak at a function she was organizing to raise awareness about the women of Afghanistan. I agreed and fully expected to meet a middle-aged woman with experience in the gender stakes. I was wrong. Lauryn was sixteen years old, had Kool-Aid-green dyed hair, and had borrowed her boyfriend's car to fetch me at the airport. She also packed a room with eager listeners and opened a chapter of CW4WAfghan in Vancouver that night. These activists in Calgary and Vancouver, Oakville and Kingston, Montreal and St. John never let go. While governments dithered, they pumped up awareness; their singular mission being to recast the status of women and girls in Afghanistan.

Eisenhauer is the full-time volunteer coordinator for the project that has at different times been both frustrating and frightening, empowering and rewarding. Combining temerity with collegiality, she invariably rallies more people to the cause when she addresses a crowd. In Ottawa, she thanked Oda and said:

> We all know there are many challenges facing women
> and girls in Afghanistan, particularly in terms of access to
> education and basic human rights. We are very proud to
> mark our tenth International Women's Day on March 8,
> 2008, working in solidarity, in partnership, and in friend-
> ship with women in Afghanistan. Our goals are to
> advance and protect human rights for Afghan women
> and girls. Each year, March 8 allows us an opportunity to
> celebrate these goals, and demonstrate our long-term
> commitment to the women of Afghanistan.

She and her band of change-makers have provided sustain-able funding for Afghan partner projects, to help bear the cost of an orphanage, community schools, books, stationery, heating bills for classrooms, library resources, transportation, medical supplies, and skills development.

Alaina Podmorow stood beside her at the Ottawa event, the quintessential Canadian girl, her wavy hair tied up in a ponytail, seemingly nonplussed by the considerable fuss around her, a ten-year-old who decided she would be part of the solution to crack a human rights problem for girls her age on the other side of the world. "Lainy," as she's known to her friends, is a pint-sized humanitarian, a soccer player, a kid who snowboards, tap dances, and performs in musical theatre. Her mom, Jamie, says:

> As far as her work goes, that comes from a different place. She is able to be very serious about what is going on there. She gathers the information, processes it, and decides how she is going to help. We talk about the issue, and then she is off playing or doing homework or dancing. That I believe is her special gift—the processing and letting go.

Jamie tells a story that best describes her remarkable daughter's unvarnished attitude:

> After an event in Calgary, the speakers were mingling about, talking to audience members that had joined them on stage. I watched as a woman slowly approached Alaina, her head veiled with a black scarf. She took Alaina's face in her hands, and with tears trickling down her cheeks, she said, "Thank you for what you are doing for my country. Thank you for what you are doing for my people." Alaina's answer was pure: a simple "You're welcome."

She and her team of preteen dynamos have held bottle drives, silent auctions, donut sales, and car washes; new chapters of Little Women for Little Women in Afghanistan have sprouted up from Mayne Island in British Columbia to Newfoundland. They have raised $22,000 to hire teachers in Afghanistan and realize Alaina's dream to make peace through education. "I want to build a bridge of peace," she says. The logo she chose is Education = Peace.

ONE OF THE RECIPIENTS OF THE PROGRAMS being celebrated in Ottawa is Shegofa Mehri, who comes from Sunge-e-Masha in Jaghori district. It is serendipitous that her name means "blossom" because she is leading the pack in 2008, the first of the Jaghori students to graduate and go to university, proof that the world the girls so badly want to join is available to them. I met her first in 2002, when she was a student at Shuhada High School. Her father, Engineer Akram Mehri (engineers in Afghanistan take their profession as titles just as doctors do), invited me to join the family at home one night after dinner. The blind corners on the dirt roads in the pitch-black night made me wonder why roads are being paved in other places, but Jaghori is not on the reconstruction map. The U.N. employee in charge of the district quipped: "They don't need roads in Jaghori; they have electricity and Sima Samar." Once at the two-storey home of the Mehri family, Shegofa acts as host, shyly introducing a stranger to her six brothers and sisters and her mom, Homina. The conversation is all about education: getting it, using it, finding the way out of the troublesome past. "I want my daughters to be doctors, engineers, politicians," her father said. "They can make this country a better place and stand on their own feet." His progressive view is unusual, even here in Jaghori, where Shuhada's schools have been open since 1991.

Today Shegofa is a second-year student at Bolzano University in Italy, one of three girls from Jaghori who won scholarships that cover tuition, as well as room and board and travel. This is the opportunity her parents had hoped for, and one her younger brothers and sisters aim to replicate.

Several international organizations have joined the effort to educate girls in Afghanistan by partnering with Shuhada. In Ghazni province, more than twenty-five thousand girls and boys are attending thirty-four different schools. As early as 2003, three hundred students had passed the university entrance exams, the highest number of successful candidates of any district in Afghanistan. But it is the success of the girls' schools in Jaghori that brings a triumphant grin to the face of Sima Samar. "Eighty-six of my girls graduated from Kabul University this year. They are the first. They studied science and literature, social science and journalism."

The Taliban still skirt the area, delivering their cowardly night letters to villagers and sending suicide bombers to terrify both the local population and the humanitarians who work here. You still need to dodge the Taliban hideouts when driving to Jaghori, but once there, the progress in the towns is apparent: The hospital is running at full capacity; the library has been rebuilt and stocked with more than five thousand volumes; the children at the orphanage are attending school; the fields that were drought-ravaged when I first visited in 2002 are now ripe with grain; and the apple and grape orchards that had succumbed to the devastation of war are heavy with fruit. The cows, sheep, and goats that have been part of the landscape for centuries are grazing in the fields and wandering onto the roads and between the stalls of merchants in Sunge-e-Masha, oblivious to the metamorphosis around them. In many ways, the villages also cling to the customs of bygone times.

When the afternoon shift at Shuhada School empties this day and the kids start their long trek back over the hills and through the valleys to their mud-brick homes, the sun is already low on the horizon. It casts yellow streaks of light and long blue shadows on the rocky ranges as I watch them walk away. Filtered through the dust that lingers from the drought, the light creates muted hues that colour the countryside now splashed with the black-and-white figures of the students, who still have homework to do and chores to tend to before dark descends.

By the time I return to the town where I am staying, fires have been lit in the hearths, everyone is preparing for dinner— "breaking bread," I think. Some are at the river that gurgles through the village, filling buckets of water, hauling them up the steep hills. A couple of chickens swing from a schoolboy's back. Shepherds are herding their goats nearer to home. A muffled echo of children's laughter reminds me that during the Taliban regime, they were not allowed to play. A gentle peace descends as the light spills through the trees and around the hills. Calm settles on the hamlets, the sort of quiet that comes from a day fulfilled, a day that brings hope for tomorrow. And although the future is still uncertain, the girls in Jaghori are dreaming big dreams. Everyone is going to be a "somebody."

CHAPTER 11

SURVIVAL

If you have come to help me, you are wasting your
time. But if you have come because your liberation is
bound up with mine, then let us struggle together.

—Attributed to Lila Watson, Australian Aboriginal activist

FATIMA GAILANI HAS ALWAYS BEEN A "SOMEBODY" in Afghanistan. She
belongs to the chattering class—the elites, the respected
scholars, the families whose names suggest gentility. They
survive despite the thugs who grab power, the boorish
warlords, and the drug barons. Most of them leave during the
insurrections, but invariably they come back, drawn to the Old
World ways of their homeland, taking a visceral flyer on the
future.

Fatima holds a master's degree in Islamic jurisprudence and is
the daughter of Pir Sayyid Ahmad Gailani, the spiritual leader of
the Sunni Muslims. I met her in London, England, where she

and her daughter were in exile in 1997. She said at that time: "A woman with a covered head is not more honourable than a woman without a covered head." Divorced from her husband, she moved in powerful circles and travelled with her father to Rome, the same year I met her, to meet with Afghanistan's King Zahir Shah, to try to find a solution to the Taliban debacle. Then she packed up and left for Providence, Rhode Island, married an Afghan who was a professor at Providence College, and lived a life of tranquility: smart cafés, theatre, women's clubs, neighbourhood walks with friends. But like so many affluent Afghans who made a life in another place—the United States, Canada, the Scandinavian countries, Australia—she came back soon after the Taliban were ousted. Now she is president of the Afghanistan Red Crescent Society (the Muslim equivalent of the Red Cross). Her husband, Anwar ul-Haq Ahady, is the minister of finance. She travels into the darkest corners of the country, including Taliban-occupied territory, because the Red Crescent is neutral and is mandated to respond to the needs of all the people. "The Taliban is the enemy of the country, but their children aren't," she says. She wears a scarf to cover her head, even while sitting behind her expansive desk in the Red Crescent office in Kabul. Her life has been immeasurably altered.

She was part of the team that wrote the constitution in 2004 and met with the Taliban, as well as the soldiers of strongman Gulbuddin Hekmatyar, a warlord who has been blacklisted by the United States as a "specially designated global terrorist." Of those conversations, she says:

> We sat in the mosques and under the trees in remote
> districts like Wardak. We had heated discussions but we
> were making progress. Then Iraq became the centre of
> attention and everything started to change. It was right
> after the constitution was written that the kidnappings
> and suicide bombs started.

It is hard to imagine the stylish, cosmopolitan Gailani on a dirt track in rural Afghanistan, having discussions with illiterate men about reforming a country, its laws, its treatment of women, its need to engage as a civil society. Her father's name provides some protection, her husband's job delivers a level of clout, but Gailani is still taking a chance. She would be a prize for any kidnappers. And the no-guns policy of the Red Crescent means she goes to work unarmed, while her cabinet minister husband has bodyguards 24/7. But she is committed to the country. "If you have the soul, you can build the body," she insists.

She treads a fine line between a life of privilege and a job that requires her to be 100 percent neutral. "When men decide to fight, it's not a choice for the women and children," she says. She is acutely aware of the danger she faces: "I lie to myself and say I have a choice, I can live elsewhere. But millions of women in this country don't have the choices I have. If we don't fix it, it will be hell again."

She was twenty-four years old when the Russians invaded and thought at the time, "Too bad, but I'm leaving. I'll send money back to help, but I'm not staying here." Like many Afghans with the means to leave, she moved to London. She kept in close touch, working with her father to negotiate a settlement from a distance. Now she is in the thick of the elusive search for peace and says, "It's too late to change course. We're all in the same boat together, rowing strongly—we have to find the shore."

A prominent women's rights activist, she calls for a brand of feminism that includes culture and religion, claiming a secular version of equality won't work here. And she is not shy about sharing her opinions. When men in the villages compliment her, as they do often, she replies, "If you want your daughter to be like me, then you have to give her the same opportunities my father gave me."

She had called a meeting for her staff at the Serena Hotel on January 14, the day the terrorists attacked. But luck was on her side: "I moved the meeting to the Intercontinental Hotel the day before because I was too cheap to pay the fee the Serena wanted." Like so many others in Afghanistan today, she can record those near-misses like appointments in her diary. She says she tries not to think about the deteriorating security. "If I got obsessed about it, I'd be too afraid to work here." Instead, she turns to the same source Afghans have used for a thousand years: "I rely on God to have mercy on me and not put me in the wrong place at the wrong time."

She picks up the framed photographs of her daughter and grandchildren who live in Dubai, looks at their sweet faces, and says, "Sometimes, I think I have to get out of here—I want to go and be a grandmother. All men and women in Afghanistan have moments of extreme discouragement, but the majority of us, we take back the heart and survive."

It is always about survival. For those without privilege, the survival stakes are higher. From finding a job to avoiding a forced marriage, the women of Afghanistan have to deal with the fractured past and the uncertain future by practising survival skills that allow them to scrounge a meal or score a cabinet post. Beating the odds in Afghanistan overrules every-thing else: it swallows passion, fidelity, even honesty. As security diminishes, the means to an end are invariably unprin-cipled: whispering about an un-Islamic act, spreading gossip about a faithless infidel, condoning a plot to unseat an enemy or even a friend, or succumbing to corruption all just become methods of survival. The gentle arts of empathy and compas-sion are traded for a better deal as a second wife or a chance to go to school. Tolerance vanishes when your daughter is bartered for blood money. Compromise doesn't work when your access to safety is cut off. The emotional landscape of Afghanistan is tough; love can seem frivolous.

People often ask about the men—the husbands and brothers whose wives and sisters live with gender apartheid. The men speak in *appeasement-ese*—a language that condones but does not endorse the unequal treatment of women. They shrug with complaisance. "It's the culture," they say. Or they shoot the messenger, saying: "This is our way and nobody else's business," as though the problem is Western interference rather than an abrogation of human rights. Even the rare men who argue for women's rights speak of their own daughters and wives more as chattels than as equals.

A select few avoid being pawns in the struggle. Adeena Niazi, who grew up in Kabul, studied in India, and now lives in Canada, says there was no violence in her family but admits it was the exception. Others such as Gailani—well educated, financially secure, belonging to a powerful family that believes in the emancipation of women—have also been spared. Sima Samar is also a "somebody" who doesn't take instruction from anyone, although her life story contains scattered examples of the same terrible experiences and is governed by the same punishing rules that most Afghan women must endure.

Afghanistan today is in many ways a contradiction in terms. It is a country that embraces religious piety but treats its citizens with brutality. It is a place with mud-brick houses on the same street as the ostentatious mansions known as "wedding-cake houses," some of them pink, which people call *narcotecture*, built with the drug barons' illicit gains. Shop windows here display Hollywood-style mannequins modelled on white women with short curly blonde hair that wear floor-length strapless gowns with huge ballroom skirts while the sidewalks are filled with women in burkas or wearing hijab. No one seems to notice the contradiction, or asks who the buyers are for these gowns. The window displays have not changed in six years.

Pop music blares from kiosks on the street while mullahs wail from the loudspeakers at the mosque across the road. You can't hear one over the other. Television programs considered un-Islamic are banned, but internet cafés are burgeoning in popularity on the streets of Kabul. The wildly popular Indian soap operas that were the evening entertainment in almost every Afghan house with a television have recently been taken off the air. So the viewers watch their favourite dramas on their computers at home, or burn DVDs on their laptops at work to watch the shows after hours. Asked about the move to ban the soaps, President Karzai told a media briefing that his government was committed to media freedom. But, he said, "We want our television broadcasting to be in line with our culture, based on our society's moral standards."

Liquor is forbidden, yet restaurants serve wine. At private parties with highly placed government officials, the booze flows right along with the contradictions. There is an expression here that, translated, goes like this: "I cannot talk because my mouth is full of water." It means, "I cannot tell the truth because it may hurt someone" or "I am not allowed to comment because of policy constraints."

Laws are written with verbal gymnastics, the language designed to dance around religious jurisprudence, in an attempt to include a modicum of human rights that pays lip service to the covenants and conventions Afghanistan signed with the rest of the world at the United Nations. There is no word for *state* in the Quran, but the government claims calling Afghanistan an Islamic state is in keeping with the Prophet's wishes. Non-governmental organizations are in business to bring aid to the people but secretly confess they have to pay a bribe to the government to get the health and education projects to their intended recipients.

Integrity Watch did a survey in 2007 that highlighted the extent of the corruption in the country: 40 percent of respondents said they had to pay a bribe to get things done with the government; 41 percent said the justice system was the most corrupt institution in the country; 60 percent said the Karzai government is more corrupt than that of the Taliban, the mujahedeen, and the communist regimes; 90 percent said that connections govern the recruitment of civil servants; and 81 percent believe that sharia law would be an effective deterrent to corruption.

But Afghanistan has charms and cultural norms that are as endearing as they are perplexing. A morning greeting, for example, requires a lengthy dissertation rather than a simple *Hi*. An oft-used formula goes, *Salaam alaikom, subh bakhair, chetor hasti, khob hastam, khob hasti*, which means, "May God be with you, good morning, how are you? Are you well? Is your family well?" The pots of tea and half-dozen plates of nuts and sweets that are prepared and served at every single meeting, whether it is at an office or someone's home, are rarely touched. They are simply the Afghan way of saying *welcome*. Even business cards include quaint additional data with the address, such as "backstreet of the National Assembly," "behind the Ministry of Commerce," or "just off Qali Musa Market, close to the British Cemetery." The loyalty and protectiveness Afghans show to a stranger are unmatched in most places around the world.

When spring comes to Afghanistan and signals the rebirth season, you can feel the collective sigh of relief, even though everyone knows the warm weather brings the terrorists out and ups the ante in the insurgency.

Spring was a particular deliverance in 2008 because the winter before it had been so harsh. Nearly one thousand people and 316,000 livestock died of exposure in villages pummelled by snow. Now the swallows and kites fill the sky again, and roses bloom in every garden. But as predictable as the relief that came with the welcome sunshine were the menacing edicts from a government that is increasingly under pressure from fundamentalists. The upcoming election in 2009 means the fundamentalists are tightening the strings on reform. The election campaign is turning into a contest between extremists, who threaten the government with disruption if they dare to alter the suffocating status of women and the reformers who need women's votes to stay in power. The president has to balance his promise to take Afghans into the twenty-first century against the demands made by a collection of power brokers whose bank accounts are fattened by the status quo. The most recent attempt to bring Karzai to heel on reform came by way of the Commission for Anti-social Behaviour and Counter-narcotics (shades of the vice-and-virtue squad), which drafted a law to "ban offensive traditions and Western culture." The rules they demand include:

- Women must not wear makeup in the workplace.
- Men must cut their hair short to avoid looking like a girl.
- Women must not speak to men in public unless they are related.
- Men must stop wearing bracelets, designer jeans, necklaces, earrings, and T-shirts.
- Pigeon flying, animal fighting, and playing with birds on rooftops will be against the law.
- There will be a ban on loud music and loudspeakers at weddings and in restaurants.
- Betting at snooker clubs will be illegal.
- Shops selling revealing clothing will be closed.
- Programs that are un-Islamic and detrimental to the young on television and radio will be forbidden.
- Anyone who sells, keeps, or imports DVDs or photos of naked or semi-naked women will be punished.
- Swearing at women and children in public will be against the law.
- Women and girls must start wearing the hijab in the Islamic way so that all the hair is covered by a shawl.

If the law passes parliament, anyone caught by the police disobeying the new rules will be fined—for instance, 1,000 afghanis (about $10) for pigeon flying, and 5,000 afghanis (about $50) for broadcasting un-Islamic programs.

The proposed law would be laughable if it wasn't for the gossip in Kabul that the government is trying to appease the Taliban in negotiations leading up to the election.

Afghanistan is at a turning point, not just for Afghans, but also for the international community that supports them. Suddenly, everyone from Kandahar to Canada is an armchair expert, poised over the petri dish that is Afghanistan. The poppy trade, for example, is the subject of much debate. Some argue the poppies should be mowed down and the fields used for saffron crops, freeing the farmers from their bondage to merciless drug barons. The Senlis Council, on the other hand, wants to select and maintain a single poppy operation, harvest the crop, make morphine tablets in local factories, and provide jobs as well as security. United Nations officials claim the plan is folly, that it would not work because the security needed for such an operation is not there. They also insist that there is no shortage of the painkilling morphine. Norine MacDonald of the Senlis Council says, "Let us do a pilot project. Let's see who's right."

There's no shortage of views on the insurgency either. Should we send more troops or bring the troops home? Both propositions have advocates. Or the government: Some argue the corruption is beyond repair, while others believe necessary changes are being made. As for the people who have to live with the decisions, there is a common denominator for survivors in war zones: When you have been in the coma of conflict for twenty-five years, you want your rescuers to ask if you have enough to eat and drink, but instead they invariably ask whose side you are on. It is hard to think about democracy when you are hungry.

It is also difficult to move forward on women's rights when the issue is muddied by those who prefer to see it in cultural or religious terms. There are a lot of highly respected diplomats and analysts, both inside Afghanistan and in the international community, who roll their eyes at the treatment of women and girls, but dismiss it as none of their business. One woman who works for CIDA was asked in a CBC radio interview about the violence against women and replied, "I know it exists but can't verify it by numbers, as no one has done the studies to prove it." There have been dozens of reports prepared by the United Nations Human Rights Commission, the Afghanistan Independent Human Rights Commission, the Women and Children Legal Research Foundation, and by dozens of NGOs, the most recent by Global Rights, a Washington-based human rights association, that surveyed fifty-seven hundred households in sixteen of the country's thirty-four provinces and found that 87 percent of the respondents reported abuse. Womankind Worldwide, a British NGO, also reported that seven years after the fall of the Taliban regime, Afghanistan is still one of the most dangerous places in the world to be a woman. Every report comes to the same conclusion: Violence against women in Afghanistan is endemic, entrenched, and very much part of the reason this country stumbles in its attempts to move forward. Yet time and again, the lives of those women are blighted by the religious and cultural interpretations of men. It is not about respecting culture and religion. It is about having the moral courage to take on the contradictions and respect international law. How can the world look the other way when women are burned alive for speaking out, when little girls are harnessed to farm equipment and used as plough horses, when all women and girls are treated as subhuman because of their gender? It is one thing for illiterate men to cling to old customs that harm women, but it is unconscionable for the international community to excuse the brutality by buying into a theory of cultural relativism.

THE LAST OF THE DAY'S SUNSHINE is casting a soft glow when Sima Samar's bodyguards bring her home. She reaches for her clippers and goes to the rose garden, a beautiful sanctuary that puts a difficult day in perspective. As she snips a wilting rose—"it'll make the new one grow"—she contemplates the one-step-forward, two-steps-backward progress for women in Afghanistan and says, "We started with no systems at all. We have accomplished a lot." She snips another rose, admires the new ones, and casually says there has been another night letter threatening to kill her and all the staff at the human rights commission. She fingers a pale green rose, comments on its originality, and turns the soil in the bed to encourage its growth. It is twilight by the time she has finished. The birds in this peaceful garden are twittering their last songs of the day. On the way into the house, she pauses and says, "It'll take more time. But I am still hopeful."

To a world still traumatized by 9/11, Afghanistan has become a story about terrorists, drug barons, and the Taliban insurgency. To me, it remains a chronicle about blameless women and girls who continue to pay an awful price for the opportunism of angry men. But I, too, am hopeful. The women activists, journalists, and change-makers are slowly breaking down the taboo around talking about the status of women and girls in Afghanistan. The uncertain fate of their sisters is in their hands.

ACKNOWLEDGMENTS

In eleven years of following the developing story of the women of Afghanistan, I have been fortunate to meet dozens of activists, diplomats, and researchers who have kindly shared their personal stories and research data with me. To each I owe my grateful thanks. First among them is Dr. Sima Samar, who has been my beacon throughout this odyssey. Her knowledge and experience can only be topped by her tenacity for changing the lives of women and her generosity to me in my quest. Her family became my home away from home. Around their *dastarkhan*, my curiosity as well as my appetite and soul were fed. I am also grateful to Christopher Alexander, the United Nations Deputy Special Representative to Afghanistan, and to Nasrine Gross at Kabultec and Hangama Anwari at the Women and Children Legal Research Foundation for their valuable input and guidance.

To my fellow travellers, Robin Benger, Alister Bell, Abdul Shokoor, Ali Adib, and the late Anna Woodiwiss from the

Turquoise Mountain Foundation who was tragically killed on April 2, 2008, many thanks. The journey would have been less without you.

My gratitude also goes to the editors and producers who sent me to Afghanistan on assignment: Craig Offman, Rona Maynard, Bonnie Baker Cowan, Mark Stevenson, and Barbara Barde. And to those who helped with the fine print, Maggie Hayes and Mary Ross Hendriks. And to the remarkable Jane McElhone, whose commitment to the advancement of women in Afghanistan has planted the seed for change.

To the women whose volunteer efforts inspired me— Canadian Women for Women in Afghanistan, Little Women for Little Women in Afghanistan, the association of Women Living Under Muslim Laws, and the Military Wives Sisterhood in Brandon, Manitoba—many thanks. And to Lauryn Oates, for squeezing into the two-foot opening at Rabbia's tomb so she could give me a bird's-eye view of the interior after my flight to Mazar-e Sharif was cancelled, a grateful *tashakoor*.

My thanks to: Dale Spender for permission to quote from her book, *For the Record: The Making and Meaning of Feminist Knowledge* (London: Women's Press, 1985); Manouchehr Saadat Noury for permission to quote his translation of Rabbia Balkhi's poem "Love"; Safia Siddiqi for permission to quote from her poetry; and Jill Frayne for permission to quote her mother, June Callwood's admonition, "If you see an injustice being committed, you're not an observer, you're a participant."

And last but by no means least, to my agent Michael Levine, and to the editors at Penguin Canada—Diane Turbide, who conceived the notion of a sequel to *Veiled Threat*, and Helen Reeves, Alex Schultz, and Jonathan Webb, who shepherded this manuscript to its completion—many thanks.

APPENDIX

AFGHANISTAN STATISTICS
SEPTEMBER/OCTOBER 2007

DEMOGRAPHICS

Population	31,889,923
Female population	49%
Population aged 15–19	51.5%
Population under 18	15,849,000
Population under 5	5,535,000

Source: SOWC 2007

CHILD HEALTH
Mortality

Under-5 mortality	257/1,000
Area average under-5 mortality, excluding Afghanistan (includes India, Pakistan, Bangladesh, Bhutan, Maldives, Nepal, Sri Lanka)	64.43/1,000
Infant mortality rate	163/1,000

Source: SOWC 2007 (Please also refer to Afghanistan U5MR for additional published numbers.)

Maternal mortality ratio	1,600/100,000
Daily deaths from pregnancy-related complications	44
Annual deaths from pregnancy-related complications	18,000

Source: "Project Proposal submitted to CIDA for Increasing Access to Maternal and Child Health Care in Mirwais Hospital—Kandahar and Southern Afghanistan," UNICEF Afghanistan, August 2007

Major Causes of Childhood Mortality

Measles
Tetanus
Diarrhea
Acute respiratory infections
Malaria
Malnutrition

Source: "Project Proposal submitted to CIDA for Increasing Access to Maternal and Child Health Care in Mirwais Hospital—Kandahar and Southern Afghanistan," UNICEF Afghanistan, August 2007

Under-5 deaths attributed to diarrhea	22% (48 per 1,000 deaths)
Chronically malnourished children	54%
Children underweight for their age	40%
Children suffering from iron deficiency	71%
Pregnant women suffering from iron deficiency	65%
School-aged children who are iodine deficient	72%
Women who are iodine deficient	42%
Population with access to clean water	23%

Source: "Project Proposal submitted to CIDA for Increasing Access to Maternal and Child Health Care in Mirwais Hospital—Kandahar and Southern Afghanistan," UNICEF Afghanistan, August 2007; UNICEF Afghanistan, "Country Programme of Cooperation 2006–2008"

Fewer than 30% of Afghan babies are exclusively breastfed, and more than two-thirds do not receive appropriate and timely complementary feeding.

Source: "Project Proposal submitted to CIDA for Increasing Access to Maternal and Child Health Care in Mirwais Hospital—Kandahar and Southern Afghanistan," UNICEF Afghanistan, August 2007

Number of Polio Cases

2000	27
2002	9
2004	4
2005	9
2006	31
2007 (to Nov. 30)	11

Measles Deaths

2001	Est. 30,000
2005	Between 100 and 2,000 (number not available)

Immunization Rates of Children under One Year of Age

	2001	2005
Tuberculosis (BCG)	54%	73%
Diptheria, Petussis, Tetanus (DPT)	44%	76%
Polio (OPV3)	45%	76%
Measles	46%	64%

Source: SOWC 2007, UNICEF Afghanistan Country Office Support to UNICEF Canada, Submission to Privy Council, January 2007; "Project Proposal submitted to CIDA for Increasing Access to Maternal and Child Health Care in Mirwais Hospital—Kandahar and Southern Afghanistan," UNICEF Afghanistan, August 2007

EDUCATION

Primary school enrolment	6 million*
Enrolment Grades 1–6	4.25 million
Percentage of girls	33%–35%*
Number of teachers	133,000

*Speech by Mohammed Haneef Atmar, Afghanistan minister of education, "The Building Blocks of a Country's Future: A Forum on Education in Afghanistan," Toronto, October 4, 2007

Children age 7–12 out of school	47%
Adult male literacy	47%
Adult female literacy	15%
Female age 15–49 literacy	14%
Female literacy in rural areas	8%

Registered schools	8,300
Satellite schools	870
Usable school buildings	2,220
Schools rehabilitated since 2000	2,000

Additional school buildings needed	4,465
Schools that need additional classrooms	1,480
Schools that are damaged	535
Schools that do not have buildings	3,930
Schools with access to safe water	Fewer than 50%
Percentage of schools with sanitary latrines	Approx. 25%
Primary school completion rate for boys	32%
Primary school completion rate for girls	13%

Source: "Best Estimates of Social Indicators for Children in Afghanistan, 1990–2005"

UNICEF OBJECTIVES TO BE ACHIEVED BY DECEMBER 2008

- Increase primary school net enrolment for girls by 20%
- Increase literacy rates of females 15–49 years of age by 50%
- 1.8 million girls to benefit from child-friendly schools
- 90,000 illiterate adults, especially women, to attend learning centres
- Mobilize decision-makers and community in favour of adult literacy, with a focus on women's literacy
- 50% of girls completing primary school to have attained acceptable levels of basic competencies

Source: UNICEF Afghanistan Annual Report 2006; "Project Proposal to UNICEF Canada from UNICEF Afghanistan for Basic Education and Gender Equality," July 2007

MAJOR INTERVENTIONS

Immunization Campaigns in 2006

- Four million children under 5 immunized against measles (72% of population under 5).
- 4.2 million women of child-bearing age immunized against tetanus.
- Five rounds of National Immunization Days (NID) conducted and close to 7 million children vaccinated in each round.
- Five rounds of Sub-National Immunization Days (SNID) conducted targeting high-risk areas. In these 5 NIDs and 5 SNIDs, children vulnerable to polio received 44.9 million cumulative doses of OPV.
- The health ministers of Pakistan and Afghanistan organized a special cross-border launch of SNID.
- Vitamin A supplementation was conducted with the spring NID, where 5.8 million children (89%) received supplementation, and in the fall NID, where 6.6 million (100%) targeted children received vitamin A supplementation.

Source: UNICEF Afghanistan, *Annual Report 2006*

Immunization Campaigns in 2007
- NID in March targeted 7.2 million children with OPV.

Source: UNICEF Canada, News Release, March 25, 2007

- NID April 22–24 targeted 7.3 million children in 34 provinces for vaccination against polio.

Source: UNICEF Afghanistan, Polio NID 22-24.04.2007

- 1.3 million children vaccinated against polio in southern and eastern regions of country, September 19–21, as part of International Day of Peace. Some of the regions accessed had not been accessible for two years due to security concerns.

Source: Roshan Khadivi, "International Day of Peace Marked with Polio Vaccination Drive in Afghanistan," **www.unicef.org**, September 20, 2007

- 1.1 million children vaccinated against polio in southern region of country, December 9–12, as follow-up from September vaccination.

Source: Afghanistan Country Visit, December 1–8, 2007

MATERNAL HEALTH IN 2006
- Training of 35 reproductive health officers in epidemiology, surveillance, data collection, management, and supervision.
- Service delivery capacity was enhanced by supporting MoPH to conduct 20 refresher courses where 171 obstetric-care providers were trained.
- Emergency Obstetric Care (EmOC) service delivery was assisted through medical consumable, operation theatre, and delivery room equipment supplies. This was provided to five Regional Referral Centres, six Comprehensive Health Centres, and five provincial hospitals.

Source: UNICEF Afghanistan, *Annual Report 2006*

MATERNAL HEALTH IN 2007
In a few short years, Afghanistan has made major strides towards creating a health system, with great improvements in the under-5 mortality rate. Malalai has become one of Afghanistan's leading training hospitals, running courses in infection prevention and emergency obstetric care.

Yet many problems continue to plague the country's efforts to slash maternal mortality—one major obstacle being the shortage of female health workers. Since it is still unacceptable for a woman to be treated by a man, this shortage contributes to Afghanistan's maternal death toll.

To address the gap, Afghanistan has launched a drive to recruit and train midwives, particularly in remote regions where the shortages are so acute. Today Afghanistan has more than 2,400 trained midwives, up from only 446 in 2002, but a far cry from the 8,000 the country needs for adequate health coverage.

Source: Mandy Cunningham, "Improving the Chances of Mothers and Babies in Afghanistan," UNICEF Intranet, Panorama, Issue 21, October 8–15, 2007

INDEX